RUDOLF WITTKOWER

ARCHITECTURAL PRINCIPLES

IN THE AGE OF HUMANISM

RUDOLF WITTKOWER

ARCHITECTURAL PRINCIPLES
IN THE AGE OF HUMANISM

ACADEMY EDITIONS

PUBLISHER'S NOTE

First published in 1949 as volume 19 of the *Studies of the Warburg Institute*. Second edition published by Alec Tiranti Ltd in 1952, followed by a third revised edition in 1962. Reprinted by Academy Editions in 1973. Fourth edition published in 1988 in a new format and with plates re-numbered and integrated within the text. It included a selection from hitherto un-published lectures and essays on proportion by Professor Wittkower kindly given to us by his widow. Sections from each manuscript had been combined and edited into one integrated essay entitled *Proportion in Art and Architecture* which was reproduced as Appendix IV. This fifth edition is intended to mark the fiftieth anniversary of the publication of the book.

Front cover: Andrea Palladio, Palazzo Chiericati, Vicenza, detail of the façade.
(The Mansell Collection, London)

Back cover: Leonardo da Vinci, Vitruvian figure.
(Accademia, Venice)

Frontispiece: Andrea Palladio, Palazzo Civena, Vicenza, project for the façade.
(The British Architectural Library, RIBA, London)

Cover design: Mario Bettella, Artmedia, London

Published in Great Britain in 1998 by

ACADEMY EDITIONS
a division of
JOHN WILEY & SONS LTD
Baffins Lane
Chichester
West Sussex PO19 1UD

ISBN 0-471-97763-2

Other Wiley Editorial Offices
New York • Weinheim • Brisbane • Singapore • Toronto

Printed in China

CONTENTS

PART I   THE CENTRALLY PLANNED CHURCH AND THE RENAISSANCE
     1. Alberti's Programme of the Ideal Church 16
     2. Centralized Churches in Later Architectural Theory 22
     3. Building Practice: S. Maria delle Carceri 29
     4. Bramante and Palladio 31
     5. The Religious Symbolism of Centrally Planned Churches 38

PART II   ALBERTI'S APPROACH TO ANTIQUITY IN ARCHITECTURE
     1. The Column in Alberti's Theory and Practice 41
     2. S. Francesco at Rimini 43
     3. S. Maria Novella 47
     4. S. Sebastiano and S. Andrea at Mantua 51
     5. The Change in Alberti's Interpretation of Classical Architecture 59

PART III   PRINCIPLES OF PALLADIO'S ARCHITECTURE
     1. The Architect as 'uomo universale': Palladio, Trissino and Barbaro 60
     2. Palladio's Geometry: The Villas 67
     3. Palladio and Classical Architecture: Palaces and Public Buildings 75
     4. The Genesis of an Idea: Palladio's Church Façades 89
     5. Palladio's Optical and Psychological Concepts: Il Redentore 97

PART IV   THE PROBLEM OF HARMONIC PROPORTION IN ARCHITECTURE
     1. Francesco Giorgi's Platonic Programme for S. Francesco della Vigna 104
     2. The Mean Proportionals and Architecture 107
     3. Alberti's 'Generation' of Ratios 111
     4. Musical Consonances and the Visual Arts 113
     5. Palladio's 'fugal' System of Proportion 119
     6. Palladio's Ratios and the Development of Sixteenth-Century Musical Theory 123
     7. The Break-away from the Laws of Harmonic Proportion in Architecture 130

APPENDIX I   Francesco Giorgi's Memorandum for S. Francesco della Vigna 138
APPENDIX II   The Problem of the Commensurability of Ratios in the Renaissance 140
APPENDIX III Bibliographical Notes on the Theory of Proportion 142
APPENDIX IV Proportion in Art and Architecture: an amalgamation of
     previously unpublished lectures by Professor Wittkower
     Part I: The Need for Order 145
     Part II: Origins of Western Proportional Systems 147
     Part III: Geometry and Mediaeval Proportions 150
     Part IV: Renaissance Proportions and Commensurability 152
     Part V: Post-Renaissance Proportioning – Dilemmas and Possibilities 154

INDEX 156

Andrea Palladio, Loggia Bernarda, Vicenza. (The Mansell Collection)

PREFACE

Despite its rather unwieldy character, this book, when it first appeared in 1949, was unexpectedly given a very friendly reception. To my surprise it caused more than a polite stir. Sir Kenneth Clark wrote in the ARCHITECTURAL REVIEW that the first result of this book was 'to dispose, once and for all, of the hedonist, or purely aesthetic, theory of Renaissance architecture', and this defined my intention in a nutshell. The book is concerned with purely historical studies of the period 1450 to 1580, but it was my most satisfying experience to have seen its impact on a young generation of architects.

The influence a book has upon its readers is to a certain extent intangible and impossible to measure precisely. Yet I may claim that within the twelve years since its appearance many of the basic tenets have been accepted, popularized, enlarged upon, transmuted, and also attacked (which is surely a fruitful way of activating and generating fresh thought). It would not serve much purpose to put this assertion fully to the present reader's test. May it suffice to indicate that such diverse publications as Walter Paatz's *Die Kunst der Renaissance in Italien* (Stuttgart, 1953), Ezra D. Ehrenkrantz's *The Modular Number Pattern: Flexibility through Standardisation* (London, 1956), and P.H. Scholfield's *The Theory of Proportion in Architecture* (Cambridge, 1958) have all taken their cue from *Architectural Principles*; that in a challenging article in the ARCHITECTURAL REVIEW of December 1955 Reyner Banham tried to assess the book's influence ('for evil as well as good') on post-war British architecture; and that Roberto Pane used the forum of the Eighteenth International Congress of the History of Art at Venice (*Venezia e l'Europa*, Venice, 1956) for a broadside against the ideas propounded by me.

It is not easy to predict when a book has run its course. My publishers believed that the time had come for a low-priced edition. The least I felt I should do to justify their optimism was to revise the book thoroughly. Many pages have been entirely rewritten, thoughts have been clarified, errors amended, and the results of new research have been incorporated. Hardly a page has survived untouched.

In a number of essays written during the last decade, I have myself continued to expand, and to comment on, the ideas in this book. The following papers are partly or wholly devoted to closely related themes: 'Systems of Proportion' in ARCHITECT'S YEARBOOK, V, 1953; 'Brunelleschi's "Proportion in Perspective" ', in JOURNAL OF THE WARBURG AND COURTAULD INSTITUTES, XVI, 1953; 'Inigo Jones, Architect and Man of Letters', in JOURNAL OF THE ROYAL INSTITUTE OF

BRITISH ARCHITECTS, LX, 1953; 'The Arts in Western Europe', in THE NEW CAMBRIDGE MODERN HISTORY, Cambridge, 1957, Vol. I; 'S. Maria della Salute: Scenographic Architecture and the Venetian Baroque', in JOURNAL OF THE SOCIETY OF ARCHITECTURAL HISTORIANS, XVI, 1957; 'L'architettura del Rinascimento e la tradizione classica' in CASABELLA, No. 234, 1959; 'The Changing Concept of Proportion' in DAEDALUS, Winter 1960. In order to preserve the original character of *Architectural Principles* I had to resist the temptation of incorporating much of the material presented in these studies.

More than once have I been criticized for not having paid sufficient attention to the manner in which the Middle Ages approached the problem of proportion. But I set out to write a book on the Renaissance and this is clearly expressed in the title. I therefore think I was justified in referring to the mediaeval position only where my argument demanded it (and this happened on many occasions). For clarity's sake I have now added as 'Appendix II' some general remarks on proportion in the Middle Ages and the Renaissance.

It is always bad policy to state what a book does not contain. But I want to avoid any misunderstanding and, therefore, wish to emphasize that I am neither concerned with a history of Renaissance architecture nor with monographic treatments of Alberti and Palladio. I am discussing the works of these architects only in so far as they are relevant to my main topic, the illumination of architectural principles at the time of the Renaissance. The structure of the book is simple. Two chapters on (what constitute in my view) the central problems of Renaissance architecture – the meaning of church architecture and the proportional organization of buildings – frame the two chapters on Alberti and Palladio who were equally great as theorists and practitioners and mark the beginning and the end of the period under review.

Some readers may take exception to the many footnotes with long quotations in languages other than English. I have decided to preserve this material also in the present edition since it provides the historical documentation to my arguments. A translation of all these texts would have swelled the size of the book unduly. But the footnotes may be left unread without disadvantage to the main argument. Foreign language quotations in the text are followed by translations. This rule has been abandoned in a few cases where the meaning is obvious.

R.W.

New York, December, 1960.

LIST OF ILLUSTRATIONS

1. Construction of square and polygons. From Bartoli's edition of Alberti's *De re aedificatoria*, 1550.
2. Francesco di Giorgio. Drawing from Codex Magliabechiano, Biblioteca Nazionale, Florence.
3. Leonardo da Vinci. Design of a church, detail. Ms.B, Institut de France, Paris.
4. Francesco di Giorgio. Studies in proportion from Codex Saluzziano, Biblioteca Reale, Turin.
5. Francesco di Giorgio. Page from Codex Ashburnham 361, Biblioteca Laurenziana, Florence.
6. Leonardo da Vinci, Vitruvian figure. Drawing, Accademia, Venice.
7. Francesco di Giorgio. Vitruvian figure, Codex Ashburnham 361, Biblioteca Laurenziana, Florence.
8. Vitruvian figure, from Cesariano's *Lucio Vitruvio Pollione de Architectura*, Como, 1521.
9. Vitruvian figure, 'Homo ad circulum'. From Fra Giocondo's *M. Vitruvius per Jocundum*, Venice, 1511.
10. Vitruvian figure, from Francesco Giorgi, *De Harmonia Mundi*, Venice, 1525.
11. Vitruvian figure, 'Homo ad quadratum'. From Fra Giocondo's *M. Vitruvius per Jocundum*, Venice, 1511.
12. Leonardo da Vinci. Designs of churches, Ms.B, Institut de France, Paris.
13. Leonardo da Vinci. Designs of churches, Bibliothèque Nationale 2037, Paris.
14. S. Maria della Consolazione, Todi, 1504.
15. Centralized plans, from Serlio's *Quinto libro dell'architettura*, 1547. From the British Architectural Library, RIBA, London.
16. Giuliano da Sangallo. S. Maria delle Carceri, Prato, 1485. Photograph: The Mansell Collection.
17. Plan of S. Maria delle Carceri, Prato. From the *Taccuino di Giuliano da Sangallo*, Biblioteca Comunale, Siena.
18. S. Maria delle Carceri, Prato. Dome.
19. S. Maria delle Carceri, Prato. Exterior. Photograph: The Mansell Collection.
20. Bramante's Tempietto. From Palladio's *Quattro Libri dell'Architettura*, Book IV, Venice, 1570. From the British Architectural Library, RIBA, London.
21. Palladio's Church at Maser. Plan. From Bertotti Scamozzi, *Le Fabbriche e i Disegni di Andrea Palladio*, Vol. IV, Vicenza, 1776. From the British Architectural Library, RIBA, London.
22. Section of the Church at Maser. From Bertotti Scamozzi, *Le Fabbriche e i Disegni di Andrea Palladio*, Vol. IV. From the British Architectural Library, RIBA, London.

23. Palladio's Church at Maser. Façade.
24. Church at Maser. View of Altar.
25. Bramante's plan of St. Peter's, Rome.
26. Bramante's St. Peter's. Foundation medal by Caradosso, 1506, British Museum, London.
27. Bramante's Dome of St. Peter's. Woodcut from Serlio's *Terzo Libro di Sebastiano Serlio Bolognese*, Venice, 1540. From the British Architectural Library, RIBA, London.
28. Raphael. S. Eligio degli Orefici, Rome. View into dome. From the Warburg Institute, London.
29. Diagrams: pillar and arch, column and arch.
30. Alberti. S. Francesco, Rimini. Façade. Photograph: The Mansell Collection.
31. S. Francesco, Rimini. South side. Photograph: The Mansell Collection.
32. Matteo de' Pasti. Medal of S. Francesco, 1450. Berlin State Museum. From the Warburg Institute, London.
33. S. Francesco, Rimini. Plan.
34. Diagram of the façade of S. Francesco, Rimini.
35. Alberti. S. Maria Novella, Florence. Photograph: The Mansell Collection.
36. S. Maria Novella, Florence. Entrance. Photograph: The Mansell Collection.
37. S. Francesco, Rimini. Entrance. Photograph: The Mansell Collection.
38. Diagram of the façade of S. Maria Novella, Florence.
39. Diagram of the façade of S. Maria Novella, Florence.
40. Alberti. Plan of S. Sebastiano, Mantua.
41. S. Sebastiano, Mantua. Present state of the façade.
42. S. Sebastiano, Mantua. Before the restoration.
43. Giacomo da Pietrasanta. S. Agostino, Rome. Façade, 1479-83. Photograph: The Mansell Collection.
44. Façade of S. Sebastiano, Mantua. Reconstruction of Alberti's 1460 project.
45. Triumphal Arch, Orange, detail. From a drawing by Giuliano da Sangallo, Vatican Library, Rome.
46. Alberti. S. Andrea, Mantua. Façade, 1470 ff.
47. Arch of Trajan, Ancona. Photograph: The Mansell Collection.
48. Alberti. S. Andrea, Mantua. Elevation of the façade. From the Warburg Institute, London.
49. Alberti. S. Andrea, Mantua. Section, interior. From the Warburg Institute, London.
50. S. Francesco, Rimini. Capital from the façade.
51. S. Maria Novella, Florence. Corner of the façade.
52. Giangiorgio Trissino. Villa Trissino, Cricoli, near Vicenza, 1530-38.
53. Villa Trissino, Cricoli. Plan. From Bertotti Scamozzi, *Le Fabbriche e i Disegni di Andrea Palladio*, Vol. II.
54. Peruzzi. Villa Farnesina, Rome, 1509-11. Plan.
55. Palladio. Villa Godi Porto at Lonedo, 1540.
56. Villa Godi Porto. Detail of plan, from Palladio's *Quattro Libri dell'Archi-tettura*, Book II.
57. Schematized plans of eleven of Palladio's Villas: Villa Thiene at Cicogna–Villa Sarego at Miega–Villa Poiana at Poiana Maggiore–Villa Badoer at Fratta, Polesine–Villa Zeno at Cessalto–Villa Cornaro at Piombino Dese–Villa Pisani at Montagnana–Villa Emo at Fanzolo–Villa Malcontenta at

Mira–Villa Pisani at Bagnolo–Villa Rotonda near Vicenza–Geometrical Pattern of Palladio's Villas.

58. Palladio's Reconstruction of the Ancient House. From Barbaro's *I Dieci Libri dell'Architettura di M. Vitruvio*, Venice, 1556.
59. Palladio. Villa Rotonda near Vicenza, 1550.
60. Palladio. Villa Malcontenta, on the Brenta, 1560.
61. Palladio. Villa Emo at Fanzolo, *c.*1567.
62. Palladio. Villa Thiene at Quinto, *c.*1550.
63. Palladio. Villa Maser near Asolo, before 1566.
64. System of Palladio's 'Basilica' at Vicenza. From Palladio's *Quattro Libri dell'Architettura,* Book III. From the British Architectural Library, RIBA, London.
65. Façade for a Venetian palace. From Serlio's *Regole Generali di Architettura*, Venice, 1537.
66. Bramante and Raphael. 'House of Raphael', Rome, after 1510. Engraving by Antonio Lafreri, Gabinetto Nazionale delle Stampe, Rome.
67. Palladio. Palazzo Porto-Colleoni, *c.*1550. Elevation of front and courtyard. Drawing, from the British Architectural Library, RIBA, London.
68. Palladio. Preparatory design for the Palazzo Porto-Colleoni. Drawing, from the British Architectural Library, RIBA, London.
69. Palazzo Porto-Colleoni. From Palladio's *Quattro Libri dell'Architettura,* Book II. From the British Architectural Library, RIBA, London.
70. Palladio. Palazzo Thiene. From Bertotti Scamozzi *Le Fabbriche e i Disegni di Andrea Palladio,* Vol. I. From the British Architectural Library, RIBA, London.
71. Palladio's reconstruction of the Roman House. From Barbaro's *I Dieci Libri dell'Architettura di M. Vitruvio*, 1556.
72. Convent of the Carità, Venice, 1561. From Palladio's *Quattro Libri dell'Architettura*, Book II. From the British Architectural Library, RIBA, London.
73. Palladio. Palazzo Antonini at Udine, 1556. From *Quattro Libri dell'Architettura*, Book II. From the British Architectural Library, RIBA, London.
74. Palladio. Palazzo Chiericati, Vicenza, 1550. Photograph: The Mansell Collection.
75. Palazzo Chiericati. From Palladio's *Quattro Libri dell'Architettura,* Book II. From the British Architectural Library, RIBA, London.
76. Detail of Palladio's 'Piazza dei Latini'. From *Quattro Libri dell'Architettura*, Book III. From the British Architectural Library, RIBA, London.
77. Palladio. Palazzo Thiene, Vicenza. Detail of ground-floor.
78. Palazzo Thiene, Vicenza. Detail of elevation. From Haupt's *Palazzi dell' Italia settentrionale e della Toscana dal secolo XIII al XVIII*, Berlin, 1907.
79. Palazzo Thiene, Vicenza. Façade *c.*1556.
80. Palladio. Drawing of the Roman arches of the Temple of Claudius at Celio, Museo Civico, Vicenza.
81. Palladio. Palazzo Valmarana, Vicenza, 1556.
82. Palazzo Valmarana, detail.
83. Palazzo Valmarana. From Palladio's *Quattro Libri dell'Architettura*, Book II. From the British Architectural Library, RIBA, London.
84. Palladio. Drawing of a Roman wall at Verona. From the British Architectural Library, RIBA, London.

85. Palladio. Loggia del Capitanio, Vicenza, 1571.
86. Side front of the Loggia del Capitanio. From Haupt's *Palazzi dell'Italia settentrionale e della Toscana, dal secolo XIII al XVIII.*
87. Detail of the side front of the Loggia del Capitanio.
88. Arch of Septimius Severus, Rome. Photograph: The Mansell Collection.
89. Palladio's decoration for Henri III's visit to Venice, 1574. Painting by Andrea Vicentino, Palazzo Ducale, Venice. Photograph: The Mansell Collection.
90. Palladio. S. Francesco della Vigna, Venice, 1562. From Bertotti Scamozzi, *Le Fabbriche e i Disegni di Andrea Palladio*, Vol. IV. From the British Architectural Library, RIBA, London.
91. Palladio. Design for S. Giorgio Maggiore, Venice. From the British Architectural Library, RIBA, London.
92. S. Francesco della Vigna: schematic representation of the two interpenetrating temple fronts.
93. Palladio. S. Giorgio Maggiore, Venice, 1566-1610. From Bertotti Scamozzi, *Le Fabbriche e i Disegni di Andrea Palladio*, Vol IV. From the British Architectural Library, RIBA, London.
94. Bramante. Design for S. Maria di S. Satiro, Milan, *c*.1480. Cabinet des dessins, Musée du Louvre, Paris.
95. Cesariano's reconstruction of the Basilica at Fano. From *Di Lucio Vitruvio Pollione de Architectura*, Como, 1521. From the British Architectural Library, RIBA, London.
96. Palladio's design of the Pantheon. From Burlington's *Fabbriche Antiche Disegnate da Andrea Palladio*, 1730. From the Warburg Institute, London.
97. Baldassarre Peruzzi (?). Cathedral at Carpi, 1515.
98. Palladio. Il Redentore, Venice, 1576-92. From Bertotti Scamozzi, *Le Fabbriche e i Disegni di Andrea Palladio*, Vol. IV. From the British Architectural Library, RIBA, London.
99. Il Redentore, Venice. Façade. Photograph: The Mansell Collection.
100. Andrea Tirali. S. Vitale, Venice, 1700.
101. Giuseppe Valadier. S. Rocco, Rome. Façade, 1834.
102. Francesco Maria Preti. Cathedral, Castelfranco. Façade, 1723.
103. Palladio. S. Giorgio Maggiore, Venice. Section, from the British Architectural Library, RIBA, London.
104. S. Giorgio Maggiore, Venice. Plan, from the British Architectural Library, RIBA, London.
105. Palladio. Il Redentore, Venice. View of the Presbytery and Nave.
106. S. Giorgio Maggiore. View of the Nave. Photograph: The Mansell Collection.
107. Il Redentore, Venice, 1576-92. Photograph: The Mansell Collection.
108 - Section and plan of Il Redentore (with visual lines drawn in). From
109. Bertotti Scamozzi, *Le Fabbriche e i Disegni di Andrea Palladio*, Vol. IV. From the British Architectural Library, RIBA, London.
110 Palladio. Plans for S. Nicola da Tolentino, Venice, 1579. Drawings, from
111. the British Architectural Library, RIBA, London.
112. Leonardo da Vinci. Study in human proportion, showing the ratios 1:3:1:2:1:2, Royal Library, Windsor.
113. Villard de Honnecourt. Page from his sketch-book, Bibliothèque Nationale, Paris.

114. Plan of S. Francesco della Vigna, Venice.
115. Diagram of the harmonic consonances. From Francesco Giorgi's *De Harmonia Mundi*, 1525.
116. Diagram showing relation between metopes and triglyphs in Solomon's Temple. From H. Prado and G. B. Villalpando's *In Ezechielem Explanationes*, Rome, 1596-1604, Vol. II.
117. Gafurio Lecturing. From Franchino Gafurio's *De Harmonia musicorum Instrumentorum*, Milan, 1518 (frontispiece).
118. Tubalcain, Pythagoras and Philolaos. From Franchino Gafurio's *Theorica Musice*, Milan, 1492 (frontispiece).
119. Pythagorean Musical Scale. Detail from Raphael's *School of Athens*, Vatican, Rome.
120. Construction of a door. From Serlio's *Primo Libro dell'Architettura*.
121. Villa Malcontenta on the Brenta. From Palladio's *Quattro Libri dell'Architettura*, Book II. From the British Architectural Library, RIBA, London.
122. Villa Thiene at Cicogna. Plan. From Palladio's *Quattro Libri dell'Architettura*, Book II. From the British Architectural Library, RIBA, London.
123. Villa Pisani at Bagnolo. From Palladio's *Quattro Libri dell'Architettura*, Book II. From the British Architectural Library, RIBA, London.
124. Villa Emo at Fanzolo. From Palladio's *Quattro Libri dell'Architettura*, Book II. From the British Architectural Library, RIBA, London.
125. Villa Sarego at Miega. From Palladio's *Quattro Libri dell'Architettura*, Book II. From the British Architectural Library, RIBA, London.
126. Villa Maser near Asolo. From Palladio's *Quattro Libri dell'Architettura*, Book II. From the British Architectural Library, RIBA, London.
127. Page from J. Gwilt's *Rudiments of Architecture*, 1825. From the British Architectural Library, RIBA, London.
128. Page from Cesariano's *Di Lucio Vitruvio Pollione de Architectura*, Como, 1521. From the British Architectural Library, RIBA, London.

We are grateful to Margot Wittkower who supplied the majority of illustrations, and to the British Architectural Library, RIBA, London, the Mansell Collection, London, and the Warburg Institute, London, for their help and for allowing us to reproduce items in their possession.

Andrea Palladio, Il Redentore, Venice, 1576-92. From Bertotti Scamozzi

PART I

THE CENTRALLY PLANNED CHURCH AND THE RENAISSANCE

Renaissance architecture is nowadays usually interpreted in terms which stress its worldliness. At best it is argued that the classical apparatus of forms was used on an equal level for sacred, profane and domestic buildings; that the classical forms were adapted for different purposes without any gradation of meaning; and that consequently, Renaissance architecture is an architecture of pure form.[1] Often in discussions of Renaissance architecture this underlying assumption is silently taken for granted. If this customary interpretation of Renaissance architecture as a profane style is correct, then what would be the essential difference between the eclecticism of the fifteenth and sixteenth centuries and that of the nineteenth century? If both are derivative styles – in the sense that they derive from classical antiquity – is the difference between them only that nineteenth-century architecture, as far as it is classical and not Gothic, is twice removed from the ancient models? The true answer appears to lie elsewhere. In contrast to nineteenth-century classical architecture, Renaissance architecture, like every great style of the past, was based on a hierarchy of values culminating in the absolute values of sacred architecture. We maintain, in other words, that the forms of the Renaissance church have symbolical value or, at least, that they are charged with a particular meaning which the pure forms as such do not contain. Both the theory and the practice of Renaissance architects are unambiguous in this respect.

Builders of fifteenth-century churches in Italy gradually turn away from the traditional Latin-Cross plan consisting of the long nave, transept and choir. Instead, they advocate centrally planned churches, and these churches have always been regarded as the climax of Renaissance architecture. But in spite of the contrary evidence of the architects themselves, in the eyes of architectural historians such plans have become something like a touchstone of Renaissance paganism and worldliness.[2] Since centrally planned churches appear to be unsatisfactory from a liturgical point of view – how can one separate in such a church clergy and laity? where is one to place the altar, etc.? – it is usually held that the craving for beauty was here given preference over the necessities of the service.[3] Thus the line art-historians have generally taken falls in with the attitude of those historians who emphasize the irreligious aspect of the Renaissance. Their interpretation derives from the simple – not to say naïve – formula that mediaeval transcendental religion was replaced by the autonomy of man in the Renaissance. A new discussion of the ideas underlying ecclesiastical

1 The extreme statement of misrepresentation will be found in Ruskin's *Stones of Venice*, Vol. III, chap iv, par. 35: 'Pagan in its origin, proud and unholy in its revival, paralysed in its old age . . . an architecture invented, as it seems, to make plagiarists of its architects, slaves of its workmen, and sybarites of its inhabitants; an architecture in which intellect is idle, invention impossible, but in which all luxury is gratified and all insolence fortified.' Geoffrey Scott in *The Architecture of Humanism*, London, 1924, attacks this view, but his results are equally disputable: 'The Renaissance style . . . is an architecture of taste, seeking no logic, consistency, or justification beyond that of giving pleasure' (p. 192).
2 P. Frankl, *Die Entwicklungsphasen der neueren Baukunst*, 1914, p. 148 ff., in his inspiring discussion of the relations between the liturgy and the Renaissance church, is still dependent on Burckhardt's conception of the Renaissance when he maintains that 'weit stärker als der christliche Zweck . . . ein heidnischer Geist die Form bestimmt . . .'(p. 151).
Burckhardt himself changed his ideas about the meaning of centrally built churches. In the *Cicerone* (9th ed., 1904, II, p 131) he says that the old ritual nave type was abandoned 'als die Renaissance sich ihrem freien Schönheitssinn überliess.' And (p. 259): 'Wenn nur etwas Schönes und Bedeutendes zustande kam, das der Bestimmung im Ganzen entsprach, so fragte der Bauherr nach keiner Tradition.' Later, in the *Geschichte der Renaissance in Italien*, he modified this opinion in the chapters which contain what is still the most important summary of centralized church architecture in Italy. 'Im Süden ist das Grosse und Schöne von selber heilig', and further: 'die Renaissance hat den Zentralbau einer künftigen Religiosität zum Vermächtnis hinterlassen' (6th ed., 1920, p. 114).
3 D. Frey, *Bramantes St. Peter-Entwurf und seine Apokryphen*, Vienna, 1915, contains many shrewd observations on the general character of Renaissance architecture. But he seems to us to go wrong in his final conclusion: 'Diese Baukunst war ebenso wenig profan als religiös; wenn sie sich heidnisch-antik gebärdete, so war das kein Bekenntnis der

15

1. Construction of square and polygons. From Bartoli's edition of Alberti's *De re aedificatoria*, 1550

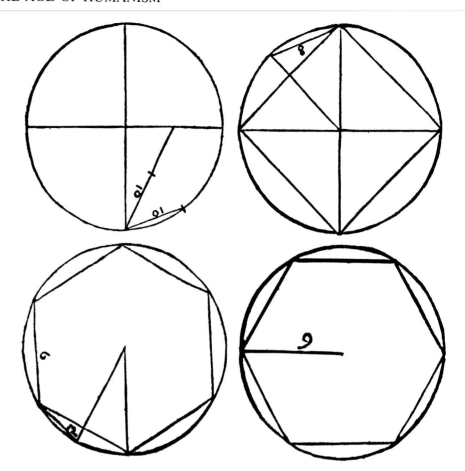

Gesinnung, kein Programm; es war im Herzen recht gut christlich gedacht und empfunden. Was sie unreligiös erscheinen lässt, ist das Fehlen eines Zweckinhalts; sie sah ebenso wenig ihre Aufgabe in der künstlerischen Gestaltung der Kultbedürfnisse als der gesellschaftlich-sozialen Lebensforderungen, sie folgte abstrakten Schönheitsnormen und versuchte in souveräner Umkehrung nach diesen das Leben zu gestalten' (p. 89).

The present position is summarized in N. Pevsner's *Outline of European Architecture*, London, 1948; he maintains that in the centralized church 'the religious meaning of the church is replaced by a human one . . .'(p. 83), that architects created the central plan for churches 'to eternalize the present' (p. 84), and that 'Man is in the church no longer pressing forward to reach a transcendental goal but enjoying the beauty that surrounds him and the glorious sensation of being the centre of this beauty' (p. 83).

Catholic authors like F.X. Kraus and J. Sauer, *Geschichte der christlichen Kunst*, Freiburg, 1908, II. 2, particularly p. 664 ff., rejected the 'pagan' interpretation of centralized church architecture (see also L. V. Pastor, *History of the Popes*, Vol. III), without, however, attempting or being able to explain its specifically 'Christian' character.

4 Cecil Grayson has recently shown convincingly (KUNSTCHRONIK, XIII, 1960, p. 359 ff. and MÜNCHNER JAHRB. DER BILD. KUNST, XI, 1960) that the bulk of the work was written between 1443 and 1452.

5 First ed. of 1485, fol. p. iiii *verso*; Ital. ed. of 1550, Bk. VII, chap. 4, p. 206.

6 At the end of this chapter Alberti introduces yet another 'temple' form which he calls the 'Etruscan Temple', following partly Vitruvius IV, 7. Cf. the illuminating remarks by Max Theuer, *Leon Battista Alberti, Zehn Bücher über die Baukunst*, 1912, p. 619 f.

architecture during the Renaissance will, it is hoped, clear the ground for a more correct understanding of the architects' intentions and, at the same time, help to elucidate the element of tradition in some important currents of Renaissance thought.

1. Alberti's Programme of the Ideal Church

The views of fifteenth- and sixteenth-century architects are available in sufficient detail to give a fairly correct picture of their ideas. In fact, the first architectural treatise of the Renaissance, Alberti's *De re aedificatoria* (written about 1450),[4] contains the first full programme of the ideal church of the Renaissance. The seventh book of this work deals with the building and decoration of sacred architecture. Alberti's survey of desirable shapes for temples – his synonym for churches – begins with a eulogy of the circle. Nature herself, he declares, enjoys the round form above all others as is proved by her own creations such as the globe, the stars, the trees, animals and their nests, and many other things.[5] Alberti recommends nine basic geometrical figures in all for churches: apart from the circle, he lists the square, the hexagon, the octagon, the decagon and the dodecagon. All these figures are determined by the circle and Alberti explains how to derive the lengths of their sides from the radius of the circle into which they are inscribed (Fig. 1). In addition to these six figures he mentions three developments from the square, namely the square plus one-half, the square plus one-third and the square doubled.[6]

These nine basic forms can be enriched by chapels. For plans derived from the square Alberti suggests one chapel at the far end, or, in addition, a central chapel at each side, or an odd number of chapels at each side. Circular plans may be given six or eight chapels; polygonal ones may either have a chapel to each wall or to alternate walls. The shape of the chapels should be rectangular or semi-circular; both types may alternate. It is evident that by adding small geometrical units to the basic figures of circle and polygon a great variety of composite geometrical configurations can be produced which all have the one element in common; that corresponding points on the circumference have exactly the same relation to the focal point in the centre.

Alberti does not directly express preference for any of the shapes recommended by him. But a bias in favour of the round form seems to be implied, judging from his remarks about nature's love for the round. For nature aspires to absolute perfection,[7] she is the best and divine teacher of all things[8] – 'la natura, cioè Idio . . .'[9]

It is well known that for his ideas on centralized planning Alberti, like other architects after him, was inspired by classical structures, though hardly by classical temples.[10] Yet, it is true, that Renaissance architects believed many of the vast number of circular and polygonal ancient ruins to have been temples in antiquity[11] and, in addition, they regarded such Early Christian buildings as Sto. Stefano Rotondo, Sta. Costanza, the octagonal Baptistery near the Lateran and even the twelfth-century octagon of the Florentine Baptistery as Roman temples turned into Christian churches. It can therefore be inferred that Alberti saw here – in spite of Vitruvius' relative silence about centralized plans of temples[12] – a continuity from ancient sacred architecture to the Early Christian church, and took this as historical justification for advocating a return to the venerable forms of temples of the ancients. Alberti was consciously linking his own ideas with those of the early Christians. Emperor Constantine's Rome had a particular attraction for him and other men of his time, because it was then, and only then, that pagan antiquity was blended with the spirit of faith and purity of the early Church. Thus Alberti makes a strong plea for going back to the liturgical usage of the period when churches had only one altar 'to celebrate only one Sacrifice in a Day'.[13] But whatever his reasoning, the stress he laid on circular and polygonal churches reveals his passion for the centralized geometrical plan.

A controversy during the erection of the choir of the SS. Annunziata in Florence shows that opinions on classical centralized structures were by no means unanimous. Work on this building had been interrupted for fifteen years and when, in 1470, Alberti carried on Michelozzo's unfinished choir, fashioned after the 'temple' of Minerva Medica, a 'reactionary' critic turned against continuing this copy after the antique. His argument was exactly the reverse of that which recommended Michelozzo's design to Alberti, for he alleged that such classical buildings had not been temples in antiquity but tombs of emperors, and were therefore unsuitable as models for churches.[14] It was this liturgical unsuitability of Michelozzo's plan which had been severely censured about twenty-five years before by the aged Brunelleschi.[15] And precisely this question of suitability was approached from a new angle during the second half of the fifteenth century. Alberti's silence on this point suggests that he did not

7 *De re aed.*, Bk. IX, chap. 5. Cf. below Part IV, p. 109.

8 Alberti, *I primi tre libri della famiglia*, ed. F.C. Pellegrini, Florence, 1911, p. 188: '. . . natura optima e divina maestra di tutte le cose.'

9 *Della famiglia, ed. cit.*, p. 236: 'Fece la natura, cioè Idio, l'uomo composto parte celeste e divino, parte sopra ogni mortale cosa formossissimo et nobilissimo.' We may translate somewhat freely: 'Nature, that is, God, united in Man celestial and divine elements with those that make him the best shaped and noble among things mortal.' This remark should not be interpreted as a pantheistic confession; cf. Paul-Henri Michel, *La pensée de L.B. Alberti*, Paris, 1930, p. 536 ff., who devotes a penetrating analysis to this passage.

10 With the exception of the Pantheon, which was and remained of course the most influential classical building, and the two small peripteral temples at Rome and Tivoli, no round or polygonal classical temple survives.

11 Above all, the nymphaeum of the Orti Liciniani, then and still known as the temple of Minerva Medica. Alberti's inclusion of the decagon among his shapes for churches is, no doubt, due to this prototype. See also p. 32, note 102.

12 There is no mention of round temples in Vitruvius' Third Book amongst his seven classes of temples. Round temples appear together with Tuscan temples as a kind of appendix to Book IV.

13 Bk. VII, chap. 13. In spite of his assertion that he leaves it to the judgment of others whether there should be one or more altars in a church, he has some sharp words about contemporary abuses in placing in a church as many altars as possible.

14 Cf. Gaye, *Carteggio inedito d'artisti . . .*, Florence, 1839, I, p. 232, also p. 226 ff.; L.H. Heydenreich, 'Die Tribuna der SS. Annunziata in Florenz,' in MITTEILUNGEN DES KUNSTHIST. INST. IN FLORENZ, III, 1930, p. 277 ff. – In a recent paper S. Lang submitted the hypothesis that the SS. Annunziata was planned as an imitation of the Holy Sepulchre (JOURNAL OF THE WARBURG AND COURTAULD INST. XVII, 1954, p. 288 ff.)

15 Braghirolli, 'Die Baugeschichte der Tribuna der SS. Annunziata in Florenz', in REPERTORIUM F. KUNSTW., II, 1879, p. 272; Heydenreich, *loc. cit.*

acknowledge the existence of the problem.[16]

It is strange that the normal and traditional type of church, the basilica, was not among those recommended by Alberti. The fact that churches were built in the form of the basilica appears only incidentally when Alberti explains that the habit was introduced by the early Christians who used private Roman basilicas as their places of worship.[17] This is the only mention of basilicas in the chapters about 'temples'. But Alberti made his position clear in the introductory chapter of the same book: the basilica, as the seat of jurisdiction in antiquity, is for him closely related to the temple. Justice is a gift of God: man obtains divine justice through piety and exercises human justice through jurisdiction. Thus temple and basilica as the seats of divine and human justice are intimately related, and in that sense the basilica belongs to the domain of religion.[18] In keeping with this, Alberti explains in a later chapter on basilicas that the basilica partakes of the decoration belonging to temples. However, the beauty of the temple is more sublime, and cannot and should not be rivalled by that of the basilica.[19] Thus in Alberti's system the time-honoured form of the church, the basilica, has been relegated from its divine to a human function, and it is evident that Alberti must exclude the basilica from being used for churches.

Alberti is explicit about the character of the ideal church. It should be the noblest ornament of a city and its beauty should surpass imagination. It is this staggering beauty which awakens sublime sensations and arouses piety in the people. It has a purifying effect and produces the state of innocence which is pleasing to God.[20] What is this staggering beauty that has so powerful an effect? According to Alberti's well-known mathematical definition, based on Vitruvius, beauty consists in a rational integration of the proportions of all the parts of a building in such a way that every part has its absolutely fixed size and shape and nothing could be added or taken away without destroying the harmony of the whole.[21] This conformity of ratios and correspondence of all the parts, this organic geometry should be observed in every building but above all in churches.[22] We may now conclude that no geometrical form is more apt to fulfil this demand than the circle or forms deriving from it. In such centralized plans the geometrical pattern will appear absolute, immutable, static and entirely lucid. Without that organic geometrical equilibrium where all the parts are harmonically related like the members of a body,[23] divinity cannot reveal itself.

Consequently we find minute guidance for all the proportions of the ideal church. Alberti discusses, for instance, the size of the chapels in relation to the central core of the building and in relation to the wall space between them, or the height of the structure in relation to the diameter of the ground plan. To give at least one concrete example: the height of the wall up to the vaulting in round churches should be one-half, two-thirds or three-quarters of the diameter of the plan.[24] These proportions of one to two, two to three, and three to four conform to the all-pervading law of harmony as Alberti demonstrates in his ninth book.[25]

It is obvious that such mathematical relations between plan and section cannot be correctly perceived when one walks about in a building. Alberti knew that, of course, quite as well as we do. We must therefore conclude that the harmonic perfection of the geometrical scheme represents an absolute value, independent of our subjective and transitory perception. And it will be seen later that for Alberti – as for other Renaissance artists – this man-created harmony was a visible echo of a celestial and universally valid harmony.

16 Alberti is, however, concerned with the position of the altar. He wants to have the main chapel one-twelfth larger ('dignitatis gratia') than the other chapels (VII, chap. 4). There should be only one altar in the main chapel (VII, chap. 13); cf. p. 17, note 13.

17 Bk. VII, chap. 3.

18 Bk. VII, chap. 1. This important passage has been misinterpreted. The original text, fol. o viii verso, runs: 'Quae pietas una est primaria iustitiae pars: ac iustitiam quidem ipsam per se divinum quoddam esse munus quis non assentiatur. Et iustitiae pars etiam est huic superiori finitima et dignitate praecipua superisque multo gratissima ac perinde sacratissima: qua erga homines pacis tranquillitatisque gratia utimur: dum esse pro meritis quibusque retributum velimus: idcirco basilicam ubi vis dandum sit religioni adiudicabimus.'

19 Bk. VII, chap. 14.

20 Summary of the beginning of Bk. VII, chap. 3. Cf. the good characterization of Alberti's prescriptions for religious buildings in Paul-Henri Michel, op. cit., p. 542. ff.

21 Cf. below Part II, p. 41.

22 Bk. VII, chap. 5, ed. 1485, fol. p vi: 'Sed quemadmodum in animante caput, pes: et qualecunque velis membrum ad caetera membra atque ad totum reliquum corpus referendum est: ita et in aedificio maximeque in templo conformandae universae partes corporis sunt: ut inter se omnes correspondeant: ut quavis una illarum sumpta eadem ipsa caeterae omnes partes dimetiantur.'

23 Cf. note 22.

24 Bk. VII, chap. 10. Alberti gives here also a ratio of 11:4 which has not been satisfactorily interpreted; an attempt by Theuer, op. cit., p. 628. But recently V. Zoubov (in BIBLOTHÈQUE D'HUMANISME ET RENAISSANCE, XXII, 1960, 56) has suggested an acceptable explanation.

25 For a detailed discussion cf. below Parts II and IV, pp. 50, 105, 111 f.

26 Bk. VII, chaps. 3 and 5.

27 Bk. VII, chap. 5. Alberti obviously had in mind the two classical types of the Pantheon and the Vesta temple.

28 Bk. VII, chap. 6. Cf. below, p. 42, note 12.

29 Bk. VII, chap. 11, ed. 1485, fol. r ii: 'Templis tectum dignitatis gratia atque etiam perpetuitatis maxime esse testudinatum velim.'

30 Bk. VII, chap. 10, ed. 1485, fol. r i: 'Mihi quidem perfacile persuadebitur coloris aeque atque vitae puritatem et simplicitatem superis optimis gratissimam esse.'

31 ibid., and fol. r i v.

32 ibid. 'Sed velim in templis cum pariete tum et pavimento nihil adsit quod meram philosophiam non sapiat.'

33 ibid. 'Maximeque pavimentum refertum velim

Apart from this concern for proportion, Alberti's advice embraces everything from the general appearance of the church down to the details of the decoration. A church should not only stand on elevated ground, free on all sides, in a beautiful square, but it should also be isolated by a substructure, a high base, from the everyday life that surrounds it.[26] The façade should be formed by a portico in the ancient manner, and round churches should also be given such a portico or be surrounded by a colonnade.[27] Arches are used in theatres and basilicas, but they do not accord with the dignity of churches; for these, only the austere form of columns with straight entablature is appropriate.[28] In contrast to basilicas, and in keeping with their dignity, churches must be vaulted; moreover, vaults guarantee perpetuity to churches.[29] The chastity of the church should not be compromised by lax appeals to the senses. There should be splendour, particularly in the use of precious materials. But just as Cicero, following Plato, thought that white was the colour for temples, so Alberti was 'entirely convinced that purity and simplicity of colour – as in life – is most pleasing to God'.[30] Pictures are preferable to frescoes, and statuary is preferable to pictures,[31] but whatever decoration is used on walls and pavement should pertain to 'pure philosophy'.[32] Thus there should be inscriptions admonishing us to be just, modest, simple, virtuous and pious, and the pavement, above all, should show 'lines and figures pertaining to music and geometry so that everywhere the education of the mind is stimulated'.[33] This last recommendation sounds particularly strange and it can only be understood if we are aware that for Alberti – who follows here a tradition unbroken from classical times – music and geometry are fundamentally one and the same; that music is geometry translated into sound, and that in music the very same harmonies are audible which inform the geometry of the building.[34] Finally, windows should be so high that no contact with the fleeting everyday life outside is possible and that one can see nothing but the sky.[35] The most dignified ornaments for vaults and domes are coffers in the manner of the Pantheon, but a cosmic significance for the dome is also suggested by a painted representation of the sky.[36] A cosmic interpretation of the dome was common from antiquity onwards and was kept alive, above all, in the Eastern Church.[37]

Alberti gives here a complete picture of the humanist conception of ecclesiastical architecture; it is apparent that for him humanism and religion were entirely compatible. And let it be said emphatically: it is a serene, philosophical and almost puritanical architecture that his descriptions conjure up before us. This was clearly felt in his own day by people who cherished the old traditions. The critic of the centralized choir of the SS. Annunziata, who has been quoted before, protests also against Alberti's wish to paint the whole choir white and leave it without any ornament whatsoever. The church, in his view, would appear 'poor and desolate'.[38] But Alberti set the standards for generations of architects with a classical bias who made his ideas and stipulations their own. For them the new forms of the Renaissance church embodied sincere religious feeling no less than did the Gothic cathedral for the mediaeval builder.

*   *   *   *   *

Filarete shows in his picturesque treatise, written shortly after the *De re aedificatoria*, that he had read Alberti to advantage,[39] and in some respects he

esse lineis et figuris: quae ad res musicas et geometricas pertineant: ut omni ex parte ad animi cultum excitemur.'

34 Cf. Part IV for the Renaissance interpretation of music and geometry.

35 Bk. VII, chap. 12; ed. 1485, fol. r iii: 'Apertiones fenestrarum in templis esse oportet modicas et sublimes: unde nihil praeter caelum spectes: unde et qui sacrum faciunt qui ve supplicant nequicquam ab re divina mentibus distrabantur.'

36 Bk. VII, chap. 11 (fol. r ii *v* and r iii). For the parallelism of dome and sky cf. also Bk. III, chap. 14 (fol. g iii).

37 The dome as symbol of the sky has a long pedigree. The material for the celestial character of domes in antiquity has been collected in an exemplary manner by Karl Lehmann, 'The Dome of Heaven', ART BULLETIN, XXVII, 1945, p. 1 ff. For Dio Cassius' comparison of the dome of the Pantheon with the sky cf. *ibid*., p. 22 (see also Robert Eisler, *Weltenmantel und Himmelszelt*, 1910, p. 614, with further examples of cosmic interpretations of vaulting). Lehmann followed the conception up into the Western, Islamic and Byzantine worlds. A Syriac seventh-century hymn about the destroyed church of Santa Sophia at Edessa with a description of the dome as a symbol of the sky, was unknown to him; cf. A. Grabar, 'Le témoignage d'une hymne Syriaque sur l'architecture de la Cathédrale d'Edesse au VIe siècle et sur la symbolique de l'édifice Chrétien', CAHIERS ARCHÉOLOGIQUES, II, 1947, p. 41 ff. Grabar has shown the dependence of the symbolism of this hymn on Dionysius the Areopagite whose mystical neo-Platonism, alive throughout the Middle Ages, was revived by Nicholas of Cusa and the Florentine Platonists. A cosmic interpretation of the dome remained common well into the eighteenth century. Cf. also the stimulating book by Louis Hautecœur, *Mystique et architecture. Symbolisme du cercle et de la coupole*, Paris, 1954.

It is worth pointing out that the Latin term *coelum* for roof or ceiling (cf. Lehmann, p. 27) was adopted by the Italians, cf. e.g. Serlio, *Terzo libro*, etc., ed. 1600, p. 52: 'essa volta o vogliamo dire cielo'.

38 Gaye, *op. cit.*, p. 232: '... se questa tribuna si facessi tutta bianca senza altri ornamenti dalle capelle in su, parrà una cosa povera e spogliata ...'

39 Filarete, *Tractat über die Baukunst*, ed. W. von Oettingen, Vienna, 1890 (Eitelber-Ilgs Quellenschr. N.F. Vol. 3), pp. 39, 47. Filarete's treatise was written *c*.1457-64 for Francesco I Sforza, but dedicated after the latter's death to Piero de' Medici. John R. Spencer (RIVISTA D'ARTE, XXXI, 1956, p. 93 ff.) argues with good reason that the treatise was composed between May 1461 and the end of 1462.

throws a rather unexpected light on the emotional reaction of Renaissance people to certain forms. He must have had the Renaissance dome in mind when he said: 'We Christians build our churches high, so that those who enter feel themselves elevated and the soul can rise to the contemplation of God'.[40] We also hear about the soothing effect of the circle; for 'in looking at a circle the glance sweeps round instantaneously without interruption or obstacle'.[41] So Alberti's cosmic philosophical consideration of the round form is here supplemented by a psychological and visual approach. And from now on the geometry of the circle plays an ever more prominent part.

Francesco di Giorgio based his advice to church builders on empirical deduction: he argued that the innumerable types of churches in existence can be reduced to three principal ones:[42] first, the round form which he declared to be the most perfect; secondly, the rectangular; and thirdly, a composite of both forms. To the first type belong all the polygons, the second type is the nave type of church comprising all the figures deriving from the rectangle, and the third type combines the nave with a centralized arrangement for crossing, choir and transept. The latter type is composite in the proper sense of the word, for each of the two parts follows the rules and norms of the type to which it belongs.

The composite type had a long monumental history in Italy, from the Cathedrals at Pisa, Siena and Florence, to the Chiesa della Casa Santa at Loreto and the Cathedral at Pavia. If completed, Alberti's S. Francesco at Rimini (Fig. 31) would have been a composite church with a dome area of staggering dimensions. Francesco di Giorgio demonstrates by means of the inscribed human figure how to weld together organically the centralized and the longitudinal parts of such a church design (Fig. 2).[43] The centralized eastern end is developed from the basic geometrical figures of circle and square. Leonardo shared Francesco di Giorgio's views on the composite church: in one of his theoretical designs the centralized part is constructed *per se* according to the 'proper rules and norms' (Fig. 3).[44] These drawings illustrate the overwhelming importance which the centralized part of such designs held for Renaissance architects: nothing could be more significant than the meeting of all the radii in the ideal centre of Francesco di Giorgio's design or the closely knit geometrical pattern of Leonardo's plan.

Francesco di Giorgio's keen interest in centralized plans becomes apparent when turning over the pages of his manuscripts; the example here shown (Fig. 5) displays systematic evolutions of the circle with and without portico, the square with inscribed circle and circular chapels, and the octagon with attached circular chapels.[45] In all these designs the integrity of each geometrical form is carefully preserved. Moreover, Francesco di Giorgio reiterates, with a strong Aristotelian bias, Alberti's ideas; there are full statements on the theory of organic proportion and minute directions are given for 'simmetria' and 'commensurazione' from the general planning down to doors and windows.[46] There is a philosophical discourse on the hierarchy in building culminating in the house of God which must be worthy of the perfection of God Himself.[47] Among his complex requirements for churches we find the postulate of the semi-circular dome, and we find, above all, a discussion of the liturgical problem of assigning the proper place for the altar in the centralized church.[48]

It will be remembered that Alberti was silent on this important point. But in the thirty years between Alberti and Francesco di Giorgio, with centralized

40 *ibid.*, Bk. VII, p. 221.

41 *ibid.*, Bk. VIII, p. 273 f: 'Quando vedi uno archo mezzo tondo, l'occhio tuo non è impedito niente quando tu lo risguardi; così quando tu vedi uno cerchio tondo, l'occhio, o vuoi dire la vista, come tu il guardi, subito la vista lo circunda intorno al primo sguardo, et transcorsa la vista, che non à ritegnio nè ostaculo nessuno.' The same arguments are repeated for the semi-circular arch. Cf. also D. Frey, *op. cit.*, p. 74 f.

42 C. Promis and Cesare Saluzzo, *Trattato di architettura civile e militare di Giorgio Martini*, Turin, 1841, Bk. IV, chap. 2, p. 102. This treatise was probably written after 1482, but Francesco di Giorgio's literary activity began at a considerably earlier date. On the problem of dating the work, which was not finished until 1492, see Horst De La Croix, in ART BULLETIN, XLII, 1960, p. 269, note 22.

43 Illustration from Cod. Magliab. of the Bibl. Naz., Florence (Cod. II. I. 141) after Roberto Papini, *Francesco di Giorgio architetto*, Florence, 1946, II, Fig. 69. For Francesco di Giorgio's procedure, cf. now H. Millon, 'The Architectural Theory of F. di G.', ART BULLETIN, XL, 1958, p. 257 ff.

44 Paris, Inst. de France MS.B, fol. 24r; see J.P. Richter, *The Literary Works of Leonardo da Vinci*, 2nd ed., 1939, II, Pl. 96. About the relation of this drawing to the Cathedral of Pavia, cf. L.H. Heydenreich, *Die Sakralbaustudien Leonardo da Vincis* (Diss. Hamburg), 1929, p. 68 ff., with further literature and a valuable discussion of the 'composite' type of church.

45 Cf. Roberto Papini, *op. cit.*, II, Fig. 288. Bibl. Laurenziana, Cod. Ashburnham, 361, fol. 12r. See also p. 25, note 59; p. 26, note 70.

46 Bk. IV, chap. 1 ff.

47 Bk. IV, prologo.

48 Bk. IV, chap. 2, p. 103 and chap. 7, p. 115 f.

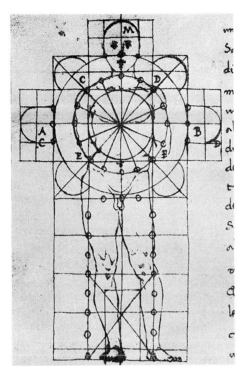

2. Francesco di Giorgio. Drawing
from Codex Magliabechiano

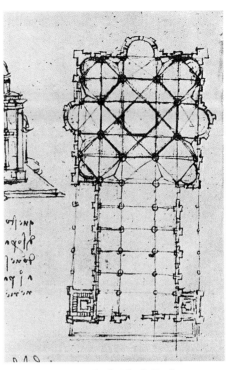

3. Leonardo da Vinci. Design
of a church (detail)

4. Francesco di Giorgio. Studies in
proportion. From the Turin Codex

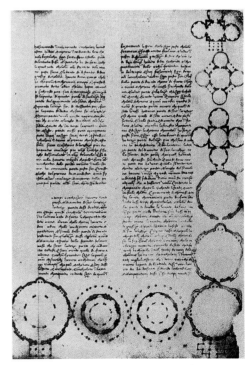

5. Francesco di Giorgio. Page from
Codex Ashburnham 361

49 *ibid.*, p. 115: 'Molti dicono che per dimostrare Dio essere in nobiltà e perfezione lungi da noi per infinita distanza, è conveniente che il simulacro sia più distante dalla porta principale che si può, e questo luogo non è se non appresso alla circonferenza opposita alla porta.' These critics also oppose the central position of the altar for practical liturgical reasons.

50 *ibid.*, p. 116: '. . . come Dio è presente in ogni luogo e creatura, e di quella cagione conservante a cui tutte le creature hanno rispetto, pare conveniente che così il sacramento o simulacro sia nel centro del tempio, come luogo più indifferente e comune a tutte le parti del tempio, e come al centro tutte le linee della circonferenza concorrono e hanno rispetto. L'altra (scil. ragione) è, come Cristo ne insegna, che dove sono più congregati nel nome Suo, Esso essere in mezzo di quelli: così è conveniente il simulacro o sacramento essere in mezzo degli uomini congregati per laudarlo nel tempio: e perchè nella circonferenza sono più luoghi comuni e di una medesima dignità, ed il luogo del centro è unico e assoluto di tutti gli altri, pare per ciò che sia conveniente, a similitudine di Colui il quale solo veramente è, e tutte le altre cose sono ombra a Lui comparate.'

51 For the tradition of Bramante as writer cf. J. Von Schlosser, *Kunstliteratur*, 1924, p. 129 f. According to A.F. Doni's *La seconda libreria* (Venice, 1555, p. 44) those who study Bramante's *Pratica* 'recognize immediately whether a building is proportioned or not, and can say of all the parts whether they form a harmonious whole'. The contemporary testimonies by Cesariano and Castiglione as to Bramante's 'illiteracy' should be taken *cum grano salis*. The well-informed Vasari evidently did not share this opinion (*Vite*, ed. Milanesi, IV, p. 164). Cf. also Geymüller, *Die ursprünglichen Entwürfe für Sanct Peter in Rom*, 1875, p. 21 ff.; Malaguzzi Valeri, *La corte di Lodovico il Moro*, 1915, II, p. 231 f. Even the notoriously learned Palladio was called 'uneducated' by more learned contemporaries; cf. below, p. 129.

52 About Peruzzi's literary plans cf. D. Frey, *op. cit.*, p. 44 f.

53 Cf. Dinsmoor, 'The Literary Remains of Sebastiano Serlio', ART BULLETIN, XXIV, 1942, p. 60, note 27. – An earlier translation by or for Francesco di Giorgio is in the codex of the Bibl. Nazionale at Florence (II. I. 141, fol. 103 ff.); cf. Vasari, ed. Milanesi, III, p. 72, Von Schlosser, *Kunstliteratur*, 1924, p. 129; Allen Stuart Weller, *Francesco di Giorgio*, Chicago, 1943, p. 272.

54 Vasari, ed. Milanesi, V, p. 472, note 1. The preface – the only existing portion – was printed by Aurelio Gotti, *Vita di Michelangelo Buonarroti*, Florence, 1876, II, p. 129 ff., and again by Paolo Fontana in *Miscellanea di storia dell'arte in onore di I.B. Supino*, Florence, 1933, p. 305 ff.

55 Cf. Claudio Tolomei's letter, in Bottari, *Lett. pitt.*, 1822, II, p. 1 ff.; Von Schlosser, *op. cit.*, p. 223.

56 Cesariano, *Di Lucio Vitruvio Pollione de Architectura*, etc., Como 1521, Bk. III, 1, fol. xlviii v: 'mi pare piu facilissima cosa circondare e construere li principali membri meniani de uno oppido:

planning coming into its own, controversies flared up which are faithfully mirrored in Francesco's text. These controversies were, however, not concerned with the liturgical suitability of centralized churches as such – which nobody seems to have doubted – but with the question whether the altar should be placed at the periphery or in the centre. Advocates of the first view argued that in order to demonstrate God's infinite distance from us the altar should be placed as far as possible from the main door, i.e. opposite it on the circumference.[49] Advocates of the second view maintained that the centre is 'one and absolute' ('unico e assoluto') and therefore like Him who alone truly is. Moreover, as God is omnipresent, the Sacrament should be in the centre upon which all the lines of the building converge (Fig. 2).[50] More directly than in Alberti's cosmic analogies, the circle and its centre are here regarded as symbols of God; it will be shown later that this conception is rooted in neo-Platonic philosophy.

2. Centralized Churches in Later Architectural Theory

Of the architectural treatises planned by the great masters of the High Renaissance none was completed, nor has enough come down to us to gauge their opinions accurately. Bramante's writings have not survived at all;[51] of Leonardo's and Peruzzi's theoretical works[52] a wealth of drawings, at least, is preserved. But light is thrown on the intentions of High Renaissance masters by their pre-occupation with, and interpretation of, Vitruvius. The intense study of Vitruvius by these masters is well known: Fra Giocondo was the first to publish the Latin text in 1511 with illustrations showing a remarkable understanding; an (unpublished) Italian translation was completed under Raphael's direction and in Raphael's house by Fabio Calvi;[53] towards the end of his career Antonio da Sangallo was engaged on an Italian edition with commentary.[54] These efforts to understand and interpret Vitruvius culminated in 1542 in the foundation of the Vitruvian Academy whose gigantic, erudite programme, however, never materialized.[55] It is through the 1521 edition of Vitruvius by Cesariano that we become acquainted with ideas current in the Milan of Bramante and Leonardo. Cesariano was a pupil of Bramante, and the fact that the first Italian edition with an extensive and learned commentary grew out of the latter's circle, is in itself highly significant. The commentary reveals again the ever present sense of an architectural hierarchy; Cesariano declares that every kind of domestic architecture is very easy in comparison with the task of erecting a sacred building 'with its fitting parts proportioned and diligently harmonized'.[56] Those architects who produce 'accurate results' appear themselves 'like demigods', 'come semidei'.[57]

What should these sacred buildings be like; when are their parts properly proportioned and harmonized? Vitruvius supplied the answer. He had introduced his third book on Temples with the famous remarks on the proportions of the human figure, which should be reflected in the proportions of temples. As a proof of the harmony and perfection of the human body he described how a well-built man fits with extended hands and feet exactly into the most perfect geometrical figures, circle and square.[58] This simple picture seemed to reveal a deep and fundamental truth about man and the world, and its importance for Renaissance architects can hardly be overestimated. The image haunted their imagination. We find it already in Francesco di Giorgio's codex in the

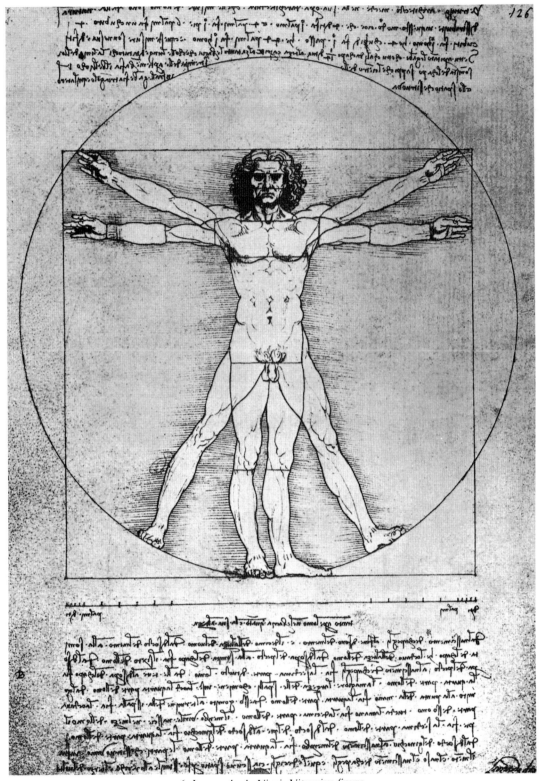

6. Leonardo da Vinci, Vitruvian figure

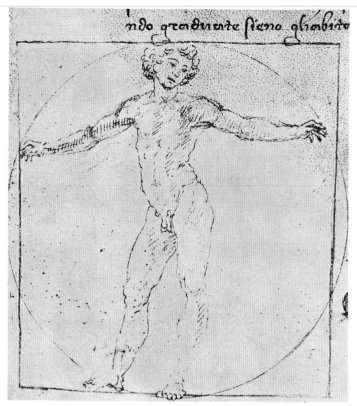

7. Francesco di Giorgio, Vitruvian figure,
Codex Ashburnham 361

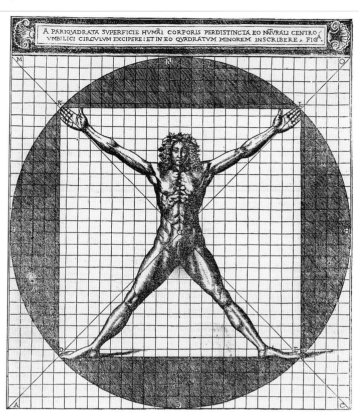

8. Vitruvian figure, from Cesariano's edition
of Vitruvius, Como, 1521

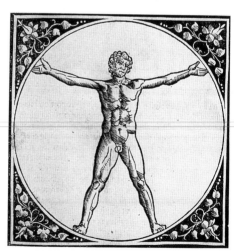

9. Vitruvian figure. From Fra Giocondo's
edition of Vitruvius, Venice, 1511

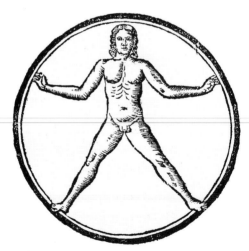

10. Vitruvian figure, from Francesco Giorgi,
De Harmonia Mundi, Venice, 1525

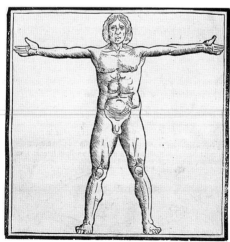

11. Vitruvian figure. From Fra Giocondo's
edition of Vitruvius, Venice, 1511

Laurenziana (Fig. 7) which was owned and annotated by Leonardo.[59] Leonardo himself interpreted Vitruvius' text more accurately in his celebrated drawing at Venice (Fig. 6),[60] and Fra Giocondo showed the 'homo ad quadratum' and 'ad circulum' on two plates of his Vitruvius edition of 1511 (Figs. 9, 11).[61] Cesariano – certainly not without knowledge of Leonardo's drawing – gave this conception two full-page illustrations (Fig. 8)[62] and accompanied it with a lengthy commentary culminating in the assertion that with the Vitruvian figure one can define the proportions – he says 'commensurare' which implies the common measure, the harmony – of everything in the world.[63]

It can hardly be doubted that Cesariano's commentary re-echoes meditations on harmony and proportion which were discussed in Bramante's and Leonardo's circle. There is further evidence of this; it comes, above all, from Leonardo's friend, Luca Pacioli, the mathematician, for whose *De Divina Proportione* Leonardo himself had drawn the illustrations. In Pacioli's work the Vitruvian concept appears again embedded in a metaphysical context. 'First we shall talk of the proportions of man', Pacioli declares in the part on architecture appended to the *De Divina Proportione*,[64] 'because from the human body derive all measures and their denominations and in it is to be found all and every ratio and proportion by which God reveals the innermost secrets of nature'. And further: 'After having considered the right arrangement of the human body, the ancients proportioned all their work, particularly the temples, in accordance with it. For in the human body they found the two main figures without which it is impossible to achieve anything, namely the perfect circle . . . and the square.'[65] These observations lead Pacioli on to a long-winded description of the Vitruvian text.

Francesco Zorzi (or Giorgi),[66] a neo-Platonic friar, who was also closely associated with architecture, takes us a step further to his work on Universal Harmony. Here we find an illustration of the Vitruvian text – significantly only the 'Homo ad circulum' – in a chapter entitled: 'Quod Homo imitatur mundum in figura circulari' ('Why Man in the figure of the Circle is an Image of the World') (Fig. 10). The cosmic meaning of this figure could not be made clearer. But the title contains only half of the author's views. Vitruvius' figure holds for him a dual quality: it discloses through the visible, corporeal world ('homo-mundus') the invisible, intellectual relation between the soul and God; for God is the 'intelligibilis sphaera'. The author interprets the figure derived from Vitruvius in the light of the mystic geometry of neo-Platonism which had reached him through Ficino from Plotinus.[67]

With the Renaissance revival of the Greek mathematical interpretation of God and the world, and invigorated by the Christian belief that Man as the image of God embodied the harmonies of the Universe, the Vitruvian figure inscribed in a square and a circle became a symbol of the mathematical sympathy between microcosm and macrocosm.[68] How could the relation of Man to God be better expressed, we feel now justified in asking, than by building the house of God in accordance with the fundamental geometry of square and circle?

This question leads us on to the the topic of Leonardo's preoccupation with the problem of the centralized church. His many drawings of centrally planned churches are more than systematic studies by the greatest artist and thinker of the Renaissance; they are, above all, documents of Renaissance religion. Leonardo himself is almost silent about the ideas which guided him.[69] But in addition to the evidence supplied by Cesariano and Pacioli we know that he was familiar with

aut Civitate: aut tuto uno magno Castello e altri loci civili cha bene construere una sacra aede con li soi debiti membri: proportionati e diligentemente symmetriati'.

57 *ibid.*, Bk. I, fol. ii v: 'quilli Architecti che sano producere li sollerti effecti pareno come semidei perche cercano che larte si asimiglia & supplisca a la natura'.

58 Bk. III, chap. 1, i: 'Namque non potest aedis ulla sine symmetria atque proportione rationem habere compositionis, nisi uti ad hominis bene figurati membrorum habuerit exactam rationem.'

59 Cf. below, p. 26, note 70, Bibl. Laurenziana, Cod. Ashburnham 361, fol. 5r. Cf. Giuseppe Favaro, *Le proporzioni del corpo umano in un codice anonimo del Quattrocento postilato da Leonardo*, Reale Acc. d'Italia, Memorie classa scienza fisiche, etc., Vol. V, 1934, p. 592 f.

60 J.P. Richter, *op. cit.*, I, p. 255, No. 343.

61 *M. Vitruvius per Jocundum*, Venice, 1511, fols. 22r and v.

62 Fols. xlix and L (Fig. 8). Fol. xlix, not here illustrated, shows the figure in the square under the heading; 'Humani corporis mensura et ab eo omnes symmetrias eurythmiatas & proportionatas geometrico schemate invenire, ut adest figura.'
Many of the later editions of Vitruvius have illustrations, often derived from Cesariano, of the figure in square and circle (Caporali, Philander). As late as 1590 prominent illustrations appear in Gio. Antonio Rusconi, *Della Architettura . . . secondo i Precetti di Vitruvio*, Venice, 1590, p. 46: System of human proportions, p. 47: 'Homo ad circulum', p. 48: 'Homo ad quadratum'.

63 *Op. cit.*, fol. 50v.: 'Et in la supra data figura del corpo humano: per li quali symmetriati membri si po ut diximus sapere commensurare tutte le cose che sono nel mondo'. How literally this was taken can be seen from the direct application of thēhuman body to the proportioning of architectural members. Examples of this method from the fifteenth to the seventeenth century are common, cf. above all, Francesco di Giorgio's drawings (Figs. 2 and 4) and for the later period Bernini's-drawings (Brauer-Wittkower, *Die Zeichnungen des G.L. Bernini*, 1931, II, p. 54) and the latter's remarks to Chantelou.

64 Ed. C. Winterberg in Eitelberger-Ilg's 'Quellenschriften', Vienna, 1889, p. 129. About Leonardo's relation to Pacioli, cf. Müller-Walde in JAHRBUCH D. PREUSS. KUNSTSLG. XIX, 1898, p. 235 ff., and Solmi, *Le fonti dei manoscritti di Leonardo da Vinci*, 1908, p. 219 ff.

65 *Div. prop.*, ed. cit., p. 131.

66 Francesco Zorzi (or Giorgi), *De Harmonia Mundi totius*, Venice, 1525, p. C, cap. 2. About Giorgi cf. Part IV, p. 104.

67 God as 'sphaera intelligibilis' in Plotinus, *Enn.*, II, 9, 17; VI, 5, 5; VI, 9, 8. Cf. D. Mahnke, *Unendliche Sphäre und Allmittelpunkt*, 1937, p. 68.

68 Rudolf Allers, 'Microcosmus', in *Traditio*, II, 1944, shows that the microcosm conception displayed 'an unexpected vitality and achieved a dominant position in the philosophy of the Italian Renaissance, and, later, with many who were

influenced by these philosophers'. The doctrine of the mathematical correspondence between microcosm and macrocosm was, of course, one of the fundamentals of mediaeval thought. The best recent survey is in Allers' article. For the aesthetic problem cf. Edgar de Bruyne, *Etudes d'esthétique médiévale*, Bruges, 1946, II, pp. 275 ff., 350 ff., 361 ff. Even the Vitruvian image had a formative influence on mediaeval thought; see for instance, the French dialogue 'Placides et Timeo' written before 1303 where we hear that 'l'homme est un microcosme. Il est rond comme le monde car il doit avoir autant de hauteur que d'envergure en étendant les bras' (Ch.-V. Langlois, *La connaissance de la nature et du monde au moyen âge*, Paris, 1911, p. 290).

69 Hints as to the 'regole del retto edifichare' in his draft of a letter to the Opera del Duomo of Pavia: 'il modelo da me fatto avere in se quella simetrja. quella chorispondentia quela chonformjtà quale s'apartiene al principiato edifitio'. Cf. L. Beltrami, *Documenti e memorie riguardanti la vita e le opere di L. da V.*, Milan, 1919, p. 24; L.H. Heydenreich, *Die Sakralbaustudien Leonardo da Vincis*, 1929, p. 39 f.

70 It should be recalled that Pacioli was a friend of Alberti's (cf. *Div. prop.*, ed. cit., p. 317 f.). For Leonardo's knowledge and use of Alberti's writings, cf. Heydenreich, *op. cit.*, pp. 41, 82; Solmi, *Fonti, op. cit.*, p. 37 ff.; Sir Kenneth Clark, *Leon Battista Alberti on Painting* (British Academy Lecture), 1944, p. 16 f. Leonardo met Francesco di Giorgio when they were together in Pavia in 1490. He possessed and annotated the unfinished architectural treatise Bibl. Laurenziana, Cod. Ashburnham 361, the attribution of which to Francesco di Giorgio can no longer be doubted; see E. Berti in *Belvedere*, VII, 1924, p. 100 ff.

71 Richter, *Literary Works*, II, p. 27, No. 753.

72 Vasari, ed. Milanesi, IV, p. 21; cf. also Richter, *op. cit.*, II, p. 48.

73 Cf. Geymüller's grouping in Richter, *op. cit.*, II, p. 19 ff. and Heydenreich's dissertation (*op. cit.*). We are here not concerned with the stylistic development of the drawings which was aptly discussed by Heydenreich.

74 Most of the relevant drawings are in MS.B of the Institut de France. Fol. 15r: simplest additions of rectangular and segmental chapels to the square; fol. 21r: the hexagon with chapels; fol. 25v: alternating rectangular and semi-circular chapels; here also an octagon with semi-circular chapels, etc.

75 Bibl. Nat. 2037, fol. 3v.

76 Venturi, *Storia dell'arte Italiana*, XI, i, 1938, p. 25.

77 Geymüller, *Die ursprünglichen Entwürfe für Sanct Peter*, p. 96 ff.; G. Giovanoni, *Saggi sulla architettura del rinascimento*, Milan, 1931, p. 90. G. de Angelis d'Ossat (BOLLETTINO D'ARTE, XLI, 1956, p. 207 ff.) has revised many of the dates of the building history and also reaffirmed Bramante's authorship. It should be mentioned that the dome raised above the semi-circle is of later date (1606-17). The interior walls are white and the windows are in the upper tier.

78 Cf. W.B. Dinsmoor, 'The Literary Remains of Sebastiano Serlio', ART BULLETIN, XXIV, 1942, p. 62 f.

Alberti's and Francesco di Giorgio's works.[70] There is also that one sentence in which he peremptorily demands that 'a building should always be detached on all sides so that its true form may be seen'.[71] This sentence discloses the same crystalline vision of architecture, the same devotion to pure geometry which we found in Alberti, and it may well reflect a direct influence of the *De re aedificatoria*. If Vasari's report is true that Leonardo meant to lift the Baptistery of Florence and set it on a base[72] – and the extravagance of the project seems to vouch for it – he must have intended to comply with Alberti's demand that a church should be isolated from, and raised above, the surrounding everyday life, a principle to which Leonardo adhered in all his designs.

If we can infer from all this that Leonardo's ideas agreed with those of Alberti, his drawings are cumulative evidence of that community of spirit: they appear indeed like illustrations to Alberti's theories. These drawings for centralized churches,[73] which demonstrate every possible evolution of the square and the circle, from the simplest to the most complex configurations (Fig. 12),[74] never deviate from the principle of lucid grouping of elementary geometrical forms, and this basic geometry loses nothing of its clarity and effectiveness in the elevations. In an example such as that in Fig. 13[75] we can see in its unadulterated form the pure cube of the main body with the inscribed circle of the drum, the semi-sphere of the dome and the attached semi-circular chapels. In all his drawings, satellite domes and chapels accompany, and lead up to, the pure and simple form of the dominating central dome under which 'the soul rises to the contemplation of God'.

Such plans, organically composed and built up of simple geometrical forms, were more often executed than is generally realized. The creation closest to the ideal plans by Leonardo is perhaps S. Maria della Consolazione at Todi[76] which looks almost as if it had been based on the design just discussed (Fig. 14), and the crystalline quality of the geometrical pattern is here as evident as it was on paper. The church was begun by Cola da Caprarola in 1504, not from a design by Leonardo, but probably from one by Bramante[77] – one of the many proofs of the closeness of their views on architecture.

If Cesariano expressed opinions current in Milan in Bramante's and Leonardo's days, Serlio reflects Roman ideas of the beginning of the sixteenth century. It is well known that Serlio's books on architecture, which appeared from 1537 onwards, were based on material left by his great master Peruzzi.[78] Serlio's work is pedestrian and pragmatic, consisting of a collection of models rather than expressions of principle, and we cannot expect to find here any of Alberti's philosophical concepts. Yet Serlio's survey of suitable plans for churches is significant. He suggests in all twelve basic shapes: 'I begin', he says, 'with the circular form because it is more perfect than all the others.'[79] Of his twelve plans nine are developments from the circle and square (Fig. 15)[80] and only three are longitudinal. Apart from two types of circular churches, he recommends the pentagon, hexagon, octagon, the square with inscribed octagon and the square with inscribed circle and circular chapels, the Greek Cross and also the oval. This latter form, though also derived from the circle, suggests an axial direction from entrance to choir and heralds therefore a new approach to ecclesiastical architecture.[81]

Serlio in fact is still concerned with almost exactly the same problems which we found in Alberti and the Milanese circle, and this is not astonishing if we

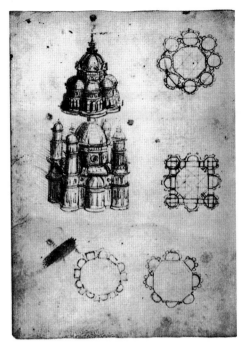

12. Leonardo da Vinci. Designs of churches

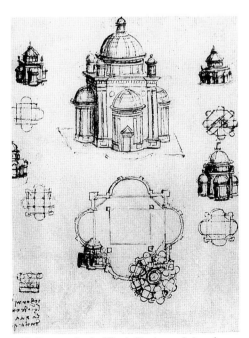

13. Leonardo da Vinci. Designs of churches

14. S. Maria della Consolazione, Todi, 1504

15. Centralized plans. From Serlio's *Fifth Book on Architecture*, 1547

remember that Bramante settled permanently in Rome shortly before 1500. But already towards the end of the fifteenth century the handing on of these ideas was no longer due to personal relations and influences alone; they had become common property, and the rigid geometry of centralized buildings had an emotional appeal not only to architects but also to sculptors and painters.[82] And a study of any architectural sketch-book of the period from the Codex Escurialensis[83] to Giuliano da Sangallo's[84] and Bramantino's sketch-books,[85] and even of the engravings of the rather belated Montano,[86] leads one forcibly to the conclusion that the geometry of the circle had an almost magical power over these men.

3. Building Practice: S. Maria delle Carceri

Building activity reflects the theoretical position. Centralized churches began to appear sporadically in the first half of the fifteenth century. The great Brunelleschi set the example in 1434 with his plan for S. Maria degli Angeli in Florence. In 1451 followed Michelozzo's choir for the SS. Annunziata. For S. Francesco in Rimini Alberti designed 'the dome of heaven to which the whole argument of the Tempio aspired'.[87] While this magnificent dome remained forever a wish-dream, he carried out the much more modest church of S. Sebastiano at Mantua over a square plan with attached rectangular chapels (Fig. 41), a plan prefiguring the later development of the Greek Cross.[88] In the last quarter of the century the examples become more numerous, particularly in northern Italy,[89] until before and after 1500 we observe a real profusion of centralized structures.[90]

Those churches whose character has not been changed by later alterations show that Alberti's postulates were regarded as binding. As an example one might quote Giuliano da Sangallo's S. Maria delle Carceri at Prato, begun in 1485 (Figs. 16-19). This church is the first Greek-Cross structure of the Renaissance, built on that plan which ideally combines the centralizing aspirations of the time with the symbolical reference to the form of the Cross.[91] Four short and equal arms are joined to the crossing which – as the plan shows – is based on the two elementary figures of square and circle. The ratios are as simple and therefore as evident as possible. The depth of the arms, for instance, is half their length and the four end walls of the cross are as long as they are high, i.e. they form a perfect square.[92] The entirely flat and plain surface of the walls and arches is framed by pilasters and simple mouldings in the joints of the building, where two surfaces meet. This structural skeleton is built in dark sandstone (pietra serena), while the walls themselves are given a white coat. Thus the dark articulations together with the white walls enhance the lucidity of the geometrical scheme. Above the entablature which runs unbroken round the whole building rise the semi-circles of the arches with the windows set into them. And above the low drum hovers the dome, again of semi-circular shape. It is important to notice that the dark ring of the drum does not touch the mouldings of the arches. The dome, the image of the sky, seems therefore magically suspended in the air as if it had no weight (Fig. 17).

Outside, the whole church is raised on a platform and is faced with white limestones slabs which are divided into geometric units by dark green framing bands.[93] Viewed from a certain distance the circle of the dome, the square of the

79 Serlio, *Quinto libro d'architettura*. In the edition of 1600, p. 202.

80 These nine plans on consecutive pages of Serlio's book have been grouped together in our Fig. 15. R. Billing, 'Die Kirchenpläne "al modo antico" von Sebastiano Serlio', *Opuscula Romana* (Acta Instituti Romani Regni Sueciae, series in 4°, XVIII), I, 1954, pp. 21-38, investigated the relation of Serlio's centrally planned churches to ancient prototypes.

81 Cf. now W. Lotz, 'Die ovalen Kirchenräume des Cinquecento', RÖMISCHES JAHRBUCH FÜR KUNSTGESCHICHTE, VII, 1955.

82 Cf. M. Ermers, *Die Architekturen in Raffaels Gemälden*, 1909; Fiske Kimball, 'Luciano Laurana and the "High Renaissance",' ART BULLETIN, X, 1927, p. 140 f.

83 H. Egger, *Codex Escurialensis*, Vienna, 1906. The group of circular buildings mainly between folios 70 and 75, all after the antique.

84 C. Hülsen, *Il libro di Giuliano da Sangallo*, Leipzig, 1910.

85 Angelo della Croce, *Le Rovine di Roma*, 1880.

86 G.B. Montano, *Scielta di varii tempietti antichi*, Rome, 1624.

87 Charles Mitchell, 'The Imagery of the Tempio Malatestiano', STUDI ROMAGNOLI, II, 1951, p. 90.

88 For the reconstruction of the interior, cf. the drawing referred to below, p. 53, note 60.

89 As we are concerned with an interpretation and not a history of centralized building we omit a discussion of the genetic derivation of centralized planning. We also omit from the following list centrally built fifteenth-century chapels and sacristies which had an important bearing on the development of centralized church design. Dates in brackets refer to the beginning of the construction: S. Maria delle Carceri, Prato (1485); Incoronata, Lodi (1488); S. Maria de' Miracoli, Brescia (1488); S. Maria della Croce, Crema (1490); S. Maria di Canepanova, Pavia (1492?); S. Maria Maggiore, Orciano near Urbino (1492); S. Maria dell'Umiltà, Pistoia (1495).

90 S. Giovanni Crisostomo, Venice (1497); Santuario, Saronno (1498, with later nave); S. Maria della Passione, Milan (1501, with later nave); Tempietto, S. Pietro in Montorio, Rome (1502); S. Magno, Legnano (1504); S. Maria della Consolazione, Todi (1504); Bramante's St. Peter's (1506); S. Giovanni Battista, Ferrara (1506); S. Maria di Loreto, Rome (1507?); Chiesa degli Innocenti, Siena (1507); S. Eligio degli Orefici, Rome (1509); Madonna di Vico near Spello (1517); Madonna di S. Biagio, Montepulciano (1518); S. Maria di Piazza, Busto Arsizio (1518); Cathedral Montefiascone (1519); S. Spirito, Ferrara (1519); S. Croce, Riva S. Vitale (c. 1520); Madonna della Steccata, Parma (1521); Madonna di Campagna, Piacenza (1522); Chiesa della Madonna, Mongiovino (1524); Chiesa della Manna d'Oro, Spoleto (1527); Cappella Pellegrini, S. Bernardino, Verona (1527-8); Cf. above all H. Strack, *Central- und Kuppelkirchen der Renaissance in Italien*, Berlin, 1882; P. Laspeyres, *Kirchen der Renaissance in Mittelitalien*, Berlin, 1882; Geymüller, *Die*

16, 17. Giuliano da Sangallo. S. Maria delle Carceri, Prato, 1485: (*above*) interior view, (*below*) plan (from the 'Taccuino')

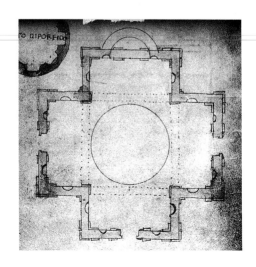

crossing and the Greek Cross of the arms appear as spatial evolutions of one geometrical concept.

This short description of S. Maria delle Carceri may have recalled to the reader Alberti's theoretical demands and shown that Giuliano da Sangallo complied with them. The church, standing here like a precious jewel, is conceived, as it were, in Alberti's spirit. Its majestic simplicity, the undisturbed impact of its geometry, the purity of its whiteness are designed to evoke in the congregation a consciousness of the presence of God – of a God who has ordered the universe according to immutable mathematical laws, who has created a uniform and beautifully proportioned world, the consonance and harmony of which is mirrored in His temple below.

4. Bramante and Palladio

Of all this we find a final and comprehensive statement in the work of the last of the great humanist architects, Palladio. The importance of his clearly arranged and lucidly written treatise, published in 1560, is comparable only with Alberti's work written more than a hundred years earlier. There is in fact a close relationship between the two treatises; for much of Palladio's thought and sometimes even his phrasing derive from Alberti.[94] Nevertheless in his economical style and with the humanist experience of four generations behind him, Palladio can often express with precision ideas which were only loosely implied by Alberti. He introduces a new clarity.

Like most Renaissance artists, Palladio, following Alberti, subscribed to the mathematical definition of beauty: 'Beauty will result from the beautiful form and from the correspondence of the whole to the parts, of the parts amongst themselves, and of these again to the whole; so that the structures may appear an entire and complete body, wherein each member agrees with the other and all members are necessary for the accomplishment of the building',[95] a formulation which closely follows Vitruvius' definition of 'symmetria'.[96] Moreover, Palladio expressed in his Fourth Book on Temples many views which stem directly from Alberti: buildings in which the supreme Being is invoked and adored should stand in the most noble part of the city, on beautiful piazzas, raised above the rest of the city. To ascend to a temple by steps inspires us with devotion and awe. Such places of worship should be of the highest perfection; they ought to be built so that nothing more beautiful could be imagined and those who enter should be transported into a kind of ecstasy in admiring their grace and beauty. Buildings dedicated to the omnipotent God should be strong and everlasting. And in order to honour divinity as much as possible, the most beautiful orders and the most excellent and precious materials should be used. White is the colour for churches, for as the colour of purity it is most akin to God. Nothing in a temple should distract the mind from the contemplation of the Divine, and the decoration should inflame us to the service of God and good works.[97] So far there is complete correspondence with Alberti's ideas.

But Palladio goes on to explain more fully what Alberti only adumbrates. For he states authoritatively which form is most worthy for the house of God. 'The most beautiful and most regular forms' – he says – 'and from which the others receive their measure are the round and the quadrangular.' And of these two he singles out the round form 'because it is the only one among all the figures that is

18. S. Maria delle Carceri, Prato. Dome

ursprüngl. Entwürfe, op. cit., p. 10 ff. and passim; Malaguzzi Valeri, *La corte di Lodovico il Moro*, Vol. II.

91 Two studies for the Madonna della Carceri, attributed by Geymüller to Giuliano da Maiano (*Architektur der Renaissance in Toscana*, Vol. XI, Figs. 33, 34) are pure octagons.

92 For more details about the proportion cf. Geymüller, *ibid.*, Vol. V, p. 8.

93 The exterior remained unfinished. The history of the building is fully discussed in Giuseppe Marchini, *Giuliano da Sangallo*, Florence, 1942, p. 87.

94 This can escape nobody who reads the beginning of Palladio's Fourth Book. Cf. below, pp. 64, 108, 109.

95 Bk. I, chap. 1.

96 I, ii, 4.

97 These sentences are an epitome from the preface and chapters i and ii of Palladio's Fourth Book.

19. S. Maria delle Carceri, Prato. Exterior

98 *ibid.*, chap. ii.

99 *ibid.* Attention to this passage was first drawn by Anthony Blunt, *Artistic Theory in Italy*, 1450-1600, Oxford, 1940, p. 129.

100 Bk. IV, Preface. The whole passage runs as follows: 'E veramente considerando noi questa bella machina del Mondo di quanti merauigliosi ornamenti ella sia ripiena, & come i Cieli co'l contínuo lor girare vadino in lei le stagioni secondo il natural bisogno cangiando, & con la soauissima armonia del temperato lor mouimento se stessi conseruino non possiamo dubitare, che douendo esser simili i piccioli Tempii, che noi facciamo; à questo grandissimo dalla sua immensa bontà con vna sua parola perfettamente compiuto, non siamo tenuti à fare in loro tutti quelli ornamenti, che per noi siano possibili.'

101 *Timaeus*, 33 B ff. The knowledge of this passage may have reached Palladio with the broad current of Renaissance Platonism.

102 Bk. IV, p. 37: the Minerva Medica as 'Tempio vulgarmente detto le Galluce'; p. 59: Baptistery of Constantine: 'Questo Tempio per mia opinione è opera moderna fatta delle spoglie de edificij antichi'; p. 83: S. Constanza: 'Io credo, ch'egli fosse una sepoltura'; others believed that it was a temple of Bacchus (see e.g. Serlio, Bk. III, fol. 56v), 'e perchè questa è la commune opinione, ... io l'ho posto infra i tempij'; p. 86: Sepulchral temple of Romulus, son of Maxentius, near S. Sebastiano fuori le Mure, not named by Palladio.

simple, uniform, equal, strong, and spacious. Therefore let us make our temples round.'[98] The context in which this important passage occurs is on the conformity between the place of worship and the character of the particular god venerated in it, in other words on the old question of agreement between content and form. Vitruvius (I, 2) explains that the form of the temple should be 'analogous to the character of the divinity', and, following him, Palladio comments that the ancients built the temples dedicated to Sun and Moon round, 'because they continually revolve round the world'; the same applies to temples dedicated to Vesta, Goddess of the Earth, 'which we know is a round body'. Thus for Palladio the particular fitness of the circle for churches consists in the fact that 'it is enclosed by one circumference only, in which is to be found neither beginning nor end, and the one is indistinguishable from the other; its parts correspond to each other and all of them participate in the shape of the whole; and moreover every part being equally distant from the centre such a building demonstrates exremely well the unity, the infinite essence, the uniformity and the justice of God'.[99] If we add to this remarkable passage Palladio's statement on the macrocosm-microcosm relation between the universe and the temple – 'We cannot doubt, that the little temples we make, ought to resemble this very great one, which, by His immense goodness, was perfectly completed with one word of His'[100] – we have an epitome of what Renaissance church builders endeavoured to achieve: for them the centrally planned church was the man-made echo or image of God's universe and it is *this* shape which discloses 'the unity, the infinite essence, the uniformity and the justice of God'.

These last words provide the key to the whole concept, for they lead us back to Plato's *Timaeus*, where Plato describes in words, which Palladio directly or indirectly borrowed from him,[101] the world as a sphere 'equidistant every way from centre to extremity, a figure the most perfect and uniform of all' so that the world which the Demiurge brought into being 'was a blessed God'. The Renaissance conception of the perfect church is rooted in Plato's cosmology. Earlier writers had adumbrated more or less clearly the Platonic substance of their thought and it is this knowledge that enables us fully to appreciate the strength which prompted the aesthetic aspirations of a whole century, since Alberti's day, as well as the persistence with which the centralized form was advocated for churches.

Palladio's Fourth Book from which we have quoted consists of measured drawings and descriptions of ancient temples which – even by modern standards – are not unsound. Although he shows, apart from the Pantheon and the Vesta temples in Rome and Tivoli, a few centralized structures which were then believed to have been temples in antiquity,[102] the impression one carries away is that the standard type of the ancient temple had a rectangular *cella*. Thus his introduction culminating in the praise of the round temple is a challenge to his contemporaries rather than the result of an analysis of ancient temple architecture. This can be illustrated by a curious interpolation in Palladio's survey of classical temples. He shows half-way through the book the plan and elevation of Bramante's Tempietto in Rome and explains in the text: 'Since Bramante was the first who brought good and beautiful architecture to light, which from the time of the ancients to his day had been forgotten, it seemed to me reasonable that his work should have a place among the ancients.' Bramante's Tempietto (Fig. 20) appears here as visible evidence for Palladio's programme. This circular

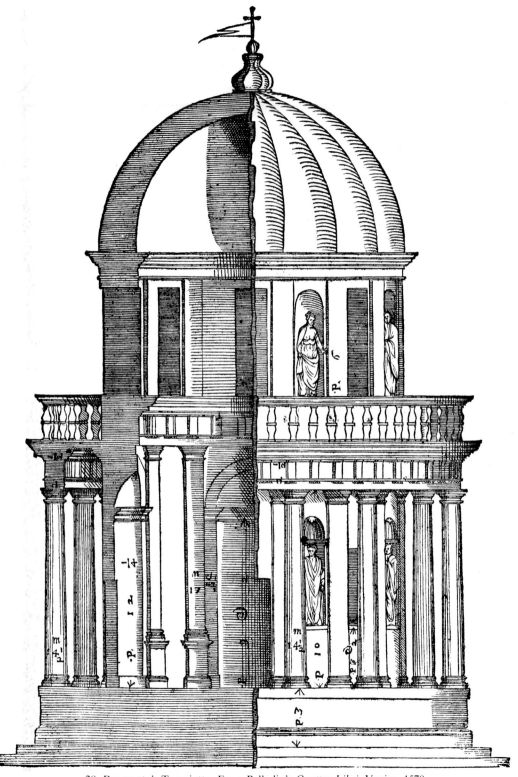

20. Bramante's Tempietto. From Palladio's *Quattro Libri*, Venice, 1570

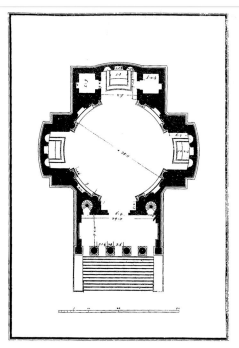

21. Palladio's Church at Maser. Plan. From Bertotti Scamozzi

structure is for Palladio *the* building which demonstrates most perfectly – to use his words again – 'the unity, the infinite essence, the uniformity and the justice of God.'

The Tempietto fulfils every demand Alberti had made for the ideal church; it was planned in the centre of a beautiful square, it is free on all sides, it stands isolated on a high platform; the perfect roundness, the quiet semi-circle of the dominating dome,[103] the austere Doric order with horizontal entablature, the abstention from painted decoration and the planned use of statues (which, characteristically, Palladio included on his plate): all this – and more could be added – shows Bramante in line of descent from Alberti as the executor of Alberti's fondest ideas. Bramante, chronologically and artistically the mediator between Alberti and Palladio,[104] represents at the same time the apex of this trio of great humanist architects.

Palladio himself tackled the problem of the centralized church at the end of his life. His little church at Maser with the austerely classical portico follows the model of the Pantheon, the most perfect centralized building of antiquity (Figs. 21, 22). In plan a complete circle with chapels in the four axes, the cylinder is vaulted by the tranquil heaven of the semi-circular dome. By excluding a drum, Palladio, unlike Bramante in the Tempietto, reduced the design to an unadulterated union of the two elementary forms, cylinder and semi-circle. The walls are white, there are no paintings, and decoration consists of statuary (Fig. 24). Alberti's directions for the perfect temple are still valid, and we can say without danger of misinterpretation that, in spite of stylistic changes, this is exactly the kind of church the beauty of which would have conjured up before Alberti, had he been able to see it, the presence of the Divine and filled his heart with deep piety.

In retrospect, it would almost seem an historical necessity that the mother church of Christianity, St. Peter's, was planned by Bramante, and planned as a centralized building. One might even go so far as to say that in the year 1505 the holiness and singularity of this church could not have been expressed by any other type of plan. I am well aware of the fact that not everybody will agree with this verdict, for there are good reasons to presume that Bramante planned, in fact, a Latin-Cross Church. But I have arrived at my conclusions after carefully weighing all the available evidence.[105]

By choosing the Greek-Cross type of plan (Fig. 25)[106] Bramante combined – like Giuliano da Sangallo and others before him – the symbol of the Cross with the symbolic values of centralized geometry. But, as is well known, this plan deviates from the simple Greek Cross of the Madonna delle Carceri. The dominating figure of the Greek Cross with its dominating dome is accompanied in the diagonal axes by small repetitions of the same figure, and to these are added in the same axes four rooms of square shape. The whole is confined within a large square from which only the four apses project. The integrity of each of these geometrical figures is carefully preserved and the transitions from one geometric unit to the other are extremely subtle. Once the intrinsic logic of the plan has been understood, its precision, its geometrical economy and its symphonic quality will be perceived.[107] The plan is, in fact, the supreme example of that organic geometry, that kind of proportionally integrated 'spatial mathematics', which we have recognized as a distinguishing feature of humanist Renaissance architecture.

The only record of an elevation reminiscent of this plan is to be found on Caradosso's famous foundation medal of 1506 (Fig. 26).[108] Here the dominant

103 The lantern is, of course, of later date. For Bramante's original intention cf. his drawing, illustrated in Venturi, STORIA DELL'ARTE, XI, i, Fig. 62.
104 For Bramante's formative influence on Palladio cf. Part III, p. 75 ff.
105 I have to resist the temptation of laying this evidence before the reader. Three points may, however, be mentioned in support of a Greek-Cross design: (1) Michelangelo later declared that all the architects who departed from Bramante's plan (to which he, Michelangelo, returned with his Greek-Cross plan) had departed from the truth (letter to Ammanati, 1555); (2) Egidio da Viterbo's contemporary report which proves that Bramante had centralized concepts on his mind (Pastor, *History of the Popes*, III, 2, p. 1140); (3) the spate of later Greek-Cross churches would be difficult to account for without Bramante's great example.
106 The plan here illustrated is a modern interpretation of Bramante's famous plan on parchment in the Uffizi (Florence), which shows only half the design and would also permit a different reconstruction.
107 A few of the most important ratios may here be given. The main dome is related to the satellite domes as 2:1; the arches of the crossing to the arches of the arms as 2:1; the diameter of the crossing to the length of the arms as 1:1. Cf. also T. Hofmann, *Entstehungsgeschichte des St. Peter in Rom*, 1928, p. 66.
108 It will be noticed that the elevation does not entirely correspond to the plan.

22-24. Church at Maser: (*above*) section (from Bertotti Scamozzi), (*below left*) façade, (*below right*) view of altar

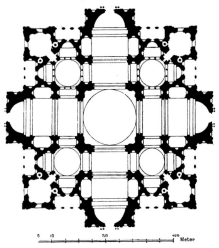

25. Bramante's plan of St. Peter's, Rome

Vesto è il diritto dentro e di fuori de la pianta passata, dal qual si puo comprendere la gran massa, & il gran peso che saria questo edificio sopra a quattro pilastri di tanta altezza: la qual massa (sì come io dissi auanti) doueria mettere pensiero ad ogni prudente Architetto a farla al piano di terra, non che in tanta altezza: e però io giudico, che l'Architetto dee esser piu presto alquanto timido che troppo animoso: perche se farà timido; egli farà le sue cose ben sicure, & ancho non si sdegnera di uolere il consiglio d'altri, e così facendo rare uolte perirà: ma se sara troppo animoso; egli non uorrà l'altrui consiglio, anzi si considera solamente nel suo ingegno, onde spesse uolte precipitaranno le cose da lui fatte: e però io concludo, che la troppo animosità proceda da la psuntione, e la prosuntione dal poco sapere, ma che la timidità sia cosa uirtuosa, dandosi sempre a credere di sapere o nulla o poco. Le misure di tutta questa opera si troueranno con i palmi piccioli, che sono qui adietro.

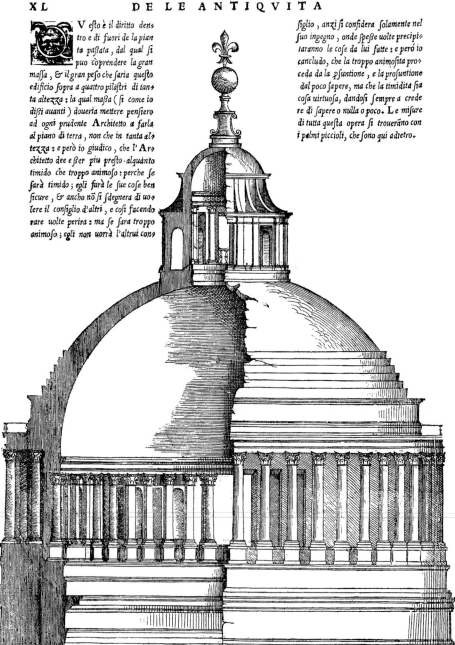

26. Bramante's St. Peter's. Foundation medal
by Caradosso, 1506

27. Bramante's Dome of St. Peter's. Woodcut from Serlio

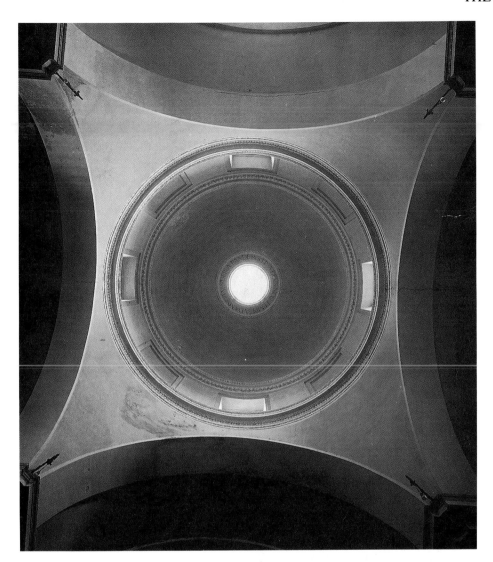

rôle of the dome is manifest, and the whole sub-structure appears to lead up to it. This church was to be crowned with the loftiest dome, an overwhelming image of the macrocosm. Its form, which we know from Serlio's woodcut (Fig. 27),[109] was to consist of the pure cylinder of the drum surmounted by the undisturbed and entirely balanced semi-sphere of the vault – the whole a monumental and simplified re-creation of Bramante's own Tempietto. It is this serenity of the structure expressed through the divine stillness of the geometry of the circle which leads man to God.

Although Bramante's plan underwent many and decisive changes, it remained a tremendous stimulus to architects all over Italy, and churches with the high dome over the Greek Cross rose everywhere.[110] Raphael himself followed the lead in the little church of S. Eligio degli Orefici in Rome (Fig. 28), which in its pure whiteness, its austerity of forms, and the abstract clarity of its geometrical scheme combines the expression of the religious feeling of the Renaissance with that of the Counter-Reformation.[111]

109 *Libro terzo*; in the edition of 1600, fol. 66*v*.
110 Cf., above all, Steccata, Parma; Madonna di Campagna, Piacenza; Chiesa della Madonna, Mongiovine; S. Maria Nuova, Cortona; S. Maria di Carignano, Genova; S. Maria della Vergine, Macerata; Madonna della Ghiara, Reggio; Cathedral, Brescia; S. Carlo ai Catinari, Rome.
111 Documents permit the conclusion that Raphael's design was adjusted and executed by Peruzzi. The dome was not finished until 1536. After 1600 Flaminio Ponzio was responsible for some important changes (1601-5); he also gave the interior its white coating; see Zocca, in *Atti I° Congresso Nazionale di storia dell'architettura*, 1938, p. 102 ff.

5. The Religious Symbolism of Centrally Planned Churches

Renaissance artists firmly adhered to the Pythagorean concept 'All is Number' and, guided by Plato and the neo-Platonists and supported by a long chain of theologians from Augustine onwards, they were convinced of the mathematical and harmonic structure of the universe and all creation.[112] If the laws of harmonic numbers pervade everything from the celestial spheres to the most humble life on earth, then our very souls must conform to this harmony. It is, according to Alberti, an inborn sense that makes us aware of harmony;[113] he maintains, in other words, that the perception of harmony through the senses is possible by virtue of the affinity of our souls. This implies that if a church has been built in accordance with essential mathematical harmonies, we react instinctively,[114] an inner sense tells us, even without rational analysis, when the building we are in partakes of the vital force which lies behind all matter and binds the universe together. Without such sympathy between the microcosm of man and the macrocosm of God, prayer cannot be effective. A writer like Pacioli goes so far as to say that divine functions are of little value if the church has not been built 'with correct proportions' ('con debita proportione').[115] It follows that perfect proportions must be applied to churches, whether or not the exact relationships are manifest to the 'outward' eye.

The most perfect geometrical figure is the circle and to it was given special significance. To understand fully this new emphasis we must turn for a moment to Nicholas of Cusa who had transformed the scholastic hierarchy of static spheres, of spheres immovably related to one centre, the earth, into a universe uniform in substance and without a physical or ideal centre.[116] In this new world of infinite relations the incorruptible certitude of mathematics assumed unprecedented importance. Mathematics is for Cusanus a necessary vehicle for penetrating to the knowledge of God, who must be envisaged through the mathematical symbol. Cusanus, developing a pseudo-hermetic formula,[117] visualizes Him as the least tangible and at the same time the most perfect geometrical figure, the centre and circumference of the circle;[118] for in the infinite circle of sphere, centre, diameter and circumference are identical.[119] Similarly Ficino, based on the authority of hermetic sources and on Plotinus, regards Him as the true centre of the universe, the inner core of everything, but at the same time as the circumference of the universe, surpassing everything immeasurably.[120]

Renaissance architects were aware of all this. Their own treatises leave not a shadow of doubt. We do not maintain that all or even many of them were familiar with the intricacies of philosophical speculation. But they were steeped in these ideas which, with the surge of Platonism and neo-Platonism in the fifteenth century, had spread quickly and irresistibly.

The geometrical definition of God through the symbol of the circle or sphere has a pedigree reaching back to the Orphic poets.[121] It was vitalized by Plato and made the central notion of his cosmological myth in the *Timaeus*; it was given pre-eminence in the works of Plotinus and, dependent on him, in the writings of the pseudo-Dionysius the Areopagite, which were followed by the mystical theologians of the Middle Ages. Why then – it may still be asked – did not the builders of the cathedrals try to give visual shape to this conception; why was it not until the fifteenth century that the centralized plan for churches was regarded as the most appropriate expression of the Divine?[122] The answer lies in the new

112 Cf. also below, Part IV.

113 Bk. IX, chap. 5, ed. 1485, fol. x viii v: 'Ut vero de pulchritudine iudices non opinio: verum animis innata quaedam ratio efficiet . . . Unde autem is animi sensus excitetur et perdeat etiam non requiro funditus.' Also y iiiii v: 'Sed nature sensu animis innato quo sentiri diximus concinnitas . . .'
All Platonic thinkers and theologians agree that beauty can only be perceived by virtue of a correspondence between the structure of the soul and the harmony in the object. Cf. for instance Ficino, according to whom the soul 'possesses the images of the divine things on which it depends itself and the concepts and originals of the lower things which in a certain sense it produces itself.' Cf. Kristeller, *Marsilio Ficino*, 1943, p. 119 f.

114 The Renaissance theory of intuition, discussed by E. Gombrich in Journal of the Warburg and Courtauld Institutes, XI, 1948, p. 170 f., is here relevant. See also the inborn judgment and its relation to the corporeal world in Cusanus' *liber de mente* (E. Cassirer, *Individuum und Kosmos in der Philosophie der Renaissance*, 1927, p. 222 ff., 226, 230 ff.).

115 *Summa de Arithmetica*, Venice 1494, dist. VI, tract. 1, artic. 2.

116 We believe that E. Cassirer's characterization of Cusanus' achievement (*Ind. und Kosmos*, chap. I) has not been seriously impaired by Duhem, Thorndike and others. The reader may also be referred to the symposium on fifteenth-century Italian science with contributions by Durand, Baron, Cassirer, Kristeller, Lockwood and Thorndike in Journal of the History of Ideas, IV, 1943.

117 *Liber XXIV philosophorum*, propos. 2: 'Deus est sphaera infinita, cuius centrum est ubique, circumferentia nullibi'; cf. Nicolai de Cusa, *De docta ignorantia*, ed. E. Hoffmann and R. Klibansky, 1932, p. 104.

118 *ibid.*, Bk. I, chap. 12; II, chaps. 11,12; pp. 25, 100, 101, 104.

119 *De docta ignor.* I, 21: 'Circulus est figura perfecta unitatis et simplicitatis . . . unitas est infinita, sicut circulus infinitus . . . Haec omnia

scientific approach to nature which is the glory of Italian fifteenth-century artists. It was the artists, headed by Alberti and Leonardo, who had a notable share in consolidating and popularizing the mathematical interpretation of all matter. They found and elaborated correlations between the visible and intelligible world which were as foreign to the mystic theology as to the Aristotelian scholasticism of the Middle Ages. Architecture was regarded by them as a mathematical science which worked with spatial units: parts of that universal space for the scientific interpretation of which they had discovered the key in the laws of perspective. Thus they were made to believe that they could re-create the universally valid ratios and expose them pure and absolute, as close to abstract geometry as possible. And they were convinced that universal harmony could not reveal itself entirely unless it were realized in space through architecture conceived in the service of religion.

The belief in the correspondence of microcosm and macrocosm, in the harmonic structure of the universe, in the comprehension of God through the mathematical symbols of centre, circle and sphere – all those closely related ideas which had their roots in antiquity and belonged to the undisputed tenets of mediaeval philosophy and theology, acquired new life in the Renaissance, and found visual expression in the Renaissance church. The man-created forms in the corporeal world were the visible materializations of the intelligible mathematical symbols, and the relationship between the pure forms of absolute mathematics and the visible forms of applied mathematics were immediately and intuitively perceptible. For the men of the Renaissance this architecture with its strict geometry, the equipoise of its harmonic order, its formal serenity and, above all, with the sphere of the dome, echoed and at the same time revealed the perfection, omnipotence, truth and goodness of God.

The realization of these ideas in the Renaissance church betrays by implication a shift in the religious feeling itself, a shift for which the change from the basilical to the centralized church is a more telling symbol than the changes in the philosophical interpretation of God and world. It should be remembered that the classical principle of analogy between form and content was never abandoned. The builders of the Middle Ages laid out their churches 'in modum crucis'[123] – their Latin-Cross plan was the symbolic expression of Christ crucified. The Renaissance, as we have seen, did not lose sight of this idea. What had changed was the conception of the godhead: Christ as the essence of perfection and harmony superseded Him who had suffered on the Cross for humanity; the Pantocrator replaced the Man of Sorrows.[124]

*   *   *   *   *

Before concluding this chapter some points require further comment. First, polygonal and Greek-Cross churches are much more frequent than churches erected over circular plans. Even if one admits that, by virtue of the reference to the Cross, the Greek-Cross plan had a particular attraction, one may wonder about the contrast between the fervent eulogy of the circle and its restricted use in practice. But Alberti had demonstrated that all polygonal figures are derived from the circle and developed from it by simple operations (Fig. 1), and in his wake Palladio and others had emphasized that regular figures receive their measure from the round and quadrangular forms. Moreover, it was the dome

ostendit circulus infinitus sine principio et fine aeternus, indivisibiliter unissimus atque capacissimus. Et quia ille circulus est maximus, eius diameter etiam est maxima. Et quoniam plura maxima esse non possunt, est intantum ille circulus unissimus, quod diameter est circumferentia. Infinita vero diameter habet infinitum medium. Medium vero est centrum. Patet ergo centrum, diametrum et circumferentiam idem esse. Ex quo docetur ignorantia nostra incomprehensibile maximum esse, cui minimum non opponitur; sed centrum est in ipso circumferentia.' (ed. Hoffmann & Klibansky, 1932, p. 42 f.).

120 References are conveniently assembled in D. Mahnke, *Unendliche Sphäre und Allmittelpunkt*, Halle, 1937, p. 59 ff.

121 Cf. Mahnke, *op. cit.*

122 For the symbolism of round and polygonal churches in the early Middle Ages, cf. R. Krautheimer, 'Introduction to an "Iconography of Mediaeval Architecture",' JOURNAL OF THE WARBURG AND COURTAULD INSTITUTES, V, 1942, p. 9.
  The impact of Greek scholars on the development of Renaissance architecture has never been investigated and would require a special study. In any case, there seems to be little doubt that the wholesale acceptance of the Greek Cross as a plan for churches belongs to the history of the Greek 'Invasion' of Italy during the fifteenth century.

123 Cf. J. Sauer, *Symbolik des Kirchengebäudes*, Freiburg i.B., 1924, p. 292.

124 Burckhardt expressed this idea in the beautiful last sentences of the *Civilisation of the Renaissance*: 'While the men of the Middle Ages look on the world as a vale of tears . . . here, in this circle of chosen spirits (i.e. the Renaissance Platonists), the doctrine is upheld that the visible world was created by God in love, that it is the copy of a pattern pre-existing in Him, and that He will ever remain its eternal mover and restorer. The soul of man can by recognizing God draw Him into its narrow boundaries, but also by love to Him itself expand into the Infinite – and this is blessedness on earth.' But it never occurred to Burckhardt to interpret Renaissance architecture as an expression of this new vision of God.

raised over the circle that epitomized the symbolism of the Renaissance church.

It has been argued persuasively[125] that High Renaissance architects shunned theory; in other words, that they were practitioners rather than thinkers. Since the great mass of centrally planned churches belong to the period 1490-1530 (see p. 29), we would have to conclude that their plans were devised from habit rather than conviction. It is impossible to affirm conclusively what goes on in a person's mind. Nor would one dare to determine the tenuous interrelation between architectural design and symbol with any degree of precision.[126] But it seems permissible to attribute the lack of architectural theory around 1500 to chance circumstances, and not to lack of theoretical interest. The material assembled by us on page 22 confirms it.

The reader may have noticed that many centralized Renaissance churches, though by no means all, are dedicated to the Virgin. The growing importance of the cult of the Virgin from late mediaeval times on is well known. In 1439 the Council of Basel encouraged the doctrine of the Immaculate Conception and in 1476 Pope Sixtus IV approved it.[127] The Reformation gave new impetus to Catholic mariological devotion. From very early times the Virgin was glorified as the Queen of Heaven and the protector of the whole universe, owing to the accretion of ideas around her burial, assumption, and coronation.[128] The martyrium erected over her tomb, the heaven in which she is received, the crown of the heavenly Queen and the crown of stars of the *Immacolata*, the roundness of the universe over which she presides – all these interrelated ideas played their part in giving preference to centralized plans of sanctuaries and churches dedicated to the Virgin. After the foregoing it is not to be wondered at that Renaissance architects, attuned to the 'divine harmony' expressed by the perfect geometry of centralized plans, were particularly responsive to this symbolism. Moreover, there always was the connotation that it was she who had reared the Child.

*   *   *   *   *

The new interpretation of religious architecture was soon to be challenged. Carlo Borromeo in his *Instructionum Fabricae ecclesiasticae et Superlectilis ecclesiasticae Libri duo*[129] of about 1572, applied the decree of the Council of Trent to church building; for him the circular form was pagan and he recommended a return to the 'formam crucis' of the Latin Cross.[130] But even amongst those who were surrounded by the fanaticism of the Catholic reform, the humanist conception of the ideal church maintained a firm grip. In his Utopian city-state of the *Città del Sole*, published in 1623, Tommaso Campanella describes thus the principal church: 'The temple is perfectly round, free on all sides, but supported by massive and elegant columns. The dome, an admirable work, in the centre or "pole" of the temple . . . has an opening in the middle directly above the single altar in the centre . . . On the altar is nothing but two globes, of which the larger is a celestial, the smaller a terrestrial one, and in the dome are painted the stars of the sky.' In spite of the Counter Reformation centralized churches played a prominent part in seventeenth- and eighteenth-century architecture: the neo-Platonic mathematical interpretation of the universe had still a long lease of life.

125 James S. Ackerman, 'Architectural Practice in the Italian Renaissance', JOURNAL OF THE SOCIETY OF ARCHITECTURAL HISTORIANS, XIII, 1954, p. 4.
126 Very rarely do we have an architect's statement that allows us to make definite assertions. For a seventeenth-century case, see my papers in JOURNAL SOC. ARCH. HIST. XVI, 1957, p. 6, and in SAGGI E MEMORIE DI STORIA DELL'ARTE, III, 1962.
127 Emile Mâle, *L'art religieux de la fin du moyen âge*, Paris, 1931, pp. 198 ff., 209.
128 R. Krautheimer, 'Santa Maria Rotunda,' in *Arte del primo millenio. Atti del Convegno di Pavia*, 1950, p. 21 ff. See also Wittkower in SAGGI E MEMORIE (*op. cit.*).
129 Ed. E. van Drival, Paris-Arras, 1885, chap. 2, p. 15 f.; cf. A. Blunt, *op. cit.*, p. 128 f.
130 Cf. also Pietro Cataneo, *I quattro primi libri di architettura*, Venice, 1554, fol. 35v ff., who demands that the cathedral should be dedicated to Christ crucified who died for mankind's redemption and that it should therefore be built in the form of the Latin Cross. But he allows centralized forms which are 'pleasing to the eye' for minor churches of a town. Cf. also the criticism in 1595 of the Greek Cross plan of St. Peter's by the Master of Ceremonies, Gio. Paolo Mucante, in M. Cerrati, *Tiberii Alpharani De Basilicae Vaticanae antiquissima et nova structura*, Rome, 1914, p. 24 f.

PART II

ALBERTI'S APPROACH TO ANTIQUITY IN ARCHITECTURE

1. The Column in Alberti's Theory and Practice

Alberti in his *De re aedificatoria* declares that the aesthetic appearance of a building consists of two elements: Beauty and Ornament. He defines Beauty, as we have seen,[1] as 'the harmony and concord of all the parts achieved in such a manner that nothing could be added or taken away or altered except for the worse'.[2] Ornament is 'a kind of additional brightness and improvement to Beauty. Beauty is something lovely which is proper and innate and diffused throughout the whole, whilst Ornament is something added and fastened on, rather than proper and innate.'[3]

Beauty is thus, according to Alberti, a harmony inherent in the building, a harmony which, as he subsequently explains, does not result from personal fancy, but from objective reasoning. [4] Its chief characteristic is the classical idea of maintaining a uniform system of proportion throughout all parts of a building.[5] And the key to correct proportion is Pythagoras' system of musical harmony.[6]

Ornament is the embellishment of the building in the widest sense of the word, ranging from the stones used for the walls[7] to the candlesticks in the building.[8] Alberti emphasizes more than once that 'the principal ornament in all architecture certainly lies in the Column'.[9] The column, then, takes up a prominent place in Alberti's aesthetic theory, and consequently large portions of the whole work deal with it.[10]

By placing the column in the category of ornament Alberti touches on one of the central problems of Renaissance architecture. Thinking in terms of the wall, the chief constituent of all Renaissance architecture, he sees the column first and foremost as decoration. Of course, Alberti imagined his theory to be in harmony with the spirit of classical architecture. He did not know Greek temples in which the column is the basic element of the building. Roman imperial architecture, his only guide, may generically be described as half-way between the Greeks and the Renaissance. It is essentially a wall architecture with all the compromises necessitated by the transformation of the Greek orders into decoration, but in many cases it still retains the original functional meaning of the orders.

The place Alberti assigns to the column is implicitly contradicted by a passage in which he defines the column as 'a certain strengthened part of the wall, carried up perpendicularly from the foundation to the top' and 'a row of columns is indeed nothing else but a wall, open and discontinued in several places'.[11] He,

1 Cf. above, p. 18.
2 English quotations are given from the still unsurpassed translation by James Leoni (*The Architecture of Leon Battista Alberti in Ten Books . . .*, London, 1726. Re-printed by J. Rykwert, London, 1955). The quotation above as well as some of the following quotations are abbreviated and slightly modernized.
  Bk. VI, chap. 2, ed. 1485, fol. vii v: 'ut sit pulchritudo quidem certa cum ratione concinnitas universarum partium in eo cuius sint: ita ut addi, aut diminui, aut immutari possit nihil, quam improbabilius reddat.'
3 *ibid.* 'erit quidem ornamentum quasi subsidiaria quaedam lux pulchritudinis, atque veluti complementum. Ex his patere arbitror, pulchritudinem quasi suum atque innatum toto esse perfusum corpore quod pulchrum sit: ornamentum autem affici et compacti naturam sapere magis quam innati.'
4 *ibid.* 'Qui ita aedificant, ut quae aedificent probari velint, quod velle debent qui salem habent hos certa sane moveri ratione. Facere quidem aliquid certa cum ratione artis est.' See also the following sentences in which Alberti attacks those who think that 'pro cuisque libidine variam et mutabilem esse formam aedificiorum nullis artium praeceptis adstringendam.'
5 Vitruvius in his *De architectura* III, i, had summarized this axiom of all classical architecture with the words: 'Proportio est ratae partis membrorum in omni opere totiusque commodulatio, ex qua ratio efficitur symmetriarum.' The same idea is covered by Alberti's central conception 'concinnitas'.
6 Bk. IX, chap. 5; cf. below Part IV, p. 104 ff.
7 Bk. VI, chap. 5.
8 Bk. VII, chap. 13.
9 Bk. VI, chap. 13, ed. 1485, fol. o vi: 'In tota re aedificatoria primarium certe ornamentum in columnis est.'
10 Chiefly Bks. VI, VII, IX.

therefore, sees the column also as a remnant of a pierced wall, a conception diametrically opposed to that of Greek architecture, according to which the column always remained a self-contained sculptural unit.

Alberti's definition of the column as part and parcel of the wall was derived from Tuscan Proto-Renaissance buildings of the twelfth century, which in their turn were in line of descent from late classical and Byzantine works. The arcade of S. Miniato al Monte can only be interpreted in this way: solid wall appears above and between the arches so that the arcade itself is, in Alberti's words, really nothing else but 'a wall open and discontinued in several places'. Buildings like S. Miniato had a formative influence on Alberti, and his definition, though a flagrant misinterpretation of the classical column, is in agreement with the traditional Christian conception of all architecture as wall architecture.

The column as ornament or as residue of the wall – these are not Alberti's only incongruous statements on columns. Actually, in spite of what has been said so far, Alberti understood more about the classical meaning of the column than any other architect of the Quattrocento. Characteristically, he does not accept the arch supported by columns, one of the key motifs introduced into Renaissance architecture by Brunelleschi and used ever since. In spite of his definition of the column as a part of a wall Alberti must have realized that there is a contradiction between the round column and the arch. The latter actually belongs to the wall of which it has been, as it were, cut out; it may be interpreted as a wall 'discontinued in several places' (Fig. 29). Thus Alberti demands, logically, the straight entablature above the column,[12] and declares that arches should be carried by 'columnae quadrangulae', i.e. pillars.[13]

In his religious buildings Alberti consistently avoided the combination of arch and column. When he used columns he did, in fact, give them a straight entablature, while when he introduced arches he made them rest on pillars with or without half-columns set against them as decoration. Alberti found the models for both forms in Roman architecture. But whereas the first motif is Greek, the Romans playing the rôle of mediators, the second is Roman. The first motif is based on the functional meaning of the column, the second on the cohesion and unity of the wall. To explain this latter point: in the Colosseum the arched pillars may be interpreted as residues of a pierced wall, with the half-columns, which carry the straight entablature, placed against them as ornament. In practice, therefore, Alberti's conception of the column is essentially Greek, while his conception of the arch is essentially Roman – in both respects he is followed by his great successors Bramante and Palladio.

But Alberti did not stop at this discrimination between the functions of arch and column. Gradually over the years he discovered the inconsistencies inherent in any combination of column and wall. For a methodical mind like his the incompatibility between the three-dimensional and plastic quality of the column and the flat character of the wall must, in due course, have become evident. In his last period he solved the theoretical contradictions by substituting pilasters for columns. The pilaster is the logical transformation of the column for the decoration of a wall. It may be defined as a flattened column which has lost its three-dimensional and tactile value.

The *De re aedificatoria* were in the main finished about 1452[14] when he was forty-eight years old. He had only just started as an architectural practitioner – his earliest plans date from the mid-forties – and his career extended over the

11 Bk. I, chap. 10, ed. 1485, fol. b vi: 'ut de columnis et de his quae ad columnas pertinent dicendum sit: quando ipsi ordines columnarum haud aliud sunt quam pluribus in locis perfixus ad apertusque paries. Quin et columnam ipsam diffinisse cum iuvet, fortassis non ineptae esse eam dicam firmam quandam et perpetuam muri partem excitatam ad perpendiculum ab solo, imo usque ad summum tecti ferendi gratia.'

12 The combination of column and arch is only acceptable for buildings of lesser importance, Bk. VII, chap. 6; ed. 1485, fol. q: 'Sed dignissimis in operibus templorum nusquam nisi trabeatae porticus visuntur.' The same is valid for private houses, Bk. IX, chap. 4; ed. 1485, fol. x vii *v*: 'Atque praestantissimorum quadem civium porticum trabeatam esse condecet: mediocrorum autem arcuatam.' See also above, p. 18.

13 Bk. VII, chap. 15; ed. 1485, fol. r vii *v*: 'Arcuatis imitationibus debentur columnae quadrangulae. Nam in rotundis opus erit mendosum . . . ' As a remedy Alberti recommends the use of a square plinth between column and arch, if columns are used, a solution which Brunelleschi

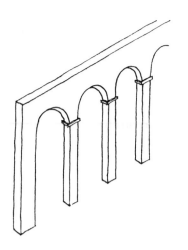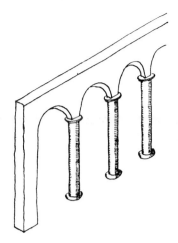

29. Diagrams: pillar and arch, column and arch

next twenty-five years. In spite of his assertion in his treatise that columns are the main ornament in all architecture, he decorated his two last façades, S. Sebastiano and S. Andrea at Mantua, with a system of pilasters. But that does not mean that Alberti had turned away from antiquity; it means rather that he had found a logical way of translating classical architecture into wall architecture proper without compromise.

Alberti's adaptation of the elements of classical architecture to a consistent wall architecture takes place in four clearly distinct stages, the mile-stones of which are his four church façades: S. Francesco in Rimini, S. Maria Novella in Florence, S. Sebastiano and S. Andrea in Mantua, which will be studied in the following pages.

2. S. Francesco at Rimini

Alberti's first ecclesiastical work, S. Francesco at Rimini (Figs. 30, 31) was executed by commission of Sigismondo Malatesta, Lord of Rimini, who wanted to turn the old thirteenth-century church into a grand memorial to himself. The work began modestly enough: between 1447 and 1449 Sigismondo had two new chapels added to the south side of the mediaeval church, and it was only in about 1450 that he conceived the idea of an entirely new exterior and of a complete transformation of the interior. Despite much research in the last decades[15] we do not know at what stage Alberti joined this enterprise, to what extent he was responsible for the interior, nor what exactly the shape and construction of the dome would have been which Matteo de' Pasti rendered in his medal (Fig. 32).[16] We do know, however, that from Rome Alberti carefully watched over the execution of the exterior which had risen to a considerable height by the winter of 1454 but remained unfinished at Sigismondo's death in 1466.

For the design of his façade Alberti borrowed from Roman antiquity the motif of the triumphal arch.[17] The large central arch opens into the church, while in the narrower side arches were to be placed the sarcophagi of Sigismondo and his

has re-introduced in his Loggia degli Innocenti. So after the first revolutionary sentence Alberti reconciles himself to tradition, but the whole passage reveals that this solution was not quite to his liking.
14 Cf. above, p. 3, note 1.
15 The classic work by Corrado Ricci, *Il Tempio Malatestiano*, Milan, 1924, has never been superseded. See also M. Salmi, in *Studi Romagnoli*, II, 1951 (with further bibliography) and *id.*, in ATTI DELL'ACCADEMIA DI SAN LUCA, 1951-52. Cesare Brandi, *Il Tempio Malatestiano*, Turin, 1956.
16 The interesting but fanciful drawing of the Tempio Malatestiano as a centrally planned building in the fifteenth-century North Italian sketchbook of the Soane Museum, London, shows a low dome over a high drum; see M. Röthlisberger, in *Palladio*, 1957, p. 96, Fig. 2.
17 Although it is undoubtedly true that for a number of details (base, half-columns, disks, mouldings) Alberti relied on the Arch of Augustus at Rimini, to which scholars always refer, the prototype for the whole system was, of course, the tripartite Arch of Constantine.

30, 31. Alberti. S. Francesco, Rimini: (*above*) façade, (*below*) south side

mistress, Isotta, whom he did not marry until 1456. With the closing of these niches Alberti's Triumph-over-Death concept has been impaired. But something of it still survives at the right (south) front, where the arches contain sarcophagi of the *uomini illustri* (Fig. 31).

To bury people under the arches of the exterior of a church was actually a mediaeval custom; examples are numerous and were well known to Alberti.[18] The tombs planned for the façade and the side fronts of S. Francesco derive from such mediaeval models. But by placing sarcophagi with classically styled inscriptions under serene Roman arches Alberti created an impressive pantheon for heroes rather than a burial-ground with its traditional funereal associations.

It is with this impression that one enters the building and here the visitor experiences an anti-climax, for he finds himself inside a Gothic church.[19] Confirmation of one's immediate reaction that the same man could not have devised both the exterior and the interior seems to be furnished by the inscriptions inside the church naming Matteo de' Pasti as architect. Yet we know that Matteo took orders from Alberti; we know that Alberti had a model made of the entire structure and that the unexecuted eastern part of the interior was designed by him. Was Matteo de' Pasti the superintendent rather than the creative architect?[20] If the ultimate responsibility lay with Alberti, he may have had reasons for not interfering too drastically with the Gothic character of the old church. We shall see how he solved a similar predicament in the façade of S. Maria Novella.

For the exterior of S. Francesco, Alberti was given a free hand. He built around the mediaeval church a shell-like structure, screening the old walls with his Roman arches (Fig. 33).[21] By placing the entire 'temple' on a high base he isolated it from its surroundings and gave it a distinct character of detachment.[22] We have seen that it was one of Alberti's theoretical requests that 'temples' be raised above the level of the common world.[23]

Quattrocento architects, faced with the problem of the church façade, found themselves in a difficult position, for there was no classical system which could be readily adapted for this purpose. S. Francesco is the first façade in the new style[24] and, by virtue of the grafting of the triumphal-arch motif upon a wall, it represents an attempt at a coherent classical solution of an intricate problem. From then on the triumphal-arch motif was repeatedly used for church façades and remained for some time one of the few effective ideas in this context.

But Alberti's recourse to a classical system for an entirely new task led to difficulties which, at this stage of his development, he could only resolve by a compromise. The Roman triumphal arch consists of one storey; the church façade, by contrast, requires two storeys when it has to screen a high nave between low aisles or chapels. This being the case in S. Francesco, Alberti had to find a way of expanding a one-storeyed into a two-storeyed system. The upper tier of the façade of S. Francesco was never finished, but its main features can be reconstructed from Matteo de' Pasti's medal of 1450 (Fig. 32). Low, curved walls over the side bays screen the roof and a full second storey over the central bay shows an arched aedicula crowned with floral ornament under which a tripartite window opens within a high niche. For this design Alberti followed a tradition well known from late Gothic churches in Venice and the *terra ferma*.[25] Recently it has been discovered that in 1454 he broke with the older tradition in one important respect, for he now planned over the side bays straight sloping walls

32. Matteo de'Pasti. Medal of S. Francesco, 1450

18 Cf. the façade of S. Maria Novella with which Alberti himself was concerned a few years later. For a full discussion of this question, cf. Ricci, *op. cit.*, p. 281 ff.

19 It should, however, never be forgotten that what we see to-day is only a fragment and that the enormous dome would have immediately engaged the beholder's attention.

20 This is (in contrast to Ricci's) Geymüller's conclusion (see Stegmann-Geymüller, *Die Architektur der Renaissance in Toscana*, Vol. III, 1885-1907, Appendix to Alberti, p. 4), and I still believe that Geymüller, despite some incorrect statements, was right in claiming Alberti as the master-mind.

21 The plan shows the new walls with seven regular niches to each side, independent of the chapel walls with their irregularly spaced windows.

22 Though the entrance door had for obvious reasons to be on the street level; cf. below, p. 55.

23 Bk. VII, chap. 5, ed. 1485, fol. p vi: 'Mea quidem sententia aream porticus et templi totius, quando id ad dignitatem vehementer faciat, exaggeratam atque a caetero urbis solo extantem esse oportet.'

24 Brunelleschi's façade of the Cappella Pazzi is actually the only Renaissance façade of importance before S. Francesco. But being conceived as part of a *chiostro* it presents a different problem from the isolated church façade.

25 Cf. the material collected by Ricci, *op. cit.*, p. 255 ff.

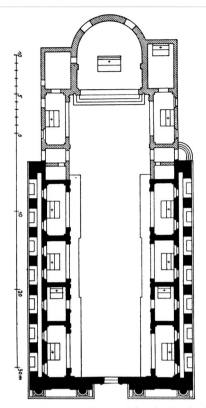

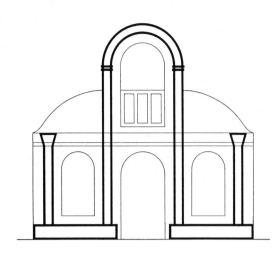

33, 34. S. Francesco, Rimini: (*above*) plan, (*right*) diagram of the façade

26 This fact can be deduced from the autograph of Alberti's famous letter to Matteo de' Pasti, lost for almost two hundred years and recently acquired by the Pierpont Morgan Library, New York. The letter, ably published by Cecil Grayson (New York, 1957) contains a small drawing by Alberti on which the above conclusions are based. In his text Grayson proved convincingly that the letter was written on 18 November 1454. See also Mario Salmi, 'La facciata de "Malatestiano",' in LA NAZIONE, 3 August, 1960.

27 Cf. the pilasters and the tripartite window replacing the traditional round one. For Alberti's rejection of the circular window, cf. Ricci, *op. cit.*, p. 259 ff.

28 It was already adumbrated in triumphal arches. Apart from the Arch of Constantine type with equal projections of the entablature above the columns, there exists another type (e.g. Arch of Titus, etc., cf. also Fig. 47) in which the projection above the two middle columns runs through uninterruptedly so that a kind of aedicula encloses the central section. The columns cannot, therefore, be seen as a simple sequence (a,a,a,a), but their rhythm must be interpreted as a,bb,a.

29 Alberti may have been influenced by the arcades of Theodoric's Tomb at Ravenna which he calls a 'nobile delubrum' (Bk. I, chap. 8).

(probably corresponding to the present ones) to be decorated with a (never executed) scroll design,[26] a forerunner of the infinitely more imposing scrolls of S. Maria Novella.

Even this belated change could not entirely harmonize the essentially mediaeval second storey with the classical main storey. While important details of the second tier were classical in design,[27] they do not conceal the fact that at this early phase Alberti was satisfied with an attempt to reconcile two systems with entirely different pedigrees.

In co-ordinating lower and upper tier the entablature projecting above each column presented a particular problem. Alberti borrowed this corollary of the blending of wall and column from triumphal arches. A straight and unbroken entablature creates a marked horizontal barrier, whereas a projection of the entablature above the columns effects a vertical continuation of the latter. The eye expects the vertical movement to run on into the upper storey. But in S. Francesco the outer columns have no crowning feature and only the two middle columns are continued in the pilasters above. Tied together by the arch topping the second storey, the columns and pilasters form a unified central motif. On the other hand, the high base on which the columns rest is interrupted by the portal and on this level each middle column is linked to an outer column by a common base. This complicated rhythm,[28] where the outer bays are closed at ground level but open and discontinued above and the central bay is open at ground level but continued and closed in the second storey (Fig. 34), resulted from a daring experiment in joining incompatible motifs and, understandably, was not repeated during the Quattrocento. But similar complexities are well known from sixteenth- and seventeenth-century architecture and their familiarity has made us disinclined to probe into their origin. In the last analysis they derived from the compromise solution almost forced upon Alberti when he chose to apply a classical system to a non-classical type of building.

Faithful to his own theory Alberti used columns as the principal ornament of the façade; and, in accordance with his demands, the arches rest on broad pillars while the columns carry a straight entablature. But theory and practice are not always good bedfellows: our analysis has shown that the blending of the columns with the wall led to difficulties which Alberti neither attempted nor was able to solve.

On the other hand, pillar and arch belong to the same domain of the wall. Nobody has ever shown this more clearly than Alberti in the side fronts of S. Francesco (Fig. 31). Here he left the pillar-and-arch motif without the ornament of the column which he reserved for the more privileged position of the façade. It is impossible to deny that Alberti logically evolved the architecture of the sides from that of the front, stripped of its columns. But, at the same time, he must have been guided by visions of Roman architecture. No later architect has come nearer to the spirit of Roman architecture, as found, say, in the inner arcades of the Colosseum.[29] Nor had any earlier architect so thoughtfully welded together an entire building by the flawless application of Pythagorean proportions.[30]

3. S. Maria Novella

At S. Maria Novella (Fig. 35) Alberti's problem was not dissimilar to that of S. Francesco. Here too a mediaeval church existed to which a façade had to be added. But the theme of S. Francesco – the screening of the old building by an entirely new and independent front – could not be repeated since parts of the façade of S. Maria Novella were standing and had to be preserved. Thus Alberti was faced with the inescapable task of having to incorporate into his design the Gothic tombs, the side doors under their pointed arches, the high blind arcades[31] as well as the large circular window in the upper tier.

Accordingly most modern critics have admired Alberti's skill in giving the façade the imprint of his style, despite all handicaps. But, frankly, at a first glance the unprejudiced beholder will rather err in the opposite direction, for he will be struck by the mediaeval appearance of the façade.[32]

This impression is due not only to the rather prominent mediaeval elements, but also to Alberti's patent wish to harmonize his own work with the parts already *in situ*. Seen in this light the façade appears as a peculiar historical paradox, for despite the fact that Alberti intended to reconcile the past and the present, he created the most important façade of the new style and set the example, as is well known, for the most common type of church façade for a long time to come.

Alberti's writings throw light on the ideas which animated him when he was faced with the problem of continuing the Gothic façade. We have seen that his basic axiom was to produce harmony and concord of all the parts in a building ('concinnitas universarum partium'). This principle also implies a correlation of qualitatively different parts – Alberti's 'finitio'[33] – and consequently a careful reconciliation of old and new. Thus the logical pursuit of the classical concept of 'concinnitas' could lead to unclassical results.[34] This is no mere theory. While engaged on the construction of S. Francesco, Alberti instructed Matteo de' Pasti with the following words in a famous letter written from Rome: 'One wants to improve what has been built, and not to spoil what is yet to be done'[35] – the inference of the first part of the sentence being that the mutual accord of old and new parts should not be lost sight of. The restrained modernization of the Gothic interior seems a perfect illustration of these words.[36]

30 The Pythagorean theme was convincingly demonstrated by Gerda Soergel, *Untersuchungen über den theoretischen Architekturentwurf von 1450-1550 in Italien*, Munich, 1958 (Dissertation), p. 11, and, abbreviated, in KUNSTCHRONIK, XIII, 1960, p. 349 f.

31 In the earlier editions of this book I submitted the hypothesis that these arcades formed part of Alberti's structure. I was led to this belief because the blind arcades constitute an anachronism at about 1350, the period of the Gothic parts of the façade. We have, however, to accept the fact that the Gothic architect had archaising tendencies and built the arcades in the style of the Florentine Proto-Renaissance of the late twelfth century (see also Paatz, *Die Kirchen von Florenz*, Frankfurt, 1952, p. 678). A renewed study of the façade revealed that Alberti placed his coupled column and pillar at the corners over the last arch of the older arcade.

32 Older authors such as Bottari, Milizia, and Quatremère de Quincy did not hesitate to draw the conclusion that the façade contained 'troppo del tedesco' (too much Gothic) to be attributed to Alberti; cf. Mancini, *op. cit.*, p. 459 f.

33 Bk. IX, chap. 5.

34 Cf. Erwin Panofsky, 'Das erste Blatt aus dem "Libro" des Giorgio Vasari', STÄDEL JAHRBUCH, VI, 1930, p. 44 ff. (English version in *Meaning in the Visual Arts*, New York, 1955, p. 191.)

35 'Vuolsi aiutare quel ch'è fatto, e non guastare quello che s'abbia a fare.' Cf. Cecil Grayson, *An Autograph Letter from L.B. Alberti to Matteo de' Pasti*, New York, 1957, p. 17.

36 Ricci (p. 255) uses Alberti's words, quoted in the last note, as confirmation of his opinion that the modernization of the interior of S. Francesco is not by Alberti. But this interpretation seems to contradict the meaning of that sentence. Geymüller, *op. cit.*, p. 4, interprets Alberti's sentence in the sense which seems to us the only possible one.

35. Alberti, S. Maria Novella, Florence

36. S. Maria Novella, Florence. Entrance

37. S. Francesco, Rimini. Entrance

It is clear then that Alberti was bent on remaining absolutely true to his own architectural principles without breaking away from the spirit of the existing portions of the façade. Since these portions already had coloured marble incrustation (white panels framed by green bands), a method of decoration which Tuscan Gothic had borrowed from the Proto-Renaissance, he seems to have felt justified in interpreting the whole façade in terms of the 'classical' Proto-Renaissance and not in those of the 'barbarous' Gothic.

In fact, the consistent incrustation alone makes Alberti's façade a posthumous member of the twelfth-century family of Proto-Renaissance buildings. Moreover, the façade contains definite elements borrowed from S. Miniato and from the Baptistery in Florence. The Baptistery supplied some details, such as the pillars at the corners with their horizontal incrustation. And S. Miniato was the model for the disposition of the façade in two storeys, of which the upper one screens only the nave and is crowned by a pediment.[37]

But it is those touches which are at first sight not so apparent and which are more difficult to define, that give the façade its new and, it may now be said, revolutionary character. First, there is the novel element of the high attic between the lower and the upper tier. It helps to overcome some of the difficulties which remained unsolved in S. Francesco at Rimini. The inner pilasters of the upper storey are placed above the columns of the lower tier, but the outer pilasters do not refer to corresponding members below. The existence of the attic conceals this discrepancy, whereas in S. Miniato, where the orders of the two storeys are independent of each other but where there is no attic, the discord is immediately apparent to a classically trained eye. The attic in S. Maria Novella is at the same time effective as a horizontal barrier and neutralizes the vertical tendency of the projecting entablature above the columns, the motif which had led to such difficulties in S. Francesco. Moreover, in contrast to S. Miniato, the façade is crowned by a classical pediment, just as the orders have classical entablatures. And the difference in width between the upper and lower storeys is bridged by the famous scrolls so that here, unlike S. Miniato, there is complete cohesion between the upper and lower parts.

Above all, Alberti again used colossal columns to articulate the main storey, for at this period columns were still for him the chief ornament of all architecture. They give the façade a powerful rhythmic accentuation; and at the same time the two outer columns, by being boldly connected with pillars, bind the whole structure together (Fig. 51).

The two inner columns frame the most elaborate part of the façade, the entrance (Fig. 36). Pilasters carrying a semi-circular arch enclose a niche just deep enough to accommodate two further pilasters at each side. The entablature above the pilasters runs right across the niche, the back wall of which up to the entablature is completely filled by the door itself.[38] The similarity of this entrance to that of S. Francesco (Fig. 37) has often been emphasized. But the portal of the earlier church lacks the compactness and precision of that of S. Maria Novella. In S. Francesco there is a vagueness about all the details[39] and a playfulness in the decorations,[40] and, above all, the door is floating, as it were, in the large space of the niche. The same difference of conception is apparent in all the other parts of the two buildings[41] and manifests itself most clearly in the crowning of S. Maria Novella by the austere classical pediment and of S. Francesco by the decorated arch which was not carried out.

37 This has, of course, often been emphasized. M. Weinberger, in JOURNAL OF THE WARBURG AND COURTAULD INSTITUTES, IV, 1940-1, p. 79, argues convincingly that Alberti's S. Maria Novella was influenced by Arnolfo di Cambio's design of the façade of the Cathedral at Florence.
38 The door was executed by Giovanni di Bertino (cf. Mancini, op. cit., p. 460) to whom some authors wrongly attributed an active part in the design of the façade.
39 The capitals, for instance, which carry the arch do not crown proper pilasters, but break into large pillars.
40 Cf. the heavy garlands which hang from the pediment of the entrance, and the coloured marble patterns under the arch.
41 Compare, e.g., the corner motif of coupled column and pilaster in S. Maria Novella with the outer columns of S. Francesco beyond which the wall runs on.

The date of the façade of S. Maria Novella has often been a matter for discussion. Relying on documentary indications some scholars date the beginning in 1448, others in 1456.[42] The latter date is much nearer the truth, for according to a document in the Rucellai Archives the façade was begun in 1458. The inscription in the upper entablature dates its completion in 1470, but the portal was still unfinished in 1478.[43] The entrance to S. Francesco, designed in 1450, is only the first step leading up to the fully developed classical composition displayed in that of S. Maria Novella.

It is characteristic that for the entrance of S. Maria Novella Alberti followed closely the main features of a work of classical antiquity, the entrance to the Pantheon. Here, too, there occurs the motif of the two pilasters placed at right angles to the doorway at each side of a deep niche; here also we find a large door with the entablature and arch above.

It is clear, then, that Alberti imbued his additions to the old façade with motifs directly derived from ancient buildings. This was for him consistent with his professed belief that it was possible to maintain continuity between the old and the new parts while at the same time improving upon the work of his predecessors – 'vuolsi aiutare quello ch'è fatto'.

All the new elements introduced by Alberti in the façade, the columns, the pediment, the attic, and the scrolls, would remain isolated features were it not for that all-pervading harmony which formed the basis and background of his whole theory. Harmony, the essence of beauty, consists, as we have seen, in the relationship of the parts to each other and to the whole, and, in fact, a single system of proportion permeates the façade, and the place and size of every single part and detail is fixed and defined by it. Proportions recommended by Alberti are the simple relations of $1:1$, $1:2$, $1:3$, $2:3$, $3:4$, etc.,[44] which are the elements of musical harmony and which Alberti found in classical buildings. The diameter of the Pantheon, for instance, corresponds exactly to its height, half its diameter corresponds to the height of the substructure as well as to that of the dome, and so forth.

Such simple ratios were used by Alberti. The whole façade of S. Maria Novella can be exactly circumscribed by a square (Fig. 38). A square of half the side of the large square defines the relationship of the two storeys. The main storey can be divided into two such squares, while one encloses the upper storey. In other words, the whole building is related to its main parts in the proportions of one to two, which is in musical terms an octave, and this proportion is repeated in the ratio of the width of the upper storey to that of the lower storey.

The same ratio of $1:2$ recurs in the sub-units of the single storeys (Fig. 39). The central bay of the upper storey forms a perfect square, the sides of which are equal to half the width of the whole storey. Two squares of that same size encase the pediment and upper entablature which together are thus exactly as high as the storey under them. Half the side of this square corresponds to the width of the upper side bays and is also equal to the height of the attic.[45] The same unit defines the proportions of the entrance bay. The height of the entrance bay is one and a half times its width, so that the relation of width to height is here two to three. Finally the dark square incrustations of the attic are one third of the height of the attic, and these squares are related to the diameter of the columns as 2:1. Thus the whole façade is geometrically built up of a progressive duplication or, alternatively, a progressive halving of ratios. It is clear then that Alberti's

42 The date 'about 1456' is given by Milanesi in his edition of Vasari, II, p. 541, note 1, and accepted for instance by Willich, *Die Baukunst der Renaissance in Italien* ('Handbuch der Kunstw.') Vol. I, p. 83. The year 1448 appears in a document published by Mancini, *op. cit.*, p. 466, and has been accepted by Baum, *Baukunst und dekorative Plastik der Frührenaissance*, Stuttgart, 1926, p. 321, and others.

43 I found these documents only after the second edition of this book had appeared. They confirm the essential correctness of my original conclusions which I had based on a hypothetical reconstruction of Alberti's development. The text of the new documents will be published elsewhere.

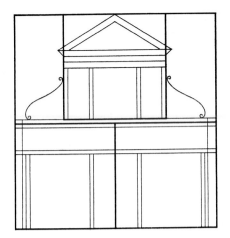 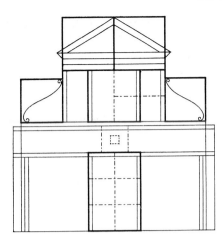

38, 39. Diagrams of the façade of S. Maria Novella, Florence

theoretical precept that the same proportion be kept throughout the building has here been fulfilled. It is the strict application of an unbroken series of ratios that marks the unmediaeval character of this pseudo-Proto-Renaissance façade and makes it the first great Renaissance example of classical *eurythmia*.[46]

4. S. Sebastiano and S. Andrea at Mantua

The complete absence of columns in the next two church façades, S. Sebastiano and S. Andrea at Mantua (Figs. 41, 46), signifies a decisive turning-point in Alberti's interpretation of architecture. It may be recalled[47] that in about 1450 Alberti considered columns to be the main ornament of architecture and that at that time he could not conceive of the noblest building, the temple or church, without this noblest form of decoration; indeed, he acted accordingly in S. Francesco and S. Maria Novella.

It is therefore fair to assume that his renunciation of the use of columns in S. Sebastiano and S. Andrea reflects a change of theory – a change that takes us beyond the position he advocated in his *Ten Books*. Although the volte-face cannot be documented by an explicit statement on his part, the evidence of his two late structures is sufficiently revealing: he must have weighed the contemporary demand of a logical wall structure against the authority of classical antiquity and decided to reject the compromise of joining column and wall – the compromise of many a Renaissance architect – in favour of a uniform wall architecture.[48]

Nevertheless, as before, his thought remained focused on the ancients but turned to the question as to how their work could be brought to bear upon modern requirements. Behind the façades of S. Sebastiano and S. Andrea lies the classical temple front with columns, entablature and pediment. But the wall of the cella has protruded, as it were, into the order which, appropriate to the character of the wall, has been changed from columns to pilasters.

44 Bk. IX, chaps. 5, 6. See Part IV.
45 The scrolls form the diagonal of a square, the side of which is related to the height of the attic as 5:3 or to the height of the upper tier as 5:6.
46 In his constructive review of the first edition of this book, James Ackerman (ART BULLETIN, 1951, p. 198) points out that Alberti's method is 'the rationalized offspring of the Gothic elevation *ad quadratum* . . . ' But it is precisely the derivation of the system from the diameter of the column (Vitruvius' module) that differentiates Alberti's approach from that of the Middle Ages. See also my discussion of proportion in Part IV of this book.
47 Cf. above, p. 41.
48 Cf. above, p. 42f.

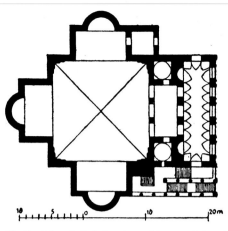

40, 41. Alberti. S. Sebastiano, Mantua: (*above*) plan, (*right*) present state of the façade

49 Cf. Rivoira, *Roman Architecture*, 1925, Fig. 182. The building has been restored and freed from mediaeval alterations.
50 The documents about S. Sebastiano were published by Braghirolli in ARCHIVIO STORICO ITALIANO IX, 1869, p. 3 ff., by F. Malaguzzi in RASSEGNA D'ARTE,I, 1901, p. 13 and by Davari, *ibid.*, p. 93 f. Cf., also Mancini, *op. cit.*, p. 392 ff.
51 Braghirolli, *op. cit.*, p. 13: 'Havemo visto quanto per la tua ne scrivi del parere de D. Baptista degli Alberti circa *il minuire quelli pillastri del portico* . . . , del che assai te commendiamo et poi chel pare cussi (così) a lui, cussi pare anche a nui (noi)'. Dated October 13, 1470. – Cf. also Lodovico Gonzaga's letter to Alberti of November 25, 1470 (Braghirolli, p. 16) in which he thanks Alberti for 'quelle misure et modi di lavorare' for the vestibule and expresses the desire to finish it quickly.
'Minuire' can mean either 'reduce in size' or 'reduce in numbers', but only the latter makes sense in our context.
52 In fact, only four of these arches had ever been given architectural facing.
53 Typical are his instructions for porticos with more than one storey. Bk. VIII, chap. 6: 'If you would make a second row of columns over the first,

Occasionally the Romans themselves had made the same adaptation of the Greek temple front, though probably not before the second century A.D., and never in temples. The tomb of Annia Regilla in the Valle Caffarella near Rome, dating from the second half of the second century A.D., is an example which was certainly known to Alberti.[49]

In S. Sebastiano as well as in S. Andrea the façade is placed in front of a vestibule, and in both façades the main proportions are identical. As in S. Maria Novella their width corresponds to their height from the level of the entrance to the apex of the pediment, so that they can be enclosed in a square, a proportion of 1:1 favoured by Alberti. But only up to this point does the conception of the two façades coincide. In most other respects they are planned on different and even opposite lines. First of all, S. Sebastiano shows as much solid wall as possible, S. Andrea as little as possible; here, apart from the enormous central arch, the side bays open into doors, niches and windows, one above the other. In S. Sebastiano an unusually heavy entablature rests on unusually thin pilasters; in S. Andrea the relation has been reversed. Finally in S. Sebastiano the central bay is remarkably narrow and the side bays are remarkably wide; again this relation has been reversed in S. Andrea. So much for the first impression produced by a comparison of these façades. It is clear that they represent two alternative schemes for reviving the classical temple front, both adapted to the needs of wall architecture.

On further investigation these façades present innumerable problems. S. Sebastiano is the earlier structure and will therefore be discussed first. The building, foreshadowing the Greek-Cross structures of the Renaissance (Fig. 40), was begun in 1460 and after a quick start progressed comparatively slowly.[50]

In 1470 the vestibule had not yet been finished. By good fortune a letter of this year has been preserved in which Lodovico Gonzaga, who had commissioned the building, wrote to Luca Fancelli, the architect in charge, expressing agreement to Alberti's proposal *to reduce the number of pilasters on the portico*.[51] Since pilasters appear only on its façade (and not in its interior) it must have been here that the reduction was made.

There existed, therefore, a project for the façade which was followed from 1460 until 1470, when Alberti proposed to alter it by the omission of pilasters. Lodovico Gonzaga's letter provides the clue for the reconstruction of the 1460 scheme. The width of the wall of each of the large outer bays of the present façade corresponds exactly to twice the width of the central bay plus one pilaster. In other words, a pilaster set up in the middle of each outer bay divides it into two equal bays, the size of the central bay. The pilaster fits exactly into the space between the arched and the adjacent rectangular opening. The result then is an equally spaced distribution of six pilasters over the plane of the façade. This should be regarded as the salient feature of Alberti's design of 1460.

But a further problem is presented by the substructure. Fig. 41 shows the façade as it appears to-day after the restoration of 1925. Three central arches now give access to a crypt which extends underneath the entire church. Two outer arches are blocked by the modern flights of stairs. Before 1925 all five arches were visible;[52] but they were walled up and their bases were hidden below the ground level (Fig.42). Prior to the modern restoration the only access to the church was a staircase to the left of the façade which leads to a small Quattrocento loggia at one end of the vestibule. The idea of attaching such a staircase, unrelated to the main structure, is as incompatible with Alberti's style as are the stylistic details of the loggia itself. This staircase, therefore, can neither belong to Alberti's project of 1460 nor to the new scheme of 1470. The modern reconstruction, however, must also be incorrect, for the arcades behind the stairs were surely built to be seen. Nor can a precedent for such a façade be found in Renaissance architecture.

But now it must be asked whether these arcades belonged to Alberti's original design. This appears to be impossible. The pilasters of the façade proper are much broader than those of the structure beneath them. This fact alone excludes Alberti's authorship, for the placing of a high and broad order above a lower and narrower one is utterly opposed to his principles.[53]

The history of the building helps to solve this problem. The façade as it existed before 1925 was not finished until long after Alberti's death. In a letter written in 1478, i.e. six years after Alberti had died, Luca Fancelli expressed his satisfaction with the stone which was being used for the vestibule.[54] In 1478 Lodovico Gonzaga died and his son Federico eventually abandoned the completion of S. Sebastiano. We still hear in May 1479 that the same Fancelli had successfully finished the difficult task of placing the two sections of the main entablature in position.[55] After this there is almost complete silence for the next twenty years.[56] Not until 1499 was the little-known architect Pellegrino Ardizoni entrusted with the completion of the building.[57]

Evidently without a knowledge of Alberti's plans, Ardizoni finished the church to the best of his poor ability. The open arcades of the substructure must be attributed to him as well as the staircase on the left; for these features are supplementary.[58] He must also have been responsible for the heavy frame of the

42. S. Sebastiano, Mantua. Before the restoration

those columns should be one-fourth part thinner and shorter than those below.'

54 Braghirolli, *op. cit.*, p. 28. The vestibule, therefore, cannot have been finished in 1472 as maintained by Braghirolli himself (p. 18), Mancini, *op. cit.*, p. 398, Stegmann, *op. cit.*, p. 7, and others.

55 Davari, *op. cit.*, p. 94: 'In questa sera abiamo tirato su tute due le chornici grandi del porticho di S. Sebastiano e gratia de dio sono fora dun grande inpacio.'

56 In 1488 the clergy of S. Sebastiano tried to finish the church, which at that time was already partly in ruins. Cf. Davari, *op. cit.*, p. 93 f.

57 Malaguzzi, *op. cit.*, p. 13.

58 As Ardizoni did not know that Alberti wanted to cover the substructure with a staircase (see below), he had to decorate the visible substructure and at the same time find a solution for the position of the staircase.

59 It had been bricked up before the restoration of 1925.

60 The parapets with putti holding the coat of arms and the emblems of the Gonzaga have been unconvincingly attributed to Luca Fancelli by Intra in ARCHIVIO STOR. LOMBARDO, XIII, 1886, p. 669, whom Mancini, *op. cit.*, p. 393, followed. They must belong to Ardizoni's period of 1499. Venturi, *Storia dell' Arte Italiana*, vi, p. 470 attributes them to a late follower of Donatello.

43. Giacomo da Pietrasanta. S. Agostino, Rome. Façade, 1479-83

central door which is partly superimposed on the adjoining pilasters. Careless and without imagination, he here copied exactly the frame of the central door which leads from the vestibule into the church. It seems that we must also ascribe to him minor details such as the straight top of the window in the central bay[59] which should probably have been arched corresponding to the windows in similar positions in the other arms of the Greek Cross.

We may therefore conclude that the modern restoration agrees neither with Ardizoni's plans – with whose arcades it interferes – nor with Alberti's project. In the first place we have no evidence that Alberti designed arcades in the substructure. Assuming that no such feature was considered by him, we are free to place his staircase where it belongs: in front of the church. It is tempting to conjecture that he planned a large staircase leading up to the level of the vestibule and extending across the whole width of the façade. A simple observation supports this hypothesis: the five openings of the façade are really doors and, obviously, doors are designed to lead somewhere. In the absence of such a staircase they had to be changed into balconies.[60]

Our assumption that a wide staircase was originally planned is above all to be derived from Alberti's own ideas and work. Churches, Alberti says,[61] ought to stand on a high base. S. Francesco at Rimini was a special case. Here he had to cut the base in the centre, for the level of the entrance was determined by that of the Gothic interior. In antiquity a broad staircase led up to the height of the portico of the temple. I have no doubt that this was in Alberti's mind when he devised the staircase for S. Andrea (begun in 1472). Echoes of his conception are to be found in some church façades, mainly in Rome, built by minor architects who in this and other respects were dependent on him (Fig. 43).[62] The precedent for all these staircases was, it can now be suggested, Alberti's project for S. Sebastiano.

As a result of this inquiry a tentative reconstruction of Alberti's design of 1460 may be undertaken (Fig. 44). His project represented a proper temple front – with due allowance, of course, for its projection on to a single wall plane.[63]

There is still one element which seems to disturb the classical harmony, namely the break in the entablature and the connection of its two halves by an arch in the pediment.[64] There existed any number of combinations of the straight entablature with the arch. Brunelleschi had introduced the motif into Renaissance architecture in his Cappella Pazzi, following such pseudo-classical mediaeval works as the façade of the Cathedral of Città Castellana near Rome. But one hesitates to accept a dependence of Alberti's severe temple front on such prototypes. On the other hand, the motif occurs frequently in Hellenistic temples and tombs in Asia Minor.[65] Although the idea is very tempting, it cannot be assumed that Alberti had any knowledge of these faraway places. The only building that could have influenced him is a monument well known to artists of the Quattrocento, namely the arch at Orange (Fig. 45),[66] the side fronts of which show the motif together with an articulation similar to our reconstruction of Alberti's S. Sebastiano.

This Hellenistic motif gives the façade of 1460 a vitality which is in contrast to its otherwise austere character. It points, still unobtrusively, to the beginning of a state of fermentation out of which a new approach to classical architecture developed. The first indication of such a change is Alberti's proposal in 1470 to alter his project of 1460 for S. Sebastiano. By omitting two of the six pilasters the

44. Façade of S. Sebastiano, Mantua. Reconstruction of Alberti's project of 1460

45. Triumphal Arch, Orange, detail. From a drawing by Giuliano da Sangallo

A drawing in the Uffizi by Labacco (published by Mancini, p. 396) shows only three doors in the portico. The drawing probably reproduces a scheme by Alberti since the dome, which was never executed, appears in it. It is the most important document for the reconstruction of the interior.
61 See above pp 18 f.
62 Cf. above all S. Maria del Popolo and S. Agostino in Rome, and the façade of the Cathedral in Turin. S. Agostino is especially important because here the stairs do not turn and run against the wall of the façade as in S. Andrea but follow the pattern of classical temples (Fig. 43).

46. Alberti. S. Andrea, Mantua. Façade, 1470 ff

63 P. Frankl, *Die Renaissancearchitektur in Italien*, Leipzig 1912, p. 36, had anticipated this reconstruction with his ingenious remark: 'Vielleicht die erste antike Tempelfront des christlichen Kirchenbaues'.
64 This motif must be attributed to Alberti, for as the letter quoted above, p. 53, note 55, shows, the entablature was put into position by Luca Fancelli who was a faithful executor of Alberti's designs.
65 Cf. the temple at Termessus, reproduced by Ricci, *Leon Battista Alberti*, 1917, Pl. 21, who was also the first to discuss Alberti's use of this motif.
66 Here illustrated after the drawing by Giuliano da Sangallo, cf. Christian Hülsen, *Il libro di Giuliano da Sangallo*, Leipzig, 1910, Pl. 25.
67 Alberti died in 1472. The building was carried out by Luca Fancelli until 1493 in accordance with Alberti's plans. The eventful history of the construction dragged on for several centuries and the interior decoration was not executed until the early nineteenth century. The best survey is given by Ritscher in *Zeitschrift für Bauwesen*, 1899, pp. 1 ff., 181 ff. For the manifold problems connected with the planning of S. Andrea, see now Erich Hubala, in KUNSTCHRONIK, XIII, 1960, p. 354 f.
68 Cf. Schumacher, *op. cit.*, p. 11.
69 Thus the simple sequence of pilasters is slightly modified (a',a,a,a'). The details of the façade make it certain that Alberti's plans were here accurately followed. (I had reached this conclusion before the last war, but Hubala, *op. cit.*, p. 356, now believes that Alberti was only responsible for the over-all project.)
70 Alberti intended to revive what he believed to have been the form of the Etruscan temple (cf. above, p. 16, note 6) as he himself explained in a letter to Lodovico Gonzaga accompanying his first

importance of the wall was emphasized and the dogmatic application of the classical temple front to his wall structure abandoned. It is this development toward a consciously unorthodox interpretation of classical architecture which marks the latest phase of Alberti's art.

Next to the revised façade of S. Sebastiano, S. Andrea, designed in the same year 1470 and begun in 1472,[67] illustrates Alberti's new approach to classical architecture (Fig. 46). Behind the façade of S. Andrea lies not only the idea of the temple front but also that of the triumphal arch.[68] The enormous central arch easily reveals its pedigree. But the model here followed was not the type of triumphal arch with three passages, used for S. Francesco at Rimini. This time Alberti chose the type of the Arch of Titus in Rome or of Trajan at Ancona (Fig. 47) with only one large passage and two small bays at the sides. In some of these triumphal arches the moulding on which the central arch rests is carried on across the narrow side bays and seems to be broken into by the large order. Alberti incorporated this motif into his façade. It strengthens the impression that the giant pilasters belong both to the triumphal arch and to the temple front. In other words, these two classical systems have here been merged in an unprecedented way.

Alberti's fusion of two systems incompatible in antiquity is thoroughly unclassical and paves the way for the Mannerist conception of architecture during the sixteenth century. It is noteworthy that Alberti tried his utmost to unify the two systems also by subtle application of detail. The mouldings and denticulation of the entablature on which the pediment of the 'temple' rests are repeated in the entablature which by rights belongs to the triumphal arch and the form of the capitals of the outer pilasters – which is not identical with that of the inner ones[69] – is echoed in the capitals of the small order.

It is now necessary to discuss for a moment the interior in so far as it has a bearing on the façade. The large vaulted hall of the nave with the three chapels opening on each side – the whole a complete and revolutionary novelty – derives from impressions which Alberti had received in Roman thermae or the Basilica of Constantine.[70] But the walls of this Roman hall are decorated in a very un-Roman manner. For here the articulation of the façade is repeated as a continuous sequence (Figs. 48, 49). Without the crowning pediment it now appears as a rhythmic alternation of narrow walls and large openings in the proportion of 3 to 4. This motif, which has been termed the 'rhythmische Travée',[71] became of the greatest importance, as is well known, after Bramante had made use of it in his Vatican buildings. In repeating the same articulation inside and outside Alberti was giving visual evidence of the homogeneity of his wall structure, but such an interpretation was inconceivable in antiquity.

It has always been noted with surprise that the façade of S. Andrea is considerably lower than the roof of the church. Alberti had to take into account the old tower in the left-hand corner of the building; it forced him to make his vestibule narrower than the church. This in itself need not have prevented him from covering the whole height of the church by a two-storeyed façade. But he wanted to emphasize the continuity of inside and outside, and went so far as to make external and internal measurements tally: the height of the façade (without the pediment) corresponds to that of the wall of the nave up to the vaulting, and its width to that of a 'rhythmische Travée' inside. Moreover, Alberti preferred to let the bare wall of the church appear above his façade rather than sacrifice the

47. Arch of Trajan, Ancona

48, 49. S. Andrea, Mantua: (*above*) elevation of
the façade, (*below*) section

colossal temple front. To do him justice it should be mentioned that all the photographs of the façade have been taken from a high point and that the wall is hardly visible from the piazza in front of the church.[72]

5. The Changes in Alberti's Interpretation of Classical Architecture

The façades discussed here – S. Francesco (1450), S. Maria Novella (1458), S. Sebastiano, first and second scheme (1460 and 1470), and S. Andrea (1470) – illustrate a development which resulted from the changes in Alberti's approach to antiquity. To his first façade, S. Francesco, Alberti applied a classical system without being able to discard problematical elements, traditional features, and Gothic reminiscences. In addition, the classical detail reveals a bias for romantic and fantastic forms which can best be illustrated by a glance at one of the capitals (Fig. 50). Antiquity is the authority which guided the architect, but his approach is emotional rather than orthodox.

The next façades, S. Maria Novella and the first scheme for S. Sebastiano, represent a change to an expurgated classicism as a result of a more purist attitude toward antiquity, which is also apparent in the detail (Fig. 51). But S. Francesco and S. Maria Novella are connected in so far as they show the compromise of wall and column, a compromise which was abandoned in S. Sebastiano. Here the compliance with the authority of classical motifs was replaced by their interpretation in terms of a consistent wall architecture. And in the second scheme of S. Sebastiano and still more in S. Andrea the purist approach to classical architecture gave way to the deliberate and free combination of its elements.

In the relatively short period of twenty years Alberti passed through the whole range of classical revivals possible during the Renaissance. He developed from an emotional to an archaeological outlook. Next he subordinated classical authority to the logic of the wall structure. And finally he repudiated archaeology and objectivity and used classical architecture as a storehouse which supplied him with the material for a free and subjective planning of wall architecture. Alberti was perhaps the only architect who progressed through all these stages, one following another in a logical evolution.

These façades must be regarded as an intellectual and artistic achievement of supreme importance. In contrast to almost all other Quattrocento architects, who preferred to avoid the problem altogether, Alberti offered a wealth of solutions – in fact, four different ones – for his successors to choose from. If one takes the trouble to survey the post-Alberti church façades, it immediately becomes evident to what considerable extent they are dependent on his work. For fully a hundred years nobody grappled equally seriously with this task. Not until Palladio designed his church façades did an architect approach the problem in a similar spirit of penetrating analysis. We shall therefore have to return to this theme in the next part of the book.

50. S. Francesco, Rimini. Capital from the façade

51. S. Maria Novella, Florence. Corner of the façade

design for S. Andrea (cf. Ritscher, *op. cit.*, p. 5). See also R. Krautheimer, in KUNSTCHRONIK, XIII, 1960, p. 364.

71 Cf. H. von Geymüller, *Die ursprünglichen Entwürfe von Sanct Peter*, 1875, p. 7.

72 The shrine-like projection above the pediment which encloses a huge window – the only direct light to the barrel vault of the nave – is, of course, visible from below. It was always believed (cf. Ritscher, *op. cit.*, pp. 185-6) that this screen was erected in the early eighteenth century in order to protect the roof of the façade pediment. But recently Wolfgang Lotz (in *Miscellanea Bibliothecae Hertzianae*, Munich, 1961, p. 171) published a drawing of the façade by Hermann Vischer the Younger, datable 1515, which shows that the screen belonged to the original design. Its present details indicate, however, that it was partially rebuilt in the course of the eighteenth-century restoration.

PART III

PRINCIPLES OF PALLADIO'S ARCHITECTURE

1. The Architect as 'uomo universale': Palladio, Trissino and Barbaro

In 1547 appeared Giangiorgio Trissino's *L'Italia liberata dai Goti*. It was the first of the great heroic epics of the sixteenth century, dogmatically based on ancient precepts. The author himself proudly repeats more than once that he had chosen Aristotle as his 'maestro' and Homer 'per duce, e per idea'. This epic had a topical interest. It tells of the expulsion of the Goths from Italy by Belisarius, Justinian's commander, a feat of arms which safeguarded the survival of classical traditions in Italy, and made Italy part of the eastern empire from which Greek civilization had sprung. But by the time the epic was written the infidels were masters of that ancient empire; the book was therefore fittingly dedicated to the emperor Charles V, the new Justinian, who would now come from the West and liberate the East.

In the course of more than twenty years, during which, as the author asserts, he skimmed through all the Latin and Greek writers, a work was completed which not only combined history with mythology and theology, but also threw much light on astronomy, medicine, alchemy, necromancy, mathematics, and, last but not least, on naval, military and civic architecture. The epic summarized Trissino's life-work and ambitions. He was an all-round humanist with an encyclopaedic knowledge, and immensely productive. He tried to revive the great Greek epic, and he introduced Greek tragedy in Italy with his *Sofonisba* (1514-5); his comedy *I Simillimi* (1548) followed Plautus, and his *Canzoni* imitated Pindar; he wrote *Eclogues* and poems in Latin and translated Horace. Linguistic problems, so much cherished by humanists of the period, attracted him particularly. He published an *Ars poetica* and books on grammar, and he is above all remembered for attempting to hellenize Italian spelling and pronunciation, and to create artificially a common Italian language. This was in opposition to the general humanist trend which with Bembo, Speroni, Varchi and so many others led to the acceptance of the *Volgare* (the Tuscan language) as the language of scholarship and learning, a movement which was crowned by the work of the Accademia della Crusca. Trissino's brand of humanism was aristocratic and in a way anachronistic; he advocated a formal, esoteric and dogmatic classicism, free from any popular tendencies.[1]

In the Fifth Book of *L'Italia liberata* is the description of a palace, which gives a good impression of the working of his mind. After a cumbersome discourse on the precincts and the entrance follows an account of the courtyard:

1 Cf. G. Toffanin, *Il Cinquecento, Storia letteraria d'Italia*, Milan, 1929, p. 448 f.

2 Work on *L'Italia liberata* was begun in 1526 and in 1529 approximately half the poem was finished; Cf. Bernardo Morsolin, *Giangiorgio Trissino*, Vicenza, 1878, p. 348. Palladio appears first with his humanist name in documents of 25th February and 10th March, 1540. In all the documents before that date he is called 'Andrea' or 'Andrea di Pietro'. Cf. Zorzi in *Archivio Veneto-Tridentino*, 1922, p. 136.

3 The old puzzle of Palladio's birth (1508 or 1518) was finally settled by documentary evidence in favour of 1508, cf. Zorzi, *op. cit.*, p. 120 ff. For the controversy about his place of birth (which turned out to have been Padua rather than Vicenza) see A.M. Dalla Pozza, *Palladio*, Vicenza, 1943, p. 9 ff., Zorzi in ARTE VENETA, III, 1949, p. 140 ff.

4 F. Lampertico, *Scritti stor. e lett.*, 1882, I, pp. 336, 366 f.

5 Zorzi, *loc. cit.* (see above, note 2), and also G. Fiocco, *Andrea Palladio Padovano*, 1933, p. 5 ff. From 1545 on Palladio is regularly named 'architetto'.

6 A document of 19th February, 1538 (cf. Zorzi, *op. cit.*, pp. 137, 143) is the first proof of familiarity between the two men.

7 The villa was built between 1530 and 1538. Cf. Rumor in *Archivio Veneto-Tridentino*, 1926, p. 202 ff. In spite of the evidence to the contrary Rumor, as well as Fiocco, *op. cit.*, p. 10, maintain the old attribution to Palladio. But other authors before them were doubtful, e.g. O. Bertotti Scamozzi, *Les Bâtiments et les desseins de André Palladio*, 1786 (2nd ed.), II, p. 32 f., and Burger, *Die Villen des Andrea Palladio*, 1909, p. 31. – Girolamo Gualdi's letter to Trissino of May 20th, 1538, seems conclusive; it mentions 'la maggior parte del disegno (*scil.* Cricoli) di Vostra Signoria' ('la maggior parte,' because older parts were left standing); cf. Morsolin, *op. cit.*, p. 230. Dalla Pozza (*op. cit.*, pp. 48, 50 ff.), using similar arguments to ours, excludes Palladio's participation in the planning of Cricoli. Zorzi (in PALLADIO, IV, 1954, p. 107) believes

A cloister runs around the little courtyard
Its spacious arches resting on round pillars
Whose height is equal to the pavement's width;
Their thickness is their height by eight divided.
Each column has a silver capital
Whose height repeats the measure of its thickness,
Whereas the shaft stands on a metal base
Which is again exactly half as high.

This account which opens up visions of an academic modular structure is a poetic paraphrase of Vitruvius; and Vitruvius was an author in whom Trissino had, as we shall see, more than a general interest. Inside the palace, by name Acrazio, are all sorts of disagreeable surprises for the conquering army; to avoid disaster God himself sent Belisarius' guardian angel to earth as guide and helpmate. It is he who renders the introductory exposition of the place, and his name is Palladio.

When the young sculptor Andrea di Pietro da Padova came into Trissino's orbit he gave him, after the fashion of humanist circles, the classical name 'Palladio', whose association with the image of Pallas indicated what he expected from the young artist. A chronological scrutiny clearly reveals that the name was first chosen for the angel of the epic, who is so well versed in architecture, and this made the conferring of the name on the architect doubly allusive.[2]

Andrea di Pietro was born in 1508.[3] At the age of sixteen, in April 1524, he was inscribed at Vicenza in the guild of the bricklayers and stonemasons.[4] For the next ten years he figures in documents as engaged on sculptural work, and in a document of 1542 he is still called 'lapicida'.[5] But some time before that, probably in 1536 or 1537, the event took place which had so far-reaching an effect on European architecture. Trissino, at that time engaged on the building of his villa at Cricoli near Vicenza, discovered the talent of the young man who worked there as a mason. Trissino was not only responsible for Palladio's change of profession, but also had a formative influence on his approach to architecture.[6]

The Villa at Cricoli has usually been attributed to Palladio, but there is strong evidence that Trissino himself was its designer.[7] Some of his architectural drawings have survived and one is inscribed: 'Alcune piante della casa di Cricoli'.[8] His keen interest in architectural problems is further documented by the existence of an undated manuscript fragment which, though very short, reveals the trend of his thought. He had undertaken, he declares, the task of writing a treatise on architecture because he had noticed that much enlightenment was needed: 'for after having read Vitruvius attentively . . . I find that those things which at his time were very familiar are now entirely-unknown . . . and that this Vitruvius is very badly understood and that he teaches nobody sufficiently in that art; therefore, while he endeavours to show that he knew things extremely well, he teaches very few of them. Leon Battista Alberti wanted to follow in his footsteps . . . but apart from the length of his treatise, it appears to me that one misses in it many things while one finds many which are superfluous.'[9]

Trissino built his Villa at Cricoli in order to realise his dream of creating a learned academy, the 'Accademia Trissiniana' as it was later called, in rural solitude. The rooms were decorated with Greek and Latin inscriptions and over three doors was written: 'Genio et studiis', 'Otio et musis' and 'Virtuti et quieti'.

that Trissino began the villa as early as 1523 and finished it before 1537.

8 In the Brera at Milan. The inscription by Trissino himself, confirms the relation of these plans to Cricoli. These drawings were discussed, but not published, by Morsolin, p. 225 f. The one published by Dalla Pozza, *op. cit.*, p. 51, shows that Trissino began his planning with a reconstruction of Vitruvius' Roman house.

9 Nozze Peserico-Bertolini, *Dell'architettura, Frammento di Giangiorgio Trissino*, Vicenza, 1878.

10 The importance of rhetoric as an incentive to political virtues in this circle was discussed by Cantimori in the JOURNAL OF THE WARBURG INSTITUTE, I, 1937-8, p. 83 ff. See also F. Gilbert, *ibid.*, XII, 1949, p. 114 ff.

11 Morsolin, *op. cit.*, p. 232 ff., gives a detailed account of the Academy, with further literature. Cf. also Lampertico, *op. cit.*, p. 154 ff. Teachers of the Academy were men of high reputation like Bernardino Donato and Bernardino Partenio. Paolo Manuzio's letter of May 20th, 1555, to Partenio about his election as teacher of the Academy gives an idea of the prestige enjoyed by that institution. Manuzio writes:' . . . con voi mi rallegro, e con quella magnifica città dell'honorato pensiero intorno all'academia: della quale usciranno, come dal cavallo Troiano, in poco tempo eccellentissimi giovani, ch'empieranno non pur Vicenza, loro patria, ma Italia tutta della gloria del nome loro . . .' (Atanagi, *Lettere di XIII uomini illustri*, Venice, 1560, p. 280).

12 'Io n'hebbi i principij dal Sig. Gio. Giorgio Trissino gentil'huomo dottissimo, e che alle molte discipline, di che egli era sicuro possessore, haveva anco aggiunta la perfetta cognitione di questa . . .'

13 Published in Giovanni Montenari, *Del Teatro Olimpico*, 1749, as the work of Giuseppe's son Paolo (1553-1621). The latter, however, seems to have made only additions to his father's notes; cf. Calvi, *Biblioteca, e storia degli scrittori di Vicenza*, 1778, IV, p. 155 ff. Gualdo's often attacked reliability has been vindicated by the more recently discovered documents. Cf. also Dalla Pozza's

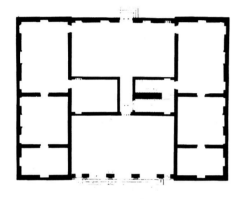

52, 53. Giangiorgio Trissino. Villa Trissino, Cricoli, near Vicenza, 1530-38: façade and plan

chapter: 'Il valore storico della biografia del Gualdo' (*op. cit.*, pp. 36-9). Giangiorgio Zorzi reprinted Gualdo's Life of Palladio with copious notes (in SAGGI E MEMORIE DI STORIA DELL'ARTE, II. 1958-9, pp. 93-104.

14 Cf. Morsolin, *op cit.*, p. 321 ff., with documents. Palladio probably accompanied Trissino to Rome also in 1541. Later, Trissino returned to Rome only once and then alone, in the year of his death, 1550. Zorzi (*I disegni delle antichità di Andrea Palladio*, Venice, 1958, pp. 20, 21) assumes that Palladio travelled briefly to Rome in 1549 and again in 1554.

On Marco Thiene, who is still remembered for his poem on Venice, cf. Morsolin in ATTI R. ISTITUTO VENETO, SERIES VII, Vol. VI., 1894-5, pp. 839-74.

15 Fiocco, *op. cit.*, p. 10, emphasized the dependence of the portico on the Loggia Cornaro in the garden of the Palazzo Giustiniani at Padua, erected by Falconetto in 1524 (see also Fiocco in DEDALO XI, 1930-1, p. 1217). This observation is only partly right; there are important differences between the two buildings: *viz.*, Ionic pilasters below, Corinthian pilasters above at Cricoli instead of Doric half-columns below and Ionic pilasters above; three large bays and one half bay at each end at Cricoli instead of five large bays; uniform entabla-

Study, Arts and Virtue – these key-words embraced the programme of the Academy. Students lived at Cricoli and their work was regulated from day-break to night-fall. Trissino seems to have wished to blend the ideals of monastic life with the traditions of the Greek schools of philosophers. Strict moral conduct as well as physical cleanliness were peremptory demands. The study of Latin and Greek, guiding the student to an accomplished Italian style, was the medium through which he hoped to infuse civic virtues into the young generation. Trissino had been an active participant in the meetings of the *Orti Oricellari* where these ideas were discussed at length among the leading Florentine humanists.[10] Here is the thread that links Trissino's enterprise to the old Platonic Academy in Florence. True to this encyclopaedic tradition the subjects of study included philosophy, astronomy, geography, and, above all, music. In the late 1530's and '40's all the young noblemen of Vicenza frequented Trissino's Academy, and though Palladio was then no longer young, nor of noble birth, he seems to have taken part in the life at Cricoli.[11]

About the very close ties between Palladio and Trissino there cannot be any doubt. In the preface to the *Quattro Libri dell'Architettura* Palladio singles him out as the 'splendore de' tempi nostri', and in the preface to his edition of Caesar he relates that it was the 'dottissimo' Trissino who taught him the secrets of ancient military science.[12] Giuseppe Gualdo, Palladio's contemporary, wrote in his reliable life of the architect,[13] that 'when Trissino noticed that Palladio was a very spirited young man with much inclination for mathematics, he decided in order to cultivate his genius to explain Vitruvius to him, and to take him to Rome three times . . .' In view of Trissino's Vitruvian record the truth of Gualdo's statement seems incontestable. We know, moreover, that Trissino, in the autumn of 1545, travelled to Rome with three of his young friends, one being the painter and poet Giambattista Maganza, the second the poet Marco Thiene and the third Palladio. Their stay lasted almost two years and they set out on their return journey in July 1547.[14]

While Trissino thus introduced Palladio to Vitruvius and to the monuments of antiquity, he himself demonstrated at Cricoli how all this knowledge should be applied in practice. Of the existing house, built after the traditional 'castello' type, he preserved the towers and linked them by a portico of Raphaelesque quality;[15] and in the ground-plan he applied those principles of symmetry and proportionate relationship of the rooms which Palladio fully developed (Figs. 52, 53).

The classical studies which he began under Trissino remained Palladio's life-long preoccupation, and his architecture cannot be dissociated from the humanist training in this circle. It always remained scientific, scholarly and to a certain degree dogmatic, and complex ideas must be taken into account in order to understand his buildings.[16]

His literary efforts were a fruit of this training. By nature Palladio seems to have been reserved and not willing to use many words where the facts speak for themselves, as is often the case with creative artists.[17] Yet his contribution to the humanities was probably greater than that of any other architect of his period, and by no means confined to architecture. The first fruits of his journeys to Rome were two small guide-books, of greater importance than their size might indicate. Both appeared in Rome in 1554.[18] One, *Le antichità di Roma*, consists of brief descriptions of the classical ruins and their history, arranged in groups, for the information of travellers. The book replaced the mediaeval *Mirabilia urbis Romae* which, as Palladio put it, were 'full of strange lies'. Classical material was now presented in accordance with the new standards of Renaissance research. 'Knowing', wrote Palladio, 'how great is everybody's wish to understand truly these antiquities' he undertook to measure the ruins and to collect reliable information about them. His scholarship is impressive; he not only used the works of the modern Roman antiquarians, Biondo, Fulvio, Fauno and Marliani, but also classical authors, Dionysius of Halicarnassus, Livy, Pliny, Plutarch, Appianus Alessandrinus, Valerius Maximus and Eutropius. By the middle of the eighteenth century Palladio's little work had gone into more than thirty editions, and had helped to shape the travellers' conception of ancient Rome for two hundred years. His second book, the *Descritione de le Chiese, Stationi, Indulgenze & Reliquie de Corpi Sancti, che sonno in la città de Roma*, also grew out of the old *Mirabilia*, which, apart from the antiquities, contained a description of Roman churches under a purely religious aspect for the use of pilgrims. Though clearly indebted to the traditional pattern, Palladio rearranged the itinerary and for the first time introduced artistic appreciations; his work was the nucleus from which, until the eighteenth century, most Roman guide-books derived.[19]

Toward the end of his career, in 1575, Palladio published Caesar's *Commentaries* with forty-one plates.[20] Indicative of his absorption in ancient writers is the fact that he studied Caesar together with his sons Leonida and Orazio, who prepared the illustrations. Both died prematurely and the father dedicated the book to their memory. He relates in the preface that for many years he had investigated ancient military science and 'read all the ancient authors and historians who had treated of it'. The preface contains an abstract of what he had found in them. He also applied his knowledge of ancient historians when illustrating Polybius, but this work, which he dedicated to the Grand Duke of Tuscany, is lost.[21]

All these publications were modest by-products in comparison with his ambitious *Quattro Libri dell'Architettura*, published in 1570, in which he set out to survey the whole field of architecture. The First Book deals with the orders and elementary problems, the Second with domestic buildings, the Third with public buildings and town-planning, and the Fourth with the temples 'without which no civilization is possible'.[22] In the dedication of the first two books to Conte Giacomo Angarano, Palladio provides a good idea of the impulses which animated his undertaking. The remains of antiquity were his constant measure of permanent values. He regarded the ancient 'enormous ruins as a shining and sublime testimony of Roman excellence (*virtù*) and grandeur', and professed to have been deeply stirred by studying that 'quality of virtue' and having concentrated all his thoughts on these studies.[23] In the preface to the Third Book he returns to the idea that 'the vestiges of so many of their sumptuous buildings' give us 'a certain knowledge of Roman virtue and greatness, which perhaps had not otherwise been believed'.[24] We are probably not wrong in concluding that for him the practice of good architecture was a moral obligation and, more than this, that in conformity with the doctrine of Trissino's Academy he regarded architecture as an important discipline of the arts and sciences the union of which embodied the ideal of *virtus*. But it is likely that architecture as a manifestation of virtue had also more specific implications for Palladio, and this will be shown later in this chapter.

ture in both tiers instead of the break in the entablature above the orders. In all these particulars Cricoli corresponds to Serlio's illustration of Raphael's loggia of the Villa Madama (Bk. III, p. 148 f.). But Serlio's third book did not appear until 1540, at a time when Cricoli was finished. Trissino had access either to Serlio's material before it was published (Serlio was in Venice from 1528 on) or brought a similar drawing back from Rome. The close relationship between Cricoli and Serlio's illustration was noticed by H. von Geymüller, *Raffaello studiato come architetto*, 1884, p. 87; cf. also Dalla Pozza, *op. cit.*, p. 53 ff.

The relationship of the humanist and philosopher Luigi (Aluise) Cornaro to his architect Falconetto (about his studies of ancient architecture in Rome cf. Vasari, ed. Milanesi, V, p. 319) anticipates that of Trissino to Palladio. On Cornaro cf. J. Burckhardt, *Die Kultur der Renaissance*, 10th ed., II, p. 56 ff. Like Trissino, Cornaro too tried his hand in writing down his ideas on architecture. His brief treatises were published by G. Fiocco, 'Alvise Cornaro e i suoi trattati sull'architettura', ATTI DELLA ACCADEMIA NAZ. DEI LINCEI, Classe di Scienze morali, storiche e filologiche, Serie VIII, Vol. IV, 1952, p. 195 ff. For Trissino's and Cornaro's different approach to architecture, cf. Von Schlosser, *Die Kunstliteratur*, Vienna, 1924, p. 222.

16 The arguments for and against Trissino's influence on Palladio's early career have both found their advocates. Dalla Pozza, in his valuable book on Palladio, unduly stresses Serlio's influence (pp. 65-87).

17 Cf. the *proemio* to the *Quattro Libri*; 'Et in tutti questi libri io fuggirò la lunghezza delle parole, & semplicemente darò quelle avvertenze, che mi parranno più necessarie.' See also the preface to the third book. In the preface to his *Antichità* he declared that he had written 'con quanta più brevità ho potuto.'

18 According to Gualdo, Palladio was in Rome in that year.

19 For the *Antichità* and the *Descritione* cf. Ludwig Schudt, *Le Guide di Roma*, 1930, pp. 26 ff., 126 ff., with complete bibliography of the editions.

20 *I Commentarij di C. Giulio Cesare, con le figure in rame de gli allogiamenti, de fatti d'arme, delle circonvallationi delle città . . .* Venezia, Pietro de' Franceschi, 1575.

21 The dedication of 1569 published by Magrini, *Memorie intorno la vita e le opere di Andrea Palladio*, Padua, 1845, appendix, p. 16. Palladio's illustrations existed in print (cf. *ibid.*, p. LI), but so far not a single copy has turned up.

22 Preface to the Third Book.

23 '. . . rendono anco nelle grandissime ruine loro chiaro, & illustre testimonio della virtù, & della grandezza Romana; in modo che ritrovandomi io grandemente esercitato, & infiammato negli ottimi studij di questa qualità di Virtù, & havendo con gran speranza messo in lei tutti i miei pensieri . . .'

24 English translations from the *Quattro Libri* are quoted, sometimes with small alterations, from Isaac Ware's edition of 1738.

25 Bk. I, p. 15.

26 *ibid.*, and I, p. 47 and *passim*. See also his dedication to the Third Book.

27 Palladio's book had long been in preparation and seems to have been ready for the press in a different form as early as before 1555. Cf. A.F. Doni, *La seconda libreria*, Venice, 1555, p. 155, who has a remarkable passage about the work which at that period had not yet a title 'ma da quello che in esso si può imparare, si puote chiamare: Norma di vera Architectura'. Daniele Barbaro, in his Commentary to Vitruvius, 1556, p. 179, says that 'presto venirà in luce un libro delle case private, composto e dissegnato dal Palladio'. About the changes in Palladio's plans for publication cf. also Tommaso Temanza, *Vita di Andrea Palladio*, Venice, 1762, p. xlii ff., Cicogna, *Iscr. Ven.*, IV, p. 408 f., Magrini, *op. cit.*, p. 105 ff., Dalla Pozza, *op. cit.*, p. 109. ff., Zorzi, *I disegni delle antichità di A.P.*, Venice, 1958, p. 148 ff.

The great majority of unpublished drawings by Palladio are now in the R. Inst. of British Architects, from the collection of Lord Burlington. About sixty of these drawings were purchased by the latter in the Villa Maser, built by Palladio for his friend Daniele Barbaro (cf. Burlington in the preface to his *Fabbriche Antiche disegnate da Andrea Palladio*, 1730). Others had been acquired by Burlington from the collection of Inigo Jones who may have got some of them in Italy (1614-15) from Scamozzi (cf. W. Grant Keith in JOURNAL R.I.B.A., XXXIII, 1925, p. 95 ff). A smaller series of drawings, possibly a portion of those mentioned by Gualdo as in the possession of Giacomo Contarini, reached the Museo Civico in Vicenza through the hands of Scamozzi, Francesco Albanese, Muttoni (cf. *Architettura di A. Palladio . . . con le osservazioni dell'Architetto N.N.* [Muttoni], 1740, I, pp. vii, xii), Temanza, Dal Peder and Pinali; cf Magrini, *op. cit.*, pp. 43, 295 ff., Giangiorgio Zorzi in *La Provincia di Vicenza*, May 17, 1910, No. 133. A few drawings are in the Pinacoteca at Brescia and one is in the Museo Civico at Verona. Four reconstructions of classical buildings, as far as we can see never before mentioned, are in the Vatican Library, cod. Vat. lat. 9838. Other series of drawings seem to be lost, e.g. twelve drawings which, in the nineteenth century, were in the collection of Giuseppe Vallardi, Milan, cf. Magrini, p. 305 ff. – In addition there are the drawings for S. Petronio in Bologna, see G. Zucchini, *Disegni . . . per la*

Palladio's plans for publication were interrupted by his death. In the preface to the first book he gave a summary of the whole scheme which was to comprise theatres, amphitheatres, arches, thermae, aqueducts, fortifications and ports. More than once he referred in his text to his forthcoming 'libri dell'Antichità'[25] or his 'libro degli Archi',[26] and, according to Gualdo, a volume containing 'Tempi Antichi, Archi, Sepolture, Terme, Ponti, Specole e altri pubblici edificii dell'antichità Romana' was left to Giacomo Contarini, Palladio's friend and patron, ready for publication. Of all this material only the Roman thermae were published, by Lord Burlington, one-hundred-and-fifty years after Palladio's death.[27]

Palladio emphasized that in preparing his book he had studied the works of those who had written on architecture before;[28] on more than one occasion he stressed the importance of Alberti, and, indeed, Alberti's influence on him was very great.[29] But above all the modern books he placed Vitruvius whom he has chosen 'per maestro, e guida'.[30] He was probably more familiar with Vitruvius than any other contemporary architect and, in keeping with Trissino's own views, he believed that Vitruvius revealed the deepest secrets of ancient architecture. His imaginative and penetrating interpretation of Vitruvius is apparent in the illustrations to Barbaro's edition of 1556. Concerning Palladio's collaboration in this work we may let Barbaro himself speak: 'For the designs of the important illustrations I used the works of Messer Andrea Palladio, architect of Vicenza, who of all those whom I have known personally or by hearsay, has according to the judgment of excellent men best understood the true architecture, having not only grasped its beautiful and subtle principles, but also practised it, whether in his most delicate and exquisite drawings of plans, elevations and sections, or in the execution and erection of many and superb buildings both in his own country and elsewhere; works which vie with the ancients, enlighten his contemporaries, and will arouse the admiration of those who come after us. And with regard to Vitruvius, the building of Theatres, Temples, Basilicas, and those things which have the most beautiful and most hidden reasons for their proportions (*compartimenti*), have all been explained and interpreted by him (Palladio), with ready skill of mind and hand; he it is who has selected the most beautiful styles of the ancients from all over Italy and has made measurements of all their works in existence.'[31]

Daniele Barbaro belonged to Palladio's generation (b. 1513) and, like Trissino, he embodied the Renaissance ideal of a comprehensive education based on classical scholarship. He was an eminent mathematician, poet, philosopher, theologian, historian and diplomatist; he founded the botanical garden at Padua and tried his hand at interior decoration. Himself one of the most outstanding personalities of the mid-sixteenth century, he was bound by close friendship to men like Aretino, Bembo, Varchi and Speroni. His report to the Venetian Senate on his mission to England, 1548-50, is a model of clarity and precision, and has gained renown as the first really comprehensive account of English life and customs by an Italian for Italians.[32] His publications ranged over a wide field; among them is a dialogue on eloquence (1557) and a treatise on perspective (1568) in which he used Dürer extensively.[33] But, like Trissino, he was above all an Aristotelian scholar.[34] He published, with a learned commentary, the Latin translation by his great-uncle Ermolao Barbaro of Aristotle's *Rhetoric* (1544) and edited Ermolao's translation of the *Nichomachean Ethics* (1544) as well as his compendium of the Aristotelian works on natural history

(1545); all this was preceded by a treatise on Porphyry's *Osagoge*, which consists of a discussion of Aristotle's categories and was traditionally published as a preface to his *Organon* (1542). Daniele Barbaro died in 1570 as Patriarch of Aquileia and left in his will to Palladio, 'nostro amorevole architetto', a token sum of fifteen ducats. It was for him and his brother Marcantonio that Palladio built the famous Villa Maser near Asolo which, decorated with Veronese's frescoes and Vittoria's statues, is one of the most perfect Renaissance creations in Northern Italy.[35]

Barbaro's commentaries on Vitruvius are most extensive and he often uses a line of the text as the starting point for long and learned expositions on a particular problem. His method reveals immediately his Aristotelian training, it is purely logical and deductive, leading from definition to definition; while his thought is often thoroughly Platonic. He begins with a preface in which he gives a philosophical definition of the arts and of architecture. First comes a definition of the arts in a general system of human pursuits, based on Aristotle's five intellectual virtues – arts, science, prudence, wisdom and intellect.[36] We need not follow Barbaro's procedure in detail and can restrict ourselves to the trend of thought which has an immediate bearing on our subject. Science and Intellect are concerned with 'certain truth' ('il vero necessario'), i.e. the truth in the objects themselves, which is found by unassailable proof. But Science is acquired, while Intellect is innate and reflects the power and virtue of the soul. The Arts are concerned with 'uncertain truth' ('il vero contingente'), i.e. the truth dependent on human will-power which is manifest in human creations. However, there is a link between the spheres of 'certain' and 'uncertain' truths. Mathematics has its life from the intellect; and those arts which are founded on numbers, geometry and the other mathematical disciplines, have greatness and in this lies the dignity of architecture.[37]

Having thus explained the close relation of the arts to other intellectual provinces, Barbaro continues with a detailed definition of the arts. With the clear-cut sentence 'nasce ogni arte da isperienza' he repeats exactly Aristotle's maxim that 'experience created art'.[38] He also follows Aristotle in his dictum that experience relies on the senses and is concerned with single instances, while the arts rest on universal principles, though these must be discovered by experience. The arts are therefore near to Wisdom, which is the virtue correlated to science and intellect as being concerned with a clear knowledge of the proofs of 'certain truth'.

The thread of these ideas is carried on in the Vitruvian text and here the Aristotelian system is given a Platonic bias. Where Vitruvius talks about the capacities an architect ought to possess (I, i, 3), Barbaro comments: 'The artist works first in the intellect and conceives in the mind and symbolizes then the exterior matter after the interior image, particularly in architecture.' Architecture, in other words, is nearer to the Platonic idea than any other art. He carries on: 'Therefore architecture above any other art signifies, i.e. represents, *le cose alla virtù*', by which he means that the form comes close to the idea. In agreement with this he affirms in another place (I, i, I): 'la virtù consiste nell' applicazione'.

Many passages show that Barbaro saw architecture not as an isolated discipline but as one of the innumerable manifestations of the human mind all of which follow the same laws. Characteristic of this, and again Aristotelian, is his comment to the second chapter where Vitruvius discusses the six categories – ordinatio, dispositio, eurythmia, symmetria, decor, distributio – of which

facciata di S. Petronio, 1933, Pls. XVI, XIX-XXI. A full statement of the history and whereabouts of Palladio's drawings (not entirely in agreement with the above summary) was given by Zorzi, *I disegni*, *op. cit.*, p. 40 ff.

28 In the dedication to the first book: 'ho rivolto con faticoso studio di molti anni i libri di coloro, che . . . hanno arricchito . . . questa scientia nobilissima.'

29 Cf. above Part I, p. 31, and below Part IV, pp. 108, 109.

30 Preface to the First Book.

31 *I dieci libri dell'Architettura di M. Vitruvio tradutti et commentati da Monsignor Barbaro*, Venice, 1556, Bk. I, chap. 6, p. 40. Barbaro pays tribute in other places to Palladio's help, particularly for the reconstruction of the Ionic volute (III, iii, p. 95, cf. Magrini, *op. cit.*, p. 30 f.) and the Roman theatre (V, viii, p. 167). Palladio, in the *Quattro Libri*, refers his readers several times to the illustrations in Barbaro's Vitruvius (cf. Bk. III, chap. 19 and Bk. IV, chap. 3). The style of the illustrations in both books is very similar and some of them are almost identical.

32 Cf. *Calendar of State Papers . . . existing in . . . Venice*, V, 1534-54, p. 338 ff.

33 A life of Daniele Barbaro has not yet been written. Most comprehensive is Giovanni Poleni, *Exercitationes Vitruvianae primae*, 1739, pp. 73-82. There are some notes in Ch. Yriate, *La vie d'un patricien de Venise au XVIe siècle* (n.y:) pp. 109 ff., 355. Barbaro's history of Venice for the years 1512-15 was published in *Arch. stor. Ital.*, 1844, p. 949.

34 According to De Thou, *Historiae sui temporis*, Geneva, 1620, II, p. 615, Barbaro used to say 'nisi Christianus esset, se in Aristotelis verba juraturum fuisse'.

35 Cf. Burger, *op. cit.*, p. 104 ff., and below Part IV, p. 125 f.

36 *Nic. Ethics*, V, 3-8.

37 Plato, *Philebos*, 34.–These are ideas which had long been current, cf. Federigo da Montefeltre's patent of 1468 for Luciano Laurano in which he speaks of 'la virtù dell'Architettura fundata in l'arte dell'aritmetica e geometria, che sono delle sette arti liberali e delle principali, perchè sono in primo gradu certitudinis, et è arte di gran scienza et di grande ingegno, et da noi molto stimata et apprezzata' (Gaye, *Carteggio*, I, p. 214).

38 *Metaphysics*, 981a.

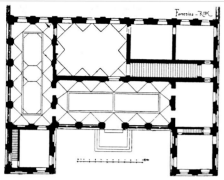

54. Peruzzi. Villa Farnesina, Rome, 1509-11. Plan

architecture consists. Barbaro declares that we find these elements in many things, and it follows that 'these terms are general and common and as such have their definition in the general and common science which is the first and is called metaphysics. But when an artist wants to apply one of those elements to his own profession, then he restricts that universality to the particular and special needs of his own art.'[39]

It would be strange if Palladio could have escaped Aristotelian influence; his practical sense seems to reflect a belief in Aristotle's doctrine of experience and his adherence to ancient prototypes a familiarity with Aristotle's doctrine of imitation; the latter, established in the *Poetics* as the supreme principle in the arts, found an intense echo in the North Italian circles from Trissino to Castelvetro. A fusion of these Aristotelian tenets with Plato's conception of ideas seems marked in Palladio's architecture; and an attentive reader will find in his *Quattro Libri* clear traces of this synthesis. In any case there is no doubt that Palladio was intimately familiar with the content of Barbaro's Vitruvian commentaries, and Barbaro's own statement is proof that many of them were even worked out in common consultation. Palladio's work embodied for Barbaro his own ideal of scientific, mathematical architecture, and it may be supposed that Palladio himself thought in the categories which his patron had so skilfully expounded. It is probable that by associating in the *Quattro Libri* virtue with architecture, Palladio like Barbaro regarded as the particular 'virtue' inherent in architecture the possibility of materializing in space the 'certain truth' of mathematics. This interpretation is supported by the title-page of the *Quattro Libri* which shows allegories of Geometry and Architecture pointing upwards to the crowned figure of Virtue ('Regina Virtus') with sceptre and book.

It may be argued that from Alberti's day onwards architecture was conceived in terms of applied mathematics; but hardly ever before Barbaro was this subject submitted to such closely-knit logical analysis. Palladio's *Quattro Libri*, almost entirely concerned with practical issues, are similarly marked by acuteness, precision, and clear and rational arrangement. And as Trissino with his application of Aristotle's *Poetics* gave structure, unity and clarity to drama and epic, so Palladio aspired to unchallengeable lucidity of architectural planning based on the authority of classical rules.

In 1555 the Accademia Olimpica was founded in Vicenza, with Palladio as one of its chief promoters. The programme was still that of the older Italian academies, the cultivation of the 'uomo universale'. And so Palladio found himself again in a circle of men who believed in the ideals which had inspired his early days in Trissino's company. Theatrical performances soon became one of the notable activities of the Academy, beginning with a memorable representation of Trissino's *Sofonisba* in 1562, in a theatre built for this purpose by Palladio inside the Sala of the Palazzo della Ragione.[40] Later on Palladio was commissioned to erect a permanent theatre. Barbaro had been dead for ten years when the foundation stone was laid on March 23rd, 1580. He rather than anyone else would have been able to appreciate Palladio's project. For to all intents and purposes it corresponded to the reconstruction of the Roman theatre which Barbaro, with Palladio's help, had published in his Vitruvius.[41] Palladio himself died six months after building had started. In 1585 the theatre was opened and, like a tribute to the *manes* of Trissino, who had introduced the taste for Greek tragedy, the first performance was Sophocles' *Oedipus Tyrannus*.

39 These indications are not meant as a summary of the complex logical structure of Barbaro's commentary. Also no attempt can here be made to trace Barbaro's sources, apart from Aristotle and Plato. Among others, he appears to have used the Aristotelian commentary of Caporali's edition of Vitruvius, Perugia, 1536.
40 Pierfilippo Castelli, *La vita di Giovangiorgio Trissino*, Venice, 1753, p. 26, believed that on that occasion the model for Palladio's Teatro Olimpico was shown. See also Calvi, *op. cit.*, IV, p. 275 ff.
41 In a brilliant study L. Magagnato (JOURNAL OF THE WARBURG AND COURTAULD INSTITUTES, XIV, 1951, p. 209 ff.) discussed the non-antique elements in the design of the Teatro Olimpico. See also *id.*, *Teatri italiani del Cinquecento*, Venice, 1954 p. 50 ff.

55, 56. Palladio. Villa Godi Porto at Lonedo, 1540: (*left*) façade, (*above*) detail of plan (from Palladio's *Quattro Libri*)

2. Palladio's Geometry: The Villas

In a chapter on abuses in architecture, Palladio remarks as follows: 'Although variety and things new may please every one, yet they ought not to be done contrary to the precepts of art, and contrary to that which reason dictates; whence one sees, that although the ancients did vary, yet they never departed from some universal and necessary rules of art, as shall be seen in my books of antiquities.'[42] He makes this statement in a definite context, but it may be generalized, and we shall now try to explore how Palladio interpreted the universal precepts of architecture. The villas in particular lend themselves to such an investigation. For the planning of his villas and palaces he followed certain rules from which he never departed. He demanded a hall in the central axis and absolute symmetry of the lesser rooms at both sides. 'And it is to be observed that those on the right correspond with those on the left, so that the building may be the same in one part as in the other.' [43]

Renaissance architects always regarded symmetry as a theoretical requirement in design, and rigidly symmetrical plans are already found in Filarete, Francesco di Giorgio and Giuliano da Sangallo.[44] But in practice this theory was rarely applied. A comparison of a Palladian plan (Fig. 56) with a typical Renaissance building such as the Farnesina in Rome (1509, Fig. 54) reveals immediately his complete break with the older tradition. It is the systematization of the ground-plan which became the distinguishing feature of Palladio's palaces and villas.[45] At Cricoli Trissino anticipated Palladio's plans; everything later undertaken by Palladio is a development of this archetype.

The earliest building which can with certainty be ascribed to Palladio is the Villa Godi Porto at Lonedo (Figs. 55, 56) for which he received payments from 1540 onwards.[46] In comparison with Cricoli this villa is retrogressive. The asymmetrical arrangement of windows in the façade can be found in innumer-

42 *Quattro Libri*, I, chap. 20, p. 48.
43 *ibid.*, I, chap. 21, p. 48.
44 Cf. Geymüller-Stegmann, *Die Architektur der Renaissance in Toscana*, Vol. XI, Gesamtüberblick, Figs. 41-49.
45 The regular plans of Roman thermae offered Palladio convincing proof that symmetry was also an indispensable requirement in ancient domestic architecture.
46 Payments continue until 1552, cf. Bertotti Scamozzi, *op. cit.*, II, p. 16, but the building seems to have been finished in the main in 1542 (date of the inscription on the façade). See also Burger, *op. cit.*, p. 16 ff. Palladio's own illustration (II, p. 63) shows a revised front.

able country-houses of the Venetian *terra ferma*, [47] and the break caused by the three-arched portico and the recessed centre are also traditional features.[48] The ground-plan too is simplified in comparison with Cricoli (Fig. 53), but with its four rooms of equal size at each side of the central axis the principle of symmetry is strictly kept.[49] This surprisingly unpretentious plan contains all the elements of Palladio's further development.

The local and traditional character which is so marked in the front of the Villa Godi disappeared completely after Palladio's stay in Rome. But the plans of the many country-houses, which he built as the fashionable architect of Vicenza from the 1450's onwards, are all different orchestrations of the same theme (Fig. 57). The pattern of these plans is founded on the straight-forward needs of the Italian villa: loggias and a large hall in the central axis, two or three living-rooms or bedrooms of various sizes at the sides, and, between them and the hall, space for small spare rooms and the staircases. An analysis of a few typical plans ranging over a period of about fifteen years will prove that they are derived from a single geometrical formula. The Villa Thiene at Cicogna,[50] built during the 1550's, shows the pattern most clearly. The rooms together with the porticos are defined by a rectangle divided by two longitudinal and four transverse lines. A variation of this type is the Villa Sarego at Miega, begun about 1564, only parts of which are preserved;[51] here the portico also extends across the width of the staircases. Before 1560 Palladio had designed a simpler version of this plan for the Villa Poiana.[52] The Villa Badoer at Fratta, Polesine,[53] c.1566, follows the same pattern, but with one portico now placed outside the cube of the building. Villa Zeno at Cessalto,[54] between 1558 and 1566, belongs to this class (reversed), but at each side of the hall two small rooms have been joined forming large rooms with their axes at right angles to the hall. We find this feature again in the Villa Cornaro at Piombino Dese,[55] mentioned in 1566, where the staircases have been transferred to the wings; the hall, which is therefore nearly square, is now the same width as the porticos. By another variation of these elements the earlier plan of the Villa Pisani at Montagnana emerges,[56] which in reverse, can be found again in the Villa Emo at Fanzolo, c.1567.[57] If the staircases of the Villa Cornaro are placed inside along the small rooms the hall acquires the cruciform shape of the Villa Malcontenta (1560),[58] a type which was varied in some other buildings, particularly in the Villa Pisani of 1561-2, at Bagnolo.[59] Finally, it will now be seen that the plan of the Villa Rotonda[60] is the most perfect realization of the fundamental geometrical skeleton.

What was in Palladio's mind when he experimented over and over again with the same elements? Once he had found the basic geometric pattern for the problem 'villa', he adapted it as clearly and as simply as possible to the special requirements of each commission. He reconciled the task at hand with the 'certain truth' of mathematics which is final and unchangeable. The geometrical keynote is, subconsciously rather than consciously, perceptible to everyone who visits Palladio's villas and it is this that gives his buildings their convincing quality.

Yet this grouping and re-grouping of the same pattern was not as simple an operation as it may appear. Palladio took the greatest care in employing harmonic ratios not only inside each single room, but also in the relation of the rooms to each other, and it is this demand for the right ratio which is at the centre of Palladio's conception of architecture. This rather complex matter will be discussed in the last part of this book.

47 It derives from the Venetian palace tradition. For fifteenth- and sixteenth-century houses with this feature, cf. Fasolo, *Ville de Vicentino*, Pls. 24-27, 32, and Giuseppe Mazzotti, *Le ville venete*, Treviso, 1954.

48 Cf. for instance Villa Ricci, Ca'Brusa, late fifteenth century, Fasolo, *op. cit.*, Pls. 14, 15.

49 In two of the rooms are small staircases which alter the shape of these rooms. But by not showing a dividing wall between the stairs and the rooms, Palladio indicated in his illustration that he wanted the ideal shape of the room to be 'read.'

50 Palladio II, p. 60. The building, which was never finished, has not survived, cf. Burger, *op. cit.*, p. 37 ff.

51 Palladio II, p. 66, Burger, p. 93, Zorzi, in ARTE VENETA, IX, 1955, p. 120 f.

52 Palladio II, p. 56, Burger, p. 98, Zorzi, *op. cit.*, p. 96.

53 Palladio II, p. 46, Burger, p. 110 ff., Mazzotti, *op. cit.*, p. 477, dates the villa 1568-70.

54 Palladio II, p. 47, Burger, p. 47 ff.

55 Palladio II, p. 51, Burger, p. 95 ff.

56 Palladio II, p. 50, Brunelli e Callegari, *Ville del Brenta*, 1931, p. 337 ff. For the date, 1553-5, see Zorzi, *op. cit.*, p. 116.

57 Palladio II, p. 53, Burger, p. 102 ff.

58 Palladio II, p. 48, Burger, p. 88 ff., Brunelli-Callegari, *op. cit.*, p. 16 ff.

59 Palladio II, p. 45, Burger, p. 40 ff. For the date, see Zorzi, ARTE VENETA, IX, 1955, p. 97.

60 Palladio II, pp. 16, 17, Burger, p. 53 ff., Zorzi, *op. cit.*, p. 100 ff. The building of the Rotonda was begun in or shortly after 1550. Magagnò's poem of 1554 (Burger p. 64) leaves no doubt about it. A much later date, still given by Roberto Pane, *Andrea Palladio*, Turin, 1948, p. 46, must therefore be refuted.

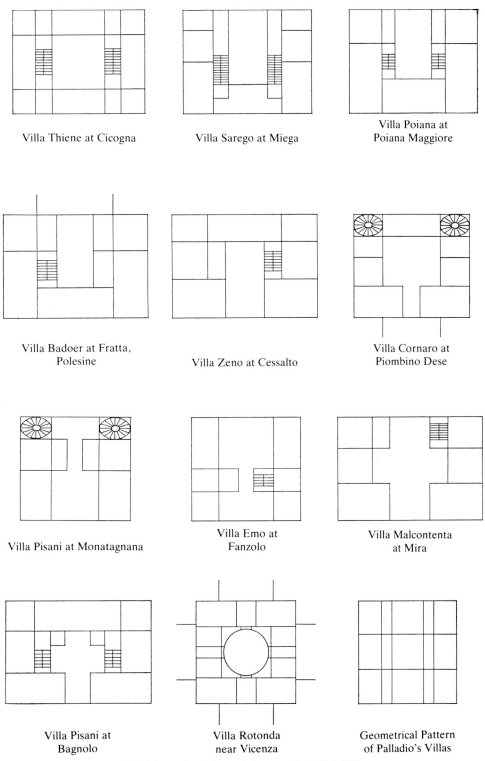

Villa Thiene at Cicogna

Villa Sarego at Miega

Villa Poiana at
Poiana Maggiore

Villa Badoer at Fratta,
Polesine

Villa Zeno at Cessalto

Villa Cornaro at
Piombino Dese

Villa Pisani at Monatagnana

Villa Emo at
Fanzolo

Villa Malcontenta
at Mira

Villa Pisani at
Bagnolo

Villa Rotonda
near Vicenza

Geometrical Pattern
of Palladio's Villas

57. Schematized plans of eleven of Palladio's Villas

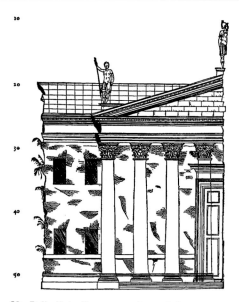

58. Palladio's Reconstruction of the Ancient House. From Barbaro's *Vitruvius*, Venice, 1556

The façades of Palladio's villas present a problem essentially similar to that of the plans. In contrast to French and English, Italian monumental architecture· is conceived, whenever feasible, in terms of a solid three-dimensional block. Italian architects strove for an easily perceptible ratio between length, height and depth of a building, and Palladio's villas exhibit this quality most lucidly. The block had to be given a façade. He turned to the classical temple front, which offered a motif associated with dignity and nobility, and invariably adapted it to the façades of his villas. The reasons for this were given by Palladio himself in a passage which shows how for him practical considerations and principles of a higher order went hand in hand. 'I have made the frontispiece (i.e. the pediment of the portico) in the main front of all the villas and also in some town-houses . . . because such frontispieces show the entrance of the house, and add very much to the grandeur and magnificence of the work, the front being thus made more eminent than the rest; besides, they are very commodious for placing the ensigns or arms of the owners, which are commonly put in the middle of the front. The ancients also made use of them in their buildings, as is seen in the remains of the temples, and other public edifices, and, as I have said in the preface to the first book, they very probably took the invention and the principles (of them) from private buildings, i.e. from the houses.'[61]

Façades of ancient domestic buildings were unknown, but with the application of the temple front to the house Palladio believed that he had re-created them in form and spirit; his reconstruction of the front of the ancient house in Barbaro's Vitruvius shows a large eight-column portico[62] (Fig. 58). His conclusion was founded on two fallacies, an erroneous theory of the development of society, and an erroneous theory of the genesis of architecture. He thought 'that man formerly lived by himself; but afterwards, seeing he required assistance of other men to obtain those things that might make him happy (if any happiness is to be found here below) naturally sought and loved the company of other men; whereupon of several houses, villages were formed, and then of many villages, cities and in these, public places and edifices were built'. Therefore, he concludes, private houses were the nuclei of public buildings; in other words, temples reflect the appearance of the ancient house.[63] The idea that the temple is a magnified house throws an interesting light on Palladio's own crystalline conception of architectural composition. He cannot think in terms of evolution, but envisages ready-made units which, under certain conditions, may be transferred from one class of building to another and may also be extended or contracted.[64] Thus to utilize the temple front for private buildings appeared to him a legitimate regression to an ancient custom. But, in fact, his peculiar reasoning led him to ennoble aristocratic domestic architecture by borrowing the principal motif from ancient sacred architecture. With this unclassical transposition, the motif acquired a new vitality which he fully exploited. He was the first consistently to graft the temple front on to the wall of the house,[65] and through him the type was most widely disseminated. The nearest approach to the classical portico with its broad and majestic staircase is to be found in the Villa Rotonda (Fig. 59); but even here the portico must be seen against the background of and in relation to, the cube of the building. The portico of the Villa Malcontenta (Fig. 60) is also free-standing; here, however, it has been integrated into the architecture of the house, for it rises above a domestic basement, while it is joined laterally by flights of stairs which are conducted along the wall of the

61 Palladio II., chap. 16.
62 Bk. VI, chap. 2.
63 Palladio I, preface. Palladio's comparison of the city with a large house and, conversely, of the house with a small city (Bk. II, chap. 12) was dictated by practical considerations. For the totality of the Palladian villa (not discussed in this book), see Fausto Franco, 'Classicismo e funzionalità della villa Palladiana "città piccola"', *Atti del I° congresso nazionale di storia dell'architettura*, Florence, 1938, 249 ff.
64 See also the statement, obviously influenced by Alberti, in Bk. II, chap. 12: 'la Città non sia altro che una certa casa grande, e per lo contrario la casa una città picciola.'
65 Attempts in this direction had been made before him, cf. for instance Giuliano da Sangallo's villa at Poggio a Caiano.

59. Palladio. Villa Rotonda near Vicenza, 1550

60. Palladio. Villa Malcontenta, on the Brenta, 1560

61. Palladio. Villa Emo at Fanzola, *c.*1567

62. Palladio. Villa Thiene at Quinto, *c.*1550

front.[66] A further step in this direction is the placing of the temple front in the plane of the wall exemplified by the Villa Emo (Fig. 61). Finally, the whole façade may be transformed into a temple front as shown in the Villa Thiene at Quinto[67] and in the Villa Maser[68] (Figs. 62, 63). The range of possibilities is very large and Palladio made full use of them. These few examples will suffice to show that he constantly varied a conception the merits of which he regarded as conclusive. While in looking at these façades nobody can escape the impression that an inexhaustible wealth of ideas has gone into their design, one should not lose sight of the fact that they are all generated from the same basic pattern.

66 The relation of this villa and of the Villa Rotonda to Palladio's reconstruction of the Temple of Clitumnus (S. Salvatore) near Trevi was discussed by Achille Bertini Calosso, 'Andrea Palladio e il Tempio del Clitunno' in *Saggi sull' architettura Etrusca e Romana*, Rome, 1940, p. 183. 67 Only a small portion of the villa, probably begun in 1549, was executed (cf. Burger, p. 68 ff. and his Pl. 24; Zorzi, ARTE VENETA, IX, 1955, p. 96). The 'temple front' illustrated in our Fig. 62 is the surviving wing of a very extensive front. It will be noted how close Palladio came here to Alberti's transformation of the ancient temple front into a consistent wall architecture, cf. above, p. 55 f. 68 Begun before 1566; see Zorzi, p. 98. R. Pallucchini (in *Palladio, Veronese e Vittoria a Maser*, Milan, 1960, p. 74) dates Veronese's frescoes as early as *c.*1560-61. The solution of the Villa Maser was anticipated in the early Villa Angarano near Bassano (1548) which was entirely rebuilt in the beginning of the eighteenth century, cf. Burger, p. 26 ff.

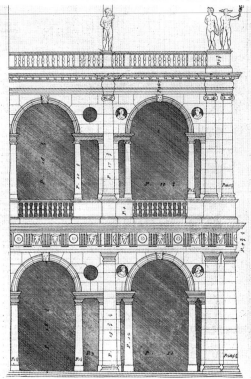

64. System of Palladio's Basilica at Vicenza.
From Palladio's *Quattro Libri*

65. Palace from Serlio's *Regole generali
di Architettura*, Venice, 1537

66. Bramante and Raphael, 'House of Raphael', Rome, after 1510. Engraving by Lafreri

3. Palladio and Classical Architecture: Palaces and Public Buildings

In the preceding section Palladio's buildings have been considered as variations on a geometric theme, different realizations, as it were, of the Platonic idea of the Villa. But it would be wrong to conclude that there was no development. This section will therefore be largely concerned with the variable factors in his architecture; and as his measure was always classical antiquity the problem of Palladio's development presents itself as an examination of his changing approach to the architecture of the ancients.[69]

Palladio's first great public success was the commission given him to support the mediaeval Palazzo della Ragione at Vicenza with a surrounding structure (Fig. 64).[70] His screen consists of an uninterrupted sequence, in two storeys, of the celebrated 'Palladio motif'. Palladio monumentalized here a conception common in Bramante's circle and later popularized through Serlio's Fourth Book on Architecture (1537) (Fig. 67).[71] When discussing the ancient basilicas in the *Quattro Libri* Palladio inserted a chapter on 'The Basilicas of our Time', in which he argued that the name can rightly be used for buildings like the Palazzo del Comune in Brescia and the Palazzi della Ragione at Padua and Vicenza, in spite of the differences in custom and building methods between ancient and modern times. There is an important *tertium comparationis* between the old and the new basilicas, for both are the seats of jurisdiction.[72] And in this chapter, following the reconstruction of the ancient basilica after Vitruvius, appear two plates of his own building at Vicenza, accompanied by these words: 'I do not doubt but that this building may be compared with the ancient edifices, and ranked among the most noble and most beautiful fabrics that have been made since the ancient times, not only for its grandeur and its ornaments, but also for the materials . . . '[73] He regarded his own building as an adaptation of the antique basilica type for modern usage. The classical forms as interpreted by Bramante were the medium through which he accomplished this revival.

According to Temanza the façade of the Palazzo Porto-Colleoni had an inscription: 'Joseph Porto MDLII'.[74] Work on the building was therefore probably begun before 1550. The derivation of the façade from a group of palaces built in Rome by Bramante and Raphael is too obvious to need any comment (Figs. 66, 67).[75] These buildings are in a class of their own and represent a climax of the High Renaissance palace between 1515 and 1520. Their functional differentiation of a rusticated ground-floor and smooth *piano nobile*, their majestic sequence of double half-columns, their use of few great forms, and their economy of detail, the organic separation of one member from another (e.g. balconies and bases of columns), the compact filling of the wall and the energetic projection of mass – all this, though unprecedented in ancient as well as modern times, gave these palaces the stamp of truly imperial grandeur. They had something of the serene and grave quality of ancient Roman buildings, and it was this palazzo type that, fused with Venetian elements first by Sanmicheli (Palazzo Pompei, Verona) and then by Palladio, was constantly imitated and varied all over Europe by architects with a classical bias.

Palladio kept more strictly to his models than Sanmicheli, but by introducing figures silhouetted against the sky, figures and festoons as decorations of the windows, and masks as keystones in the basement, he gave his building a richer and more genial appearance; all these additions are characteristic of Venice and

69 Cf. also Herbert Pée, *Die Palastbauten des Andrea Palladio*, Würzburg, 1939, and the critical review by W. Lotz in ZEITSCHRIFT FÜR KUNSTGESCHICHTE, ix, 1940, p. 216 ff.

70 Palladio received payment for four drawings on October 27th, 1545 (cf. Magrini, *op. cit.*, p. 17), at a time when he had already left for Rome together with Trissino. Almost three years later, on September 6th, 1548, his model was practically accepted for execution (*ibid.*, p. 20 ff., also for other documents on the progress of the work). Dalla Pozza, *op. cit.*, pp. 95-142, has given the history of the building with new documents.

71 In Italy the motif is therefore usually called 'Serliana'. I have discussed the genesis of this motif in a different context; cf. *England and the Mediterranean Tradition*, edited by the Warburg and Courtauld Institutes, 1945, p. 142 f.

72 Bk. III, preface, p. 1; chap. 16, p. 27; chap. 20, p. 37. For Alberti's remarks about the ancient basilica as the seat of jurisdiction, cf. above, Part I, p. 17.

73 Bk. III, chap. 20, p. 37.

74 *Op. cit.*, p. viii.

75 Palazzo Vidoni-Caffarelli, 1515, by Raphael, and the so-called Casa di Raffaello (destroyed) built by Bramante for Count Caprina, finished by Raphael in c.1517. See also Palazzo Bresciano (1515) in the Borgo (Venturi, XI, 1, p. 237), Peruzzi's Palazzo Ossoli (*ibid.*, Fig. 343), and others.

Palladio's first palace, the Palazzo Civena at Vicenza (1540-2) is even closer to this Roman palace type than the Palazzo Porto. For the attribution of the Palazzo Civena to Palladio, now generally accepted, see Zorzi, 'Una restituzione palladiana', ARTE VENETA, III, 1949, p. 99 ff.

76 Palladio never used in the first floor a Doric order which he associated with the ground-floor.

77 This is by no means the whole list of differ-

ences. We have given the description after Palladio's plate (II, p. 7). In the building figures and festoons only occur in the centre and the end bays; and instead of the crowning figures, there are two standing in front of the mezzanine right and left of the central bay. Palladio's drawing for the engraving shown in Fig. 67 (Burlington-Devonshire Coll., R.I.B.A., Vol. XVII, No. 3) is somewhat closer to the execution than the Plate of the *Quattro libri*.

78 Burlington-Devonshire Coll., Vol. XIV, 11: Casa di Raffaello; ill. Venturi, *Storia dell'Arte*, XI, 1, Fig. 189 (left half only of the drawing). The drawing has not always been accepted as by Palladio's hand. Vol. XVII, 12: Elevation with Corinthian pilasters, ground-floor with two alternatives for rustication. Two more alternative drawings for the rustication of the ground-floor are on the verso. XVII, 9 (Fig. 68): Two alternative designs, one with the mezzanine under the cornice and the other with it above the cornice similar to the execution. There can be no doubt that these drawings relate to the Palazzo Porto. Like the final design all the projects have seven bays. In addition, the measurements match almost exactly. In the left-hand design of Fig. 68 the socle under the ground-floor windows is five *palmi* high and the same height is inscribed in the plate of the palace in the *Quattro libri* (II, p. 7); the mezzanine of seven-and-a-half *palmi* is identical in both cases and so is the width of the half-columns (two *palmi*), but there is a difference of half a *palmo* in height (eighteen in the design instead of eighteen-and-a-half).

Dalla Pozza, *op. cit.*, p. 167 f., advocates a relation of this drawing to the Palazzo Poiana at Vicenza. This palace, of five not of seven bays, is dependent on the Palazzo Porto.

79 Bk. II, chap. 7, p. 32, plan, letter 'E' ('salotti di quattro colonne').

80 Reconstructed by Palladio in II, chap. 5: 'Dell' Atrio di Quattro Colonne.'

81 Bk. I, chap. 21, p. 48 about 'sale': 'quanto più si approssimeranno al quadrato, tanto più saranno lodevoli, & commode.'

82 Commentary to Vitruvius VI, chap. 3, p. 171.

83 Cf. above, p. 61. Trissino's 'colonne tonde Che son tant'alte, quanto è la larghezza Del pavimento . . .' may, however, after Vitruvius, be interpreted to mean that the height of the columns corresponds to the width of the colonnade.

84 Palladio, I, pp. 10-13. Inscriptions on façade (1556) and courtyard (1558). Cf. S. Rumor, *Il Palazzo della Banca Popolare*, Vicenza, 1912. Renato Cevese, *I Palazzi dei Thiene*, Vicenza, 1952, p. 39 ff., believes that the palace was designed as early as 1542 and that Vittoria began his interior decoration in 1547. G. Zorzi, in ARTE VENETA, IX, 1955, p. 96, does not accept Cevese's conclusions and dates the beginning of the structure c.1550-1. Only about one-third of the original plan was finished.

85 Bk. II, p. 42.

86 See e.g. the sequence of round and octagonal rooms in the Thermae of Constantine or of octagonal, apsidal and rectangular rooms in the Thermae of Diocletian. For the large apsidal hall along one side of a peristyle, cf. the Thermae of Agrippa.

the *terra ferma*, and Palladio could find most of them in Sansovino's Libreria. He also transformed the weighty double order of Doric columns into a more elegant single Ionic sequence,[76] and gave the heavy Roman rustication a light and decorative quality.[77] The keen interest which Palladio took in the Roman palaces can still be demonstrated from drawings which have survived. The Burlington-Devonshire collection contains not only a drawing by him after the Casa di Raffaello, but also three elevations which must be regarded as early designs for the Palazzo Porto, and form in various ways transitions between the Roman type and the final design (Fig. 68).[78]

Like the plans of the villas, the plan of the Palazzo Porto is without precedent in the sixteenth century (Fig. 69). It consists of two identical blocks on each side of a courtyard, only one of which, incidentally, was built. In this arrangement Palladio was following, so he says, the Greek type of private house in which the family apartments were separated from those of the guests. Each block is divided by a central axis into two symmetrical groups of rooms, and in each block the central feature is a large hall with four columns. This is the 'tetrastyle,' which plays an important part, in a central and dominating position, in Palladio's reconstruction of the Roman house.[79] The tetrastyle as the *leit-motif* of the ground-plan is one of the recurrent characteristics of Palladio's palaces. In Book II, chapter 8, he gives a large-scale reconstruction of the tetrastyle under the heading: 'Of the Halls with four columns'; and his text says: 'The following design is of the halls, which were called Tetrastili, because they had four columns. They were made square; and the columns were so placed as to make the breadth proportionable to the height, and to make the place above secure; which I have done myself in many buildings.' The ancient atrium had an open roof; since an open atrium could hardly be built by a modern architect, Palladio used the tetrastyle hall for his atrium. But he made the exchange on good authority, for among the five types of atria mentioned by Vitruvius there is one supported by four columns, i.e. a tetrastyle.[80] Palladio's preference for this atrium was based not only upon its structural solidity, but above all upon its square shape which he regarded as a perfect form.[81]

The formal quality of Palladio's plan appears perhaps most significantly in the arrangement of the staircase, which was uncomfortably placed under the portico on one side of the courtyard; Palladio explains that he did this in order to compel anyone wanting to go upstairs to admire the finest part of the building first. It is, in fact, the courtyard – the ancient peristyle – that was regarded as the most important part of the house. Barbaro, in his commentary, following Alberti's comparison between the forum of a town and the cortile of a house, says that 'si dà prima d'occhio al cortile' – one first looks at the cortile as the centre where everything comes together.[82] Palladio's cortile with its giant composite colonnade (Fig. 67) was of a grandeur hitherto unsurpassed; it meant an entirely new departure for the Italian cortile, the reverberations of which are still to be found in Bernini's Louvre project. This revolution was brought about because Palladio wanted to make the height of the columns of the peristyle correspond to its breadth – an idea which Trissino had already expressed in his description of the enchanted palace.[83] These theoretical ratios are clearly demonstrated in the illustration of the *Quattro libri*. It is not improbable that this conception was derived from a misinterpretation of Vitruvius' demand (VI, iii, 7) that the height of the columns of the peristyle should correspond to the width of the colonnade.

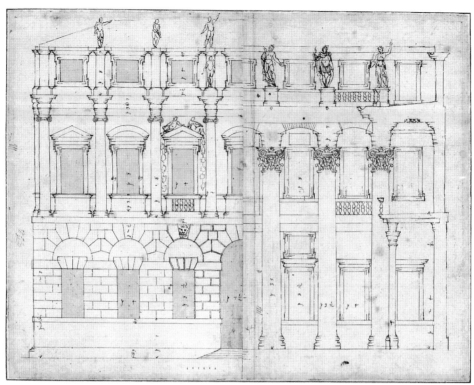

67. Palladio. Palazzo Porto-Colleoni, *c.*1550. Elevation of front (*left*) and courtyard (*right*)

68. Palladio. Preparatory design for the Palazzo Porto-Colleoni

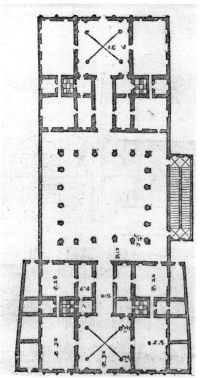

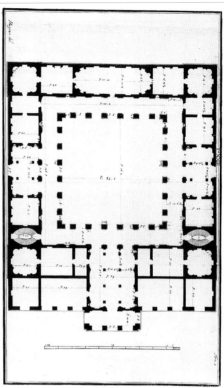

69. Palazzo Porto-Colleoni. From
Palladio's *Quattro Libri*

70. Palladio. Palazzo Thiene. From
Bertotti Scamozzi

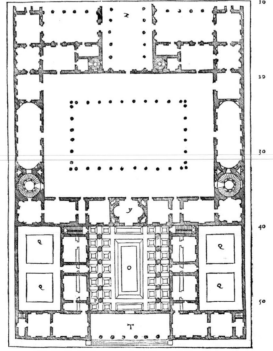

71. Palladio's reconstruction of the Roman
House. From Barbaro's *Vitruvius*

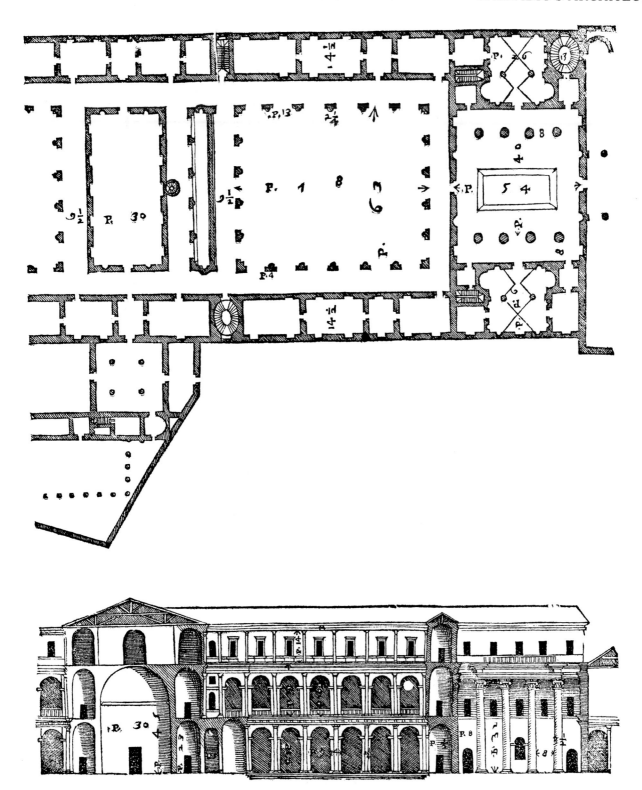

72. Convent of the Carità, Venice, 1561. From Palladio's *Quattro Libri*

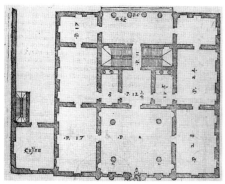

73. Palladio. Palazzo Antonini at Udine, 1556. From Palladio's *Quattro Libri*

87 Now Accademia delle Belle Arti. Only a small portion of the plan was executed. Palladio, II, chap. 6, pp. 27-30. See also Cicognara, Diedo and Selva, *Le Fabbriche e i monumenti più cospicui di Venezia*, 1840 (2nd ed.), pp. 81 ff., Pls. 207-11; F. Lazzari, *Il Convento della Carità*, 1835.

88 Vasari, ed. Milanesi, VII, p. 529.

89 The Corinthian atrium, according to Vitruvius, VI, iii, 1, has rows of columns alongside the open space.

90 One example may show how this is meant Palazzo Antonini at Udine (1556, Fig. 73, Palladio, II, p. 3) consists of a tetrastyle atrium from which one goes, as one should, straight into the tablinum; right and left from it open small rooms, Vitruvius' alae. Further on in the main axis is a narrow passage (the ancient vestibulum, shown in Palladio's reconstruction of the Greek house between the street and the atrium) with the staircases at both sides; from here one reaches the loggia which replaces the ancient œcus. There is no peristyle. The plan would therefore appear to be a contraction or abbreviation of that of the ancient house, adapted to the particular circumstances.

Burger, *op. cit.*, p. 69, has demonstrated the derivation of the Villa Thiene at Quinto from Vitruvius' description of the Greek house.

91 Palladio, II, pp. 4, 5. Now Museo Civico. The documents published by A. Magrini, *Il Palazzo del Museo Civico in Vicenza*, Vicenza, 1855, p. 67 ff., make it possible to follow up the quick progress of the building in years 1551-4. The palace was only partly finished by Palladio, the rest was executed towards the end of the seventeenth century, cf. Magrini, *ibid.*, p. 35 f., and Bertotti Scamozzi, *op. cit.*, I, p. 29 ff. The festoons along the windows and the groups at both sides of the staircase, shown in Palladio's illustration, were never executed. See also Barbieri-Cevese-Magagnato, *Guida di Vicenza*, 1956, p. 167.

In view of the evidence of the documents G. Fiocco's defence of the late date of the Palazzo Chiericati is unwarranted (in: *Primato. Lettere e Arti d'Italia*, III, Oct. 15, 1942, p. 384 f.).

92 Palladio, III, chap. 16, p. 27. Cf. Previously Alberti, Bk. VIII, chap. 6.

It is clear that, while the façade of the Palazzo Porto is still Bramantesque, the ground-plan reveals a development in a new direction. Palladio was evidently toying with the idea of re-creating the ancient house for modern use from Vitruvius' text. A further step in this development is represented by the Palazzo Thiene, built probably after 1550 (Fig. 70).[84] The group of the atrium with adjoining rooms, octagonal rooms in the corners and, next to them, spiral stairs, corresponds in essence to Palladio's reconstruction of the Roman house as published in Barbaro's Vitruvius, significantly in the year (1556) when the structure of the Palazzo Thiene was rising (Fig. 71). But a feature unknown in ancient houses was also incorporated into this plan. The wing at the far end consisting of small octagonal and retangular rooms at both sides of a centrally placed long hall with apsidal ends is a complete novelty. The long apsidal room had been used by Palladio, not only in the two side wings of the Roman house in Barbaro's illustration, but also in the similarly arranged lateral wings of the Greek house in the *Quattro Libri*[85] but in neither of them is there anything like the dynamic variety of shapes of the Palazzo Thiene. Palladio had found such sequences when studying the Roman thermae and Hadrian's Villa at Tivoli, and he believed them to be ancient domestic features.[86] At this stage of his career he had an eye for the dynamic effect of such a suite of rooms, and ancient precedents were a welcome guide to their employment. No one had hitherto thought of vitalizing ancient planning in this way. Nor can a contemporary plan be found in the whole of Italy which comes anywhere near this diversity in a sequence of rooms.

In 1561 Palladio planned and partly executed his most elaborate reconstruction of the Roman house at the convent of the Carità in Venice (Fig. 72).[87] His programme was never misinterpreted. Vasari, as early as 1568, wrote, that this building was designed 'a imitazione delle case che solevano far gli antichi' ('in imitation of the houses which the ancients used to build')[88] and Palladio himself says in his description of the building: 'I have endeavoured to make this house like those of the ancients; and therefore I have made a Corinthian Atrium to it . . .' Here, at last, he had an opportunity of building a real atrium with an open ceiling.[89] The sacristy and a corresponding small room, which both adjoin the atrium like wings, are called by him 'tablinum', the tablinum being that room of the ancient house which connects atrium and peristyle. From the atrium one proceeds into the chiostro which, being too large for one giant order, was given a system in three tiers derived from that of the Colosseum. At the far end of the cloister is the refectory, instead of the *œcus* of the ancient house.

All the other plans for palaces take their place in this evolution, and appear as partial realizations of the ideal towards which Palladio was steadily working.[90] While the planning thus became gradually more Roman, the façades tended to break away from the simple classicism of Bramante which determined the Basilica and the Palazzo Porto. Palazzo Chiericati (Fig. 74), however, probably designed shortly after the Palazzo Porto, presented a particular problem.[91] The palace was to be built along one side of a large square, and not in a narrow street. Palladio therefore visualized its façade in terms of a Roman forum and designed long colonnades in two tiers. That the idea of a forum was on his mind can be proved with his own words; he says in the chapter on 'Piazze': 'Porticoes, such as the ancients used, ought to be made round the piazze'.[92] Of course, the colonnade of the *piano nobile* is interrupted by the five slightly projecting centre bays which form a proper palazzo front derived from the same Bramantesque

74, 75. Palladio. Palazzo Chiericati, Vicenza, 1550 (drawing from Palladio's *Quattro Libri*)

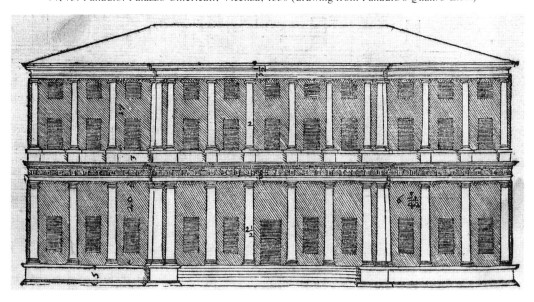

prototype as the Palazzo Porto. But this deviation from the ideal was not only an artistic necessity; it belonged to the sphere of the useful and the practicable, which play such an important part in the *Quattro libri*, and which he always strove to reconcile with his ideal demands. On the other hand, Palladio made his theoretical conception quite evident in his illustration of the whole façade (Fig. 75), for he left the orders white, and shaded all the walls in the same manner, regardless of whether they were joined to the colonnade or placed much further back, thereby giving the façade of the palace an appearance similar to that of the engraving of his 'piazza' (Fig. 76). This comparison also shows that he conceived the colonnades of the piazza with rich Ionic and Corinthian orders, while at the period of the Palazzo Chiericati a chaste Doric below and an unadorned Ionic order above were chosen. The Doric has still something of the simple grandeur of Bramante's Tempietto, and is entirely untouched by the problematic style of Michelangelo, who at exactly this period was reviving an ancient piazza in his design for the Capitol.

Gualdo reports that Palladio was in Rome in 1554. This visit must have opened his eyes to the meaning of contemporary architecture. Not only his planning but also the style of his façades went through a metamorphosis after his return. The first document of this change is the façade of the Palazzo Thiene (Figs. 77-79).[93] Although the one executed front again shows rustication below and order above, expression and emphasis are entirely different from the Palazzo Porto. Now the rustication of the basement has no longer a decorative quality; its large, rough blocks convey, on the contrary, the impression of mass and power similar to, if somewhat tamer than, the rustication of Augustus' walls round the forums which were the model for Bramante's Palazzo di S. Biagio[94] and for the other palaces of this group. The entrance gate, with its heavy, alternating small and large bosses overlapping the rustication of the wall, was a feature constantly used and varied in Italian Mannerism after Raphael had introduced it in the Palazzo Pandolfini in Florence. The wall of the *piano nobile* is not smooth as in the Bramantesque Roman palaces, but consists of sharply cut, flat rustication on which the order is superimposed. With this arrangement Palladio takes up the tradition which leads back through the Cancelleria and Alberti's Palazzo Rucellai to the top storey of the Colosseum; Palladio's own reconstruction of the exterior of the Pantheon shows that he regarded this treatment as common in antiquity. The contradiction inherent in this combination attracted Mannerist architects, and they exploited it in various ways from Giulio Romano's Palazzo del Te[95] to Alessi's Palazzo Marino in Milan. Palladio himself made the contrast between the heavy quoins and voussoirs of the window frames and the regular, flat rustication of the wall with its large smooth pilasters the main theme of the façade.

The Ionic columns of the aediculae of the windows are almost invisible under the rectangular bosses. This motif had the support of such classical structures as the Porta Maggiore in Rome.[96] But it was only in Mannerist architecture that the motif came into its own. Mannerist architects were enchanted with the 'unfinished' appearance of such an order; its many potentialities were fully exploited as the works by Giulio Romano, Sansovino, Sanmicheli, Ammanati, Dosio, Alessi, Vignola and many others demonstrate. In the case of the Palazzo Thiene the rusticated small Ionic columns and the smooth Corinthian pilasters of the large order were related in a subtle way. An entablature, that appears to run along under the pilasters, unites the small columns[97] so that a coherent small

93 I doubt that the design of the façade can be dated before Palladio's return from Rome, even though the interior was then already far advanced; see p. 76, note 84.

94 Cf. Giovannoni in BOLLETTINO D'ARTE, VIII, 1914, p. 185 ff.

95 For the use in the Palazzo Thiene of motifs deriving from Giulio Romano, cf. E. Gombrich, 'Zum Werke Giulio Romanos,' JAHRBUCH D. KUNSTHIST. SLG. IN WIEN, N.F. IX, p. 138. For a broad discussion of Giulio Romano's influence on Palladio, see R. Pallucchini, in *Bollettino del Centro Internazionale di Studi d'Architettura* I, 1959, p. 38 ff.

96 Among the drawings by Palladio in Vicenza is one showing the Porta Maggiore and on the verso are three Roman arches with a heavy rusticated Tuscan order, inscribed in Palladio's hand: 'questa opera sie a santo joane paulo . . . ' (Fig. 80). These arches belonged to the substructure of the Temple of Claudius on the Celio. Cf. Giuseppe Lugli, *Roma antica*, Rome, 1946, p. 377. According to Zorzi, *I disegni, op. cit.*, p. 60, No. 13, the drawing is by Falconetto, but inscribed in Palladio's hand.

97 The linking up of the window aediculae already occurs in the Palazzo Pandolfini, but of course without a large order cutting across the band of the string-course.

76. Detail of Palladio's 'Piazza'. From Palladio's *Quattro Libri*

77. Palazzo Thiene, Vicenza. Detail of ground-floor

78. Palazzo Thiene, Vicenza. Detail of elevation. From Haupt's *Palazzi dell'Italia*

79. Palazzo Thiene, Vicenza. Façade, *c.*1556

83

80. Palladio. Drawing of the Roman arches on the Celio, Museo Civico, Vicenza

order seems to alternate with the large one. The complicated rhythm created by the interpenetration of a small and a large order often recurs in Mannerist architecture. The horizontal course of the frieze of the small order, running across the length of the façade, has still another result; it interferes with the consistency of the rusticated wall, cutting it, as it were, in two; this same idea was introduced in the basement (Fig. 77), where two smooth courses above and below the windows contrast with the irregular surface of the rusticated blocks.[98]

In spite of such Mannerist factors as conflict and complication, we find in the building neither Michelangelo's extreme tension, nor Giulio Romano's almost pathological restlessness; it is orderly, systematic and entirely logical, and one looks at it with a disengaged curiosity rather than with that violent response which many more complex Mannerist structures evoke. And let it be said, all its details had the warrant of classical prototypes.

A further step in the direction of a Mannerist solution is the façade of the Palazzo Valmarana, built in 1566 (Figs. 81, 83).[99] It is obvious that this façade contains a reference to the problematic architecture of Michelangelo. The stimulus of the Capitoline palaces is apparent in the combined use of a giant and a small order. But apart from this basic idea the differences are considerable. In the Palazzo Valmarana the wall is almost eliminated, and the surface is crowded with motifs. The window frames in the *piano nobile* touch the entablature above, and are hemmed in at the sides by the enormous capitals. An unequal, typically Mannerist, conflict arises between the slender mouldings of the window frames and the bulky mass of the pilasters. Moreover, the treatment of the ground-floor is extremely complicated, for the small Corinthian order is not applied to a proper wall (Figs. 82, 83). The ground, to which it is attached, is rusticated, but the rustication has been given a particular meaning. The strips at the sides of the windows have been treated to look like Tuscan pilasters with their own capitals,[100] and this results in the impression of a third minute order; the relationship of the giant composite order to the small Corinthian order is repeated in the relationship of the Corinthian to the Tuscan pilasters. Above the windows are reliefs, and as they are in a deeper plane than the rustication, the latter appears like a frame to them, the lower border being at the same time the lintel of the windows. In all this, one would be inclined to believe, Palladio was going his own way, without regard to ancient models. But even for this building he reverted to classical antiquity, and found there, surprisingly enough, his justification for the extremely complicated interplay of wall and order (Fig. 84).[101]

The system of the Palazzo Valmarana is not coherent, as were all the other structures which have been discussed. It is not only broken into and interrupted by the extravagantly high entrance, but also by the complete change of treatment of the two end bays. Here the windows are framed differently and are different in height, and, above all, the colossal order is matched and balanced at the corners by a small Corinthian pilaster which carries a caryatid figure. The disquieting effect of this arrangement was observed and put on record in the eighteenth century when Temanza lamented that the corners had been weakened though these were just the points which should show the greatest strength.[102] But this was precisely what Palladio here intended to do. In no other building did he attempt an equally deliberate break with established classical conventions.

Language and patience have limits when describing a Mannerist structure, and many other features of this building may be left unrecorded. But a case of typical

98 Similar interruptions of the rustication are common with Giulio Romano; see, e.g., the Palazzo del Te and his house at Mantua.
99 Palladio II, pp. 14, 15. Generally dated 1556, but the foundation medal, reported by Magrini (*op. cit.*, p. xxiv, also p. 79), bears the date 1566. Cf. also the document of Dec. 14, 1565, published by Dalla Pozza, *op. cit.*, p. 222 f.
100 It is also irregular for these Tuscan pilasters not to carry arches; cf. Palladio I, p. 14
101 See two drawings by Palladio in the Burlington-Devonshire Coll. (Vol. X, No. 13 and XII, 22 v.) after a wall above the Roman Theatre at Verona, cf. Pirro Marconi, *Verona Romana*, 1937, p. 133, Fig. 88.
102 *Op. cit.*, p. xxv.

81. Palladio. Palazzo Valmarana,
Vicenza, 1566

82. Palazzo Valmarana. Detail

83. Palazzo Valmarana. From Palladio's
Quattro Libri

84. Palladio. Drawing of a Roman
wall at Verona

Mannerist inversion seems worth mentioning.[103] The cornice projects above each pilaster of the large order, but there is no such projection at the corners, above the atlantes; the entablature of the small order, on the other hand, is in one plane throughout, with the exception of the corners where it projects under the atlantes. A similar inversion can be found in an example of ancient 'Mannerist' architecture, the Porta de' Borsari at Verona, which was well known to Palladio, and the influence of which can be traced in other late works of his.[104] At this period Palladio was evidently attracted by the unclassical tendencies in ancient architecture. His Mannerism at this moment is a phenomenon of considerable interest since, after the 'wild' 1530's and 1540's, the prevailing tendency of the 1550's and 1560's was a return to classicism, to 'regularity, symmetry, orderliness', as Professor Lotz put it.[105]

The Palazzo Valmarana was not Palladio's last word. His most important later building at Vicenza is the Loggia del Capitanio of which only three bays were erected, in 1571 (Fig. 85).[106] As a type, the structure has its place in the long tradition of the Palazzo Communale, the Palazzo del Consiglio or del Podestà; there are always open loggias for public use below and offices above.[107] Palladio again devised the main front towards the piazza after the model of Michelangelo's Capitoline palaces. Yet he abandoned the interplay of several orders, and gave the front a most powerful accentuation of giant half-columns. The treatment of the bays themselves is remarkable: the windows cut through the entablature,[108] and very heavy balconies are resting on what can best be described as pieces of a cornice with triglyphs instead of brackets. Similar reversals of classical usage – very rare with Palladio – are first to be found in the aediculae of Michelangelo's Ricetto,[109] and had become almost a stock feature of Mannerist architecture. One of the strangest characteristics of this front is the *horror vacui*; all free wall-space disappears under a bewildering maze of stucco reliefs, some of which have now crumbled away. In addition, the small scale and flatness of these decorations is in remarkable contrast to the large-scale architecture in heavy relief. The key to this is to be found in the architecture of the side front. It is surprising, and contrary to Palladio's normal practice, that the system of the main front is not carried on at the side (Figs. 86, 87). Here there is no giant order. To be sure, this front faces on to a narrow street, but the Palazzo Valmarana shows that the narrowness of the street did not deter Palladio from using a giant order. The side front forms a unit of its own, based on the triumphal arch motif.[110] It is this motif that Palladio took up in the decoration of the main front: examples of triumphal arches of antiquity account for the *horror vacui*.

A similar crowding of the walls with reliefs is to be found on the Arch of Septimius Severus (Fig. 88) and on that at Orange (Fig. 45). Moreover, the former also shows the contrast between the smallness of the reliefs and the massiveness of the architectural members, while the latter is decorated all over with trophies, the symbols of victory. Now, with the exception of the figures in the spandrels of the arches, the reliefs of the Loggia del Capitanio represent trophies *all'antica* (Fig. 87). Palladio's building would thus appear to be a monumental symbol of victory like the triumphal arches of antiquity.

On the side of the building are six allegorical figures, and the two in the lower tier leave no doubts as to the victory, which was here commemorated. They represent Peace and Victory and have the following inscriptions: 'Belli secura quiesco' ('I rest untroubled by war') and 'Palmam genuere carinae'.[111] 'The ships

---

103 On inversion as a Mannerist principle cf. Wittkower in ART BULLETIN, XVI, 1934, p. 210.

104 It is interesting that Serlio in his Third Book commented upon the Porta de' Borsari as being licentious and a 'cosa barbara'.

105 W. Lotz, 'Architecture in the Later Sixteenth Century', COLLEGE ART JOURNAL, XVII, 1958, p. 129.

106 Documents in Magrini, *op. cit.*, p. 163 ff. and G. Fasolo in ARCHIVIO VENETO, 5TH SERIES, XXII, 1938, p. 283, ff. The Loggia was to replace an earlier dilapidated one.

107 Here the Venetian magistrate was to officiate. The office was held in 1571 by Gio. Battista Bernardo as recorded in the inscription of the cornice: 'IO BAPTISTAE BERNARDO PRAEFECTO CIVITAS DICAVIT'.

108 This feature has been interpreted by authors with an academic bias as having been done by workmen in Palladio's absence, cf. Bertotti Scamozzi, *op. cit.*, I, p. 34 f. and F.V. Mosca, *Descrizione delle Architetture, Pitture, e Scolture di Vicenza*, 1779, II, p. 17f., and others. However, Palladio proudly put his signature ANDREA PALLADIO ARCHITETTO at the side front under the arch, which almost cuts the entablature in two (see Fig. 86). Moreover, Magrini (p. 169) has shown that Palladio was at Vicenza throughout 1571.

109 Cf. Wittkower, *op. cit.*, p. 207.

110 Above the arch with its two framing composite columns is a minute order of Tuscan pilasters. The placing of the Tuscan above the Composite order as well as the proportions are quite unorthodox. It seems that the model for the proportions was again the Porta de' Borsari at Verona. The breaking of the entablature by the arch in the first storey was authorized by the side front of the triumphal arch at Orange (cf. Fig. 45).

111 In the upper tier at the two ends are Virtus as a young warrior ('Uni virtutis genio') and Honor, as on the medal of Vitellius, as a young woman with uncovered breasts, cornucopia and a helmet under one foot ('Dea nubit honoris'); cf. Ripa, *Iconologia*, 1603, p. 203 (here also is the close alliance of Honor and Virtus explained). In the most prominent position, left and right of the central arch, are the two Christian virtues Fides and Pietas. Fides with cross, flame and watering jug and a reference in the inscription to the heathen libation (Diis thure et corde libandum') and Pietas with a stork at her side and a little child on her arm who holds an elephant's head, all symbols mentioned by Ripa, p. 402. The inscription refers to the purifying power of Piety ('Sordes pietas una abluit omnes'). The programme of the figures would thus appear to be: Virtue and Honour under the flag of Faith and Piety achieved Victory and Peace.

85. Palladio. Loggia del Capitanio, Vicenza, 1571

86. Loggia del Capitanio. From Haupt's *Palazzi dell'Italia*

87. Detail of the side front of the Loggia del Capitanio

88. Arch of Septimius Severus, Rome

89. Palladio's decoration for Henri III's visit to Venice, 1574. Painting by Andrea Vicentino, Palazzo Ducale, Venice

112 On the flood of works of art celebrating this victory, cf. A. Blunt in JOURNAL OF THE WARBURG AND COURTAULD INSTITUTES, III, 1939-40, p. 63 f.
113 1It would appear that the documents speak a clear enough language. R. Pane (in *Venezia e l'Europa. Atti del XVIII Congresso Internazionale di Storia dell'Arte*, Venice, 1956, p. 410) attacked my conclusions, obviously without having taken the trouble to check how I arrived at them.
114 Palladio's decorations are shown in the picture by Andrea Vicentino in the Sala delle Quattro Porte of the Palazzo Ducale. For further references cf. Pierre de Nolhac and Angelo Solerti, *Il viaggio in Italia di Enrico III*, 1890, particularly pp. 33 ff., 36 ff., 98 ff. Cf. also L. Molmenti, *Storia di Venezia nella vita privata*, II, p. 103.
Temanza, *op. cit.*, reports that Consul Smith in Venice possessed exact drawings of these decorations by Antonio Visentini. They are now in the British Museum, King's 146, and the title to the volume of ten sheets says that they were 'diligentemente dissegnato e sopra le giuste misure prese dalla relazione di Marsilio dalla Croce eseguito da Antonio Visentini ... l'anno del Guibileo MCCL'.
115 Before 1558 Palladio was given a commission by the Patriarch Vincenzo Diedo for the façade of the church of S. Pietro di Castello at Venice. According to a document of January 7, 1558, published by Magrini, *op. cit.*, p. xvii ff., Palladio's design showed 'porte e *finestre*', '*sei* colonne grandi' and '*sei* pilastri quadri cioè tre per banda'.

which have brought victory' can only refer to Lepanto, the decisive sea-battle against the Turks won in 1571, and this reference has always been understood.[112] We can now also understand the two large allegories of victory resting on the arch of the side front, after the fashion of triumphal arches, and the figures in the spandrels of the arches of the main front. All their attributes consist of allusions to the element of water.

Documents show that the Loggia was built by the Community of Vicenza with extraordinary speed. On April 18th, 1571, building had not yet begun, but during the summer the structure rose quickly, and by the end of the year it was roofed in. The victory of Lepanto was won on October 7th. On the 18th of this month it became known at Vicenza, which, being Venetian territory, was particularly stirred by the great news. Its reverberations made themselves felt immediately in the decision of the overjoyed community, taken on October 26th, to contribute 24,000 ducats to the expenses of the campaign. Impressed by this feat of arms, Palladio must have changed his original plans for the Loggia, for it is evident that he could not have decided on the triumphal decorations of the main front before the middle of October. Nor does it seem probable that the triumphal arch motif of the side was introduced before Lepanto supplied a reason for it. Political actuality overruled considerations of artistic principle. It seems justifiable to conclude that Palladio sacrificed an originally uniform plan to the exigencies of the victory.[113]

Nevertheless, there existed for Palladio a deep affinity between the monumental loggia and the triumphal arch. He demonstrated it in the decoration he built in 1574 for the solemn visit to Venice of Henry III of France while on his way from

Poland to Paris (Fig. 89). The decoration consisted of a triumphal arch similar to that of Septimius Severus, and, behind it, a loggia of twelve colossal Corinthian columns, equal in height to the columns of the arch,[114] thereby manifesting that assembly and triumph are closely interrelated. With this festival decoration in mind, one feels entitled to say that Palladio considered it a satisfactory solution to blend a loggia and a triumphal arch in a permanent structure.

In the Loggia del Capitanio the monumental and dense quality, which was already noticeable in the Palazzo Valmarana, has become the dominant factor, and overshadows the Mannerist features. At this period, the emphasis on mass in late Roman architecture had a strong hold on Palladio's imagination. Apart from the direct influence of the Arch of Septimius Severus, the powerful remains of the ancient thermae fascinated him. But the nearest parallels to this Loggia are Hellenistic buildings, such as the Temples at Baalbek, which were unknown to him. His own development had brought him to a point where he re-created the spirit of this kind of architecture.

The Loggia del Capitanio faces Palladio's Basilica on the same square. The comparison shows clearly what had happened in the course of twenty-five years. Though deriving from similar classical sources the two buildings could not be more widely different. The early building was based on Bramante, in other words, on a contemporary interpretation of classical architecture rather than on Palladio's own. The later building is the expression of an essentially personal approach. In its design many classical conceptions are strung together; yet far from being orthodox and archaeological, it seems a free and emotional transformation of ancient models.

4. The Genesis of an Idea: Palladio's Church Façades

Rather late in life Palladio designed two large churches and one church façade in Venice.[115] The façade is that of S. Francesco della Vigna, probably begun in1562, as a front to Jacopo Sansovino's structure.[116] S. Giorgio Maggiore and Il Redentore, Palladio's two churches, followed later. The foundation stone of S. Giorgio was laid in 1566, but the front was erected between 1597 and 1610.[117] Il Redentore was dedicated during the plague of 1576, and completed in 1592, twelve years after Palladio's death.[118] In this section only the three façades will be studied (Figs. 90, 93). They follow one and the same pattern: a colossal temple front is placed before the nave and a small order carrying part of a pediment before each of the aisles. The pattern of the design may be represented as two superimposed temple fronts, a major and a minor (Fig. 92).[119] It is worth asking why Palladio had recourse to the same basic type for his three monumental façades. The answer has evidently been anticipated by our discussion of the villas.

For Renaissance architects the church façade raised one of the most intricate problems.[120] Those architects who thought in classical terms and regarded the Christian church as the legitimate successor to the ancient temple,[121] wrestled constantly with attempts to apply the temple front to the church. But unlike the ancient temple with its uniform cella, most churches were built on the basilical system with a high nave and lower aisles. How could a temple front with its simple portico and pediment be applied to such a structure? The first solution was drastic: one large temple front was made to appear as if it covered both nave and aisles. This was how Alberti tackled the problem in S. Andrea at Mantua

Vincenzo Diedo died on December 9th, 1559, possibly before building had started. The present façade was executed between 1594 and 1596 by Francesco Smeraldi who combined features from S. Francesco della Vigna and the Redentore. Since Smeraldi's façade has neither windows nor six columns and six pilasters (but only four of each kind), it cannot correspond to the original design by Palladio which we are not in a position to reconstruct. The present façade is, in fact, a *pasticcio*: it is impossible to assume that Palladio anticipated his own late style of the Redentore by almost twenty years. Pane's assertion (*Palladio*, p. 102 and Pl. 101) that the present façade was based on Palladio's design is therefore unfounded.
116 Foundation stone of the church: 1534, the date of the façade is not absolutely certain. Vasari, *Vite*, ed. Milanesi, VII, p. 529, saw the structure rising. He was at Venice in 1566. According to Tassini, *Curiosità Veneziane*, 1933, p. 284 f., it was begun in 1562. Cf. also Magrini, *op. cit.*, p. 65 ff.
117 Inscriptions of 1602 and 1610 on the façade. For the history of S. Giorgio, cf. Temanza, *op. cit.*, p. lxxi f.; Bertotti Scamozzi, *op. cit.*, IV, p. 11 f.; Francesco Sansovino, *Venezia . . . descritta*, ed. of 1668, p. 218 ff.; G.A. Moschini, *Guida per la Città di Venezia*, 1815, I, i, p. 55; Cicogna, *Isriz. Ven.* IV, pp. 265, 331, 402 ff.; Cicognara, etc., *Le Fabbriche e i monumenti cospicui di Venezia*, 1840, II, p. 15 ff., Pls. 133-7; Magrini, *op. cit.*, pp. 62, xxii (document about model built between 25th November, 1565, and 12th March, 1566). R. Gallo has shown, on the basis of newly discovered documents, that Simone Sorella *Fig* and not, as is traditionally believed, Scamozzi *Fig* was responsible for the execution of the façade. Work began in 1597, was taken up in 1607 and completed in 1610 (RIVISTA DI VENEZIA, 1955, p. 23 ff. and *Venezia e l'Europa. Atti del XVIII Congresso Internazionale di Storia dell'Arte*, Venice, 1956, p. 401).
118 Cf. Palladio's letter of 1577 with a most illuminating report about his design, in Bottari, *Racc. di lettere*, 1822, I, p. 560 ff.; Temanza, *op. cit.*, p. lxii ff; Moschini, *Guida*, II, ii, p. 343, f; Magrini, *op. cit.*, pp. 210 ff, lix (documents). Foundation stone: May 3rd, 1577. Cf. the fully documented monograph by P. Davide M. da Portogruaro in RIVISTA DI VENEZIA, 1930 (April-May).
119 It should be emphasized that Palladio wanted his façades to be seen as isolated features: they stand in brilliant whiteness in front of the red brick structures of the churches.
120 See above, p. 45.
121 They even talk about temples when they mean churches; thus Alberti in his *De re aedificatoria*; see also Serlio whose Fifth Book deals with 'diverse forme di Tempij sacri, secondo il costume Christiano, & al modo antico'; also Palladio in the preface to his Fourth Book.
The architect Fausto Rughesi, in his 'Considerationi sopra la nuova aggiunta da farsi alla Fabrica di San Pietro', correlates the term 'tempio' with centralized structures; he says that Michelangelo 'elesse la forma del tempio et non della Basilica'.

90. Palladio. S. Francesco della Vigna, Venice, 1562. From Bertotti Scamozzi

91. Palladio. Design for S. Giorgio Maggiore, Venice

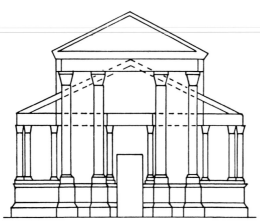

92. S. Francesco della Vigna: schematic representation of the two interpenetrating temple fronts.

93. Palladio. S. Giorgio Maggiore, Venice, 1566-1610. From Bertotti Scamozzi

(1470) (Fig. 46).[122] At the same time, by approximating his system to that of the triumphal arch with its large central bay and narrow side bays, he was able to echo in his façade the proportions of nave and aisles. But the combination of a temple front and a triumphal arch, though perfectly satisfactory in this case, was too complex and too personal to be generally acceptable. For reasons of proportion it was also often impossible to cover both nave and aisles with a single temple front.

The next step was taken by Bramante ten years after S. Andrea in a design for the façade of S. Maria di S. Satiro in Milan (Fig. 94).[123] For the first time during the Renaissance he used here parts of pediments to correspond with the aisles,[124] and created the impression of a large pediment split open by a central feature which is also crowned by a pediment. In keeping with traditional church façades Bramante planned two storeys, a major one across the whole width of the façade and, above it, a narrower one corresponding to the nave. The four large pilasters of the principal storey, though echoing in their position nave and aisles, are all the same size and in the same plane. So one unifying system without 'joints' binds nave and aisles together. The whole height of the nave is divided in two parts by the broad entablature, and the somewhat isolated second tier with its circular window has a typical Quattrocentesque character. In contrast to Palladio's design, the order determined by the aisles is the dominating motif of the front. From Palladio's standpoint such a façade was not an organic and 'antique' answer to the problem. Bramante, however, regarded his design as warranted by antiquity.

It was logical for an architect with classical tendencies to investigate what kind of façade the ancients had used for their basilicas, because, like churches, these structures had a nave and lower aisles. The answer was given in Vitruvius' obscure words about the 'double arrangement of gables' in the Basilica of Fano.[125] That Bramante endeavoured in his design for S. Satiro to interpret this passage can be proved indirectly, for his pupil Cesariano, in his edition of Vitruvius (1521), illustrated the Basilica of Fano with a design deriving from Bramante's project (Fig. 95).[126]

A further step towards Palladio's solution was taken by Peruzzi in the façade to the old Cathedral at Carpi, built in 1515 (Fig. 97).[127] The connection with Bramante's design is obvious. But Peruzzi took the decisive step of using a giant order for the nave and a small order for the aisles; thus he almost anticipated Palladio's scheme. However he did not carry his novel design to its logical conclusion. Like Alberti, he again fused the temple front with the triumphal arch motif. He therefore failed – Palladio might have argued – to develop a uniform system of design. Nor did he safeguard the uniformity of the side bays, for no properly finished half-pilasters correspond on the inside to the Corinthian pilaster outside.

Palladio accomplished what his predecessors had begun. He was intent on preserving the pure temple front before the nave: S. Francesco della Vigna and S. Giorgio are prostyles, Il Redentore is a temple *in antis*, all of them of course projected on to a wall. The small bays corresponding to the aisles at each side of the slightly projecting central part are clearly defined and bound together by orders outside and inside. Moreover, the rhythm of the small order penetrates into the main temple front not only with the order framing the central door but also with the entablature, the continuity of which is suggested right across the whole façade. Thus the two orders are firmly linked. But their calculated

(M. Cerrati, *Tiberii Alpharani De Basilicae Vaticanae antiquissima et nova structura*, Rome, 1914, p. 203 ff.).

122 Cf. the detailed analysis above, p. 56 ff.

123 First published by Beltrami in RASSEGNA D' ARTE, I, 1901, p. 33 ff.

124 This motif also appears in the late-fifteenth-century Florentine engraving of the Presentation in the Temple (Hind B. I. 4), probably based on Vitruvius' description of the Basilica at Fano (see below).

125 Cf. Vitruvius, V, i, 10: 'Ita fastigiorum duplex tecti nata . . .'

126 The same design was copied in the editions by Caporali (1536) and Philander (1544); the latter was used for our illustration.

127 Vasari, ed. Milanesi, IV, p. 598. The attribution to Peruzzi is not undisputed, cf. W. Winthrop Kent, *The Life and Works of Baldassare Peruzzi*, New York, 1925, p. 28, Pl. 30; also article in Thieme-Becker, and Venturi, *Storia dell'arte*, XI, 1, p. 392, who believes that the façade is of Lombardo-Bramantesque origin. The context in which the façade is shown in the present study would seem to strengthen the old attribution to Peruzzi. Proof of Peruzzi's authorship in C.L. Frommel's *Farnesina* (Berlin, 1961, p. 145 ff.), a work which has come to hand at the very last moment.

94. Bramante. Design for S. Maria di S. Satiro, Milan, *c*.1480

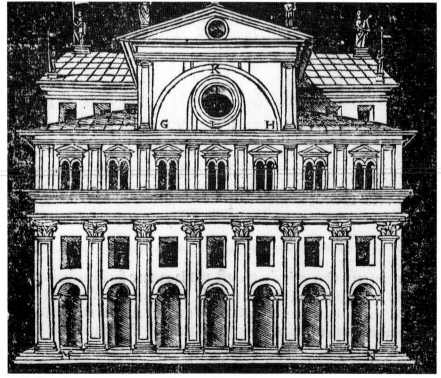

95. Cesariano's reconstruction of the Basilica at Fano. From Philander's *Vitruvius*, 1544

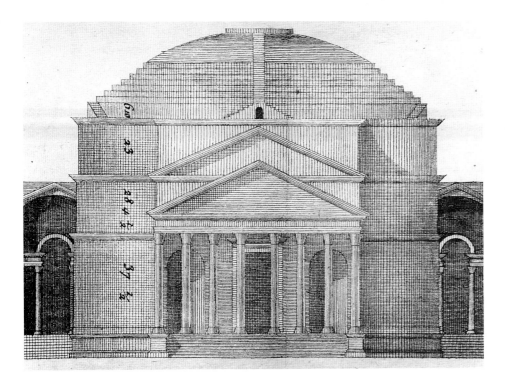

96. Palladio's design of the Pantheon. From Burlington's *Fabbriche Antiche*, 1730
97. Peruzzi (?). Cathedral at Carpi, 1515

interlocking makes the 'reading' of such a façade no easy matter. The sophistication and intellectualism of the design are truly Mannerist, far removed from what might be called Renaissance naïveté. Yet in contrast to Michelangelo's deeply disturbing Mannerism, Palladio's is sober and academic: it is hardly ever concerned with detailed forms; capitals, tabernacles and entablatures retain their classical significance, shape and ratio. It is the interplay of entire classical units that accounts for the Mannerist character of the whole.

Palladio's use of two pediments in the same façade was legitimized not only by the problematical Basilica at Fano, but, above all, by their co-existence in the most venerable ancient temple, the Pantheon, where one pediment crowns the portico, while the other, further back, is attached to the high attic which projects from the rotunda (Fig. 96). It is from here also that Palladio derived his attic for the Redentore.

Almost all the measured drawings of the Pantheon made during the later sixteenth century show the two pediments, and Palladio himself drew it twice with them, once for the *Quattro Libri*, and a second time in the series of thermae which were published by Lord Burlington (Fig. 96). The men who interpreted the front of the Pantheon in this way thought in terms of complicated wall arrangements, and took it for granted, therefore, that the two pediments belonged to a homogeneous classical design. The views of the Pantheon drawn in the fifteenth and early sixteenth centuries show only one pediment. These views are also accurate if it is considered that from a near distance the second pediment is invisible. The men of the Quattrocento, thinking and seeing in terms of simple wall arrangements, assume this near distance.[128] In the seventeenth century a more detached archaeological approach led Carlo Fontana to conclude that the portico was a later addition to the original Pantheon, and he reconstructed it in its supposed simplicity without a portico.[129] Following the precedent of the

128 Only one pediment is shown, for instance, in the Codex Escurialensis (cf. H. Egger's edition, 1905, fol. 43v.), by Cronaca (drawing, Uffizi, illustr. in Lukomski, *I maestri della architettura classica*, 1933, p. 293); and still later by Heemskerck (Egger-Hülsen, *Die römischen Skizzenbücher von Marten van Heemskerck*, Berlin, 1913, I, fol. 10.) and Serlio (Bk. III). By contrast Dosio's drawings (Uffizi, cf. Bartoli, *Monumenti*, V, Figs. 848, 881) show two pediments.
129 C. Fontana, *Templum Vaticanum*, 1694, p. 457.

98. Palladio. Il Redentore, Venice, 1576-92. From Bertotti Scamozzi

Pantheon, and with Vitruvius' description of the Basilica of Fano in mind, Palladio gave intersecting pediments to the front of the Basilica of Constantine,[130] which for him was the 'Tempio della Pace'. It is evident that he regarded this motif as well established in classical antiquity.

* * * * *

So far we have only considered Palladio's three façades in the light of their fundamental uniformity. Although in all three cases the system is identical, there are still important differences. S. Francesco and S. Giorgio, near in time, show also a close resemblance (Figs. 90, 93). It must, however, be said that S. Giorgio as we see it today does not seem to correspond to Palladio's intentions. The two orders do not rise from the same level. The large half-columns stand on high pedestals, while the small pilasters rise almost from the ground. This discrepancy in level, which is particularly unfortunate where the high pedestals cut into the adjoining pilasters, is not the only fault in this façade.[131] Palladio's original design has been preserved in a measured drawing (Fig. 91)[132] which allows us to assess the later alterations. The drawing proves that he wanted the large and small orders to rise from the same level and, no doubt, he must have regarded this as essential to the unity of his design.[133] A comparison of S. Francesco and S. Giorgio must take this drawing into consideration. It appears then that in spite of the similarity in general treatment there is a development in these façades. The small order has gained in importance as compared with S. Francesco and the relationship between the small and the large order is now close to that of the late Redentore. This change makes the visual impression of an interpenetration of two temple fronts more convincing. There is another point worth mentioning about the drawing. It is unfinished and it is just this fact which throws a light on Palladio's thought. The large order, standing out before a wall on which no detail has yet been drawn, is closely reminiscent of the portico of a Corinthian temple.

The relation of S. Francesco and S. Giorgio to the Redentore (Figs. 98, 99) can be compared with that of the Palazzo Valmarana to the Loggia del Capitanio. In the late façade of the Redentore there is, above all, a new and powerful concentration; the large temple motif dominates and no distracting details appear in the outer bays, while the entrance bay is filled entirely by the simple columned aedicula framing the door. In addition, the wide staircase, imitating that of ancient temples, ties together the three bays of the colossal order. But with the greater concentration goes a complexity which did not appear in the earlier façades. The interplay of the two temple systems is now emphasized by peculiar repetitions. The large pediment is repeated in the door pediment, and the parts of pediments of the side bays are repeated higher up on a deeper plane; the top pediment is bisected by a rectangular attic, which was derived, as we saw, from the Pantheon.[134] It hardly needs emphasizing that the intricate classicism of the Redentore is far removed from the simple and unsophisticated classicism of Palladio's early period.

* * * * *

Although Palladio's intersecting temple fronts must be regarded as typical late-sixteenth-century interpretations of ancient architecture, they fulfil the basic requirements of all classical architecture since the days of anitquity. By using

130 Bk. IV, p. 11.

131 The socles under the aediculae of the outer bays correspond in height to the pedestals of the giant order and are disproportionately high in relation to the aediculae. Moreover, the pilasters of the small order between the tabernacles and the half-columns appear almost crushed.

132 R. Inst. of British Architects, Burlington-Devonshire Coll., Vol. XIV, No. 12.

The relation of the drawing to S. Giorgio Maggiore is placed beyond dispute by the aedicula with the small sarcophagus in the side bay. The sarcophagi and busts of the executed front were erected in honour of the doges Tribuno Memmo and Sebastiani Ziani, one the mythical founder of the monastery, the other its benefactor. The drawing shows that the memorials were planned from the beginning. It should also be noted that the proportions of Palladio's design correspond almost exactly to those of the actual façade (height of aisle and nave and width of aisle), and therefore, in reconstructing the façade, one must assume that it was intended to stand on the lowest possible base.

99. Il Redentore, Venice. Façade

The idea of placing the columns on the pavement without a high base was particularly dear to Palladio. In Bk. IV, chap. 5, he said concerning this point: 'Ma però nei Tempi Antichi non si veggono Piedestalli, ma le colonne cominciano dal piano del Tempio; il che molto mi piace: si perchè con i piedestali si impedisce molto l'entrata al Tempio; si anco perchè le colonne, le quali da terra cominciano, rendono maggior grandezza, e magnificenza.'

133 All the problems apparent in the existing front are here solved. E.g., the relationship of the socle to the aedicula is proportionate.

134 Palladio's problem was here similar to Alberti's in S. Andrea at Mantua. The nave was too high to be covered by one temple front; the attic was therefore a necessary expedient. The parts of pediments running into it were also structurally necessary. They are buttresses: each side of the high wall of the nave is supported by four pairs of such buttresses. But like every great architect, Palladio made such structural features serve his aesthetic ends.

temple motifs in front of the nave and aisles, i.e. motifs of the same species, and by carrying the theme through with absolute consistency, he achieved congruity of all the parts, *dispositio* in Vitruvius' terminology. Moreover, his structures also obey Vitruvius' all-important postulate of *symmetria*, which is the fixed mathematical ratio of the parts to each other and to the whole.

The façade of S. Francesco della Vigna may be used for a demonstration. In accordance with Vitruvius, a unit of measurement, the *modulus*, was applied to all dimensions in the façade. The diameter of the small columns which is two feet (*piedi*) constitutes the basic unit. The diameter of the large order is two moduli, i.e. four feet. The height of the small columns is twenty feet (ten moduli), that of

100. Andrea Tirali. S. Vitale, Venice, 1700

101. Giuseppe Valadier. S. Rocco, Rome, 1834

102. Francesco Maria Preti. Cathedral, Castelfranco, 1723

the larger ones forty feet (twenty moduli). In both cases the ratio of diameter to height is 1:10 and that of the small order to the large order is 1:2. The width of the intercolumniation of the centre bay is again twenty feet (ten moduli). Even without charting all the dimensions, we may conclude that, just as in Alberti's S. Maria Novella, simple ratios of the same modulus are effective throughout the building. But this is not the whole story. The centre part of the façade in front of the nave is twenty-seven moduli wide. Is this strange figure fortuitous or was it not rather arrived at as a result of careful considerations? We have good reasons to believe that *symmetria* for Palladio meant more than applying a simple system of commensurable ratios. In the next section the philosophical issues will be discussed which will throw light on Palladio's choice of the figure 'twenty-seven'. But we may anticipate the conclusion by pointing out that he, as heir to a long tradition, regarded *symmetria* as a meaningful relationship of numbers, in tune with that cosmic order which Pythagoras and Plato had revealed.

With his scheme for the church façades Palladio had solved one of the great problems of Christian architecture. From a classical point of view one cannot go beyond his solution and this is the reason why Palladio himself repeated the same type in his three façades for basilical churches.[135] Once the problem was solved he could vary the answer without changing its essence. Whatever one may think about Palladio's façades, it must be admitted that they represent the climax of a development to which, significantly, the great classical architects Alberti, Bramante, and Peruzzi had contributed.[136] It is not surprising, therefore, that Palladio's design proved to be outstandingly successful and was adapted and copied for two hundred and fifty years (Figs. 100-102).

5. Palladio's Optical and Psychological Concepts: Il Redentore

The interiors of Palladio's principal churches lend themselves to a discussion of certain aspects of his architecture which have not yet been mentioned. His latest church, the Redentore, is evidently in a class of its own. But even the earlier S. Giorgio Maggiore (Figs. 103, 104, 106) displays some unusual features which may be briefly enumerated: (1) the plan consists of three clearly isolated units, the Latin Cross with a short nave and an impressive domed area; the rectangular presbytery with isolated columns in the re-entrant angles; and the choir separated from the presbytery by an imposing screen of columns. (2) These three units are also separated by steps: the floor of the presbytery lies three steps above the floor of the nave, and the floor of the choir is elevated four steps above that of the presbytery. (3) The high altar is placed in front of the two pairs of columns through which a vista opens into the choir. (4) The articulating members become more potent in the vicinity of the high altar. (5) Colouristic differentiation confirms the definition of spaces: the half-columns of grey stone in the nave are placed against whitewashed pilasters;[137] by this device Palladio pulled the nave together as a rhythmically divided unit and contrasted its longitudinal direction with the transverse direction of the aisles and shallow chapels. (6) The architectural system changes in the choir. Instead of continuing the large order, Palladio gave a sequence of small-scale alternating niches and aediculae, an articulation derived from classical models.[138] (7) The mullioned, semi-circular windows in the vault, the chapels, and the presbytery guarantee uniformity of the

135 In his memorandum of 1567 he suggested it also for the front of the Cathedral at Brescia; cf. Magrini, *op. cit.*, Appendix, p. 13. His designs for the façade of S. Petronio at Bologna, particularly that of 1578, follow the same pattern (Museo di S. Petronio, No. 20, cf. Zucchini, *op. cit.*, pl. 21).

136 My interpretation of Palladio's church façades has aroused some violent criticism (see, above all, Pane, *loc. cit.*, above p. 88, note 112). It seems that my diagram Fig. 92 was the cause of some misunderstanding. I therefore wish to emphasize that this diagram was never intended as a reconstruction of Palladio's creative procedure. My text makes it sufficiently clear that in my view Palladio was striving for an organic and uniform solution which had the authority of classical antiquity and that he fulfilled, within the time-bound stylistic possibilities, the Vitruvian demand of *dispositio* and *symmetria*.

137 In the course of the recent restoration, the pilasters of the small order were painted grey and the old colour contrast has thus disappeared.

138 See the court of the Jupiter temple on the Quirinal, ill. in Palladio's *Quattro Libri* (IV, Pl. 26).

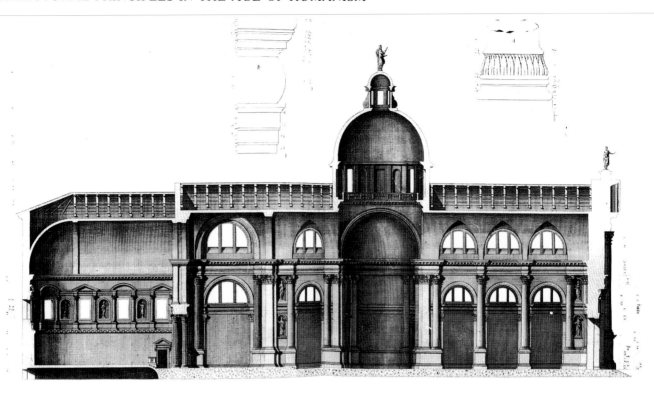

103, 104. Palladio. S. Giorgio Maggiore, Venice: (*above*) section, (*below*) plan

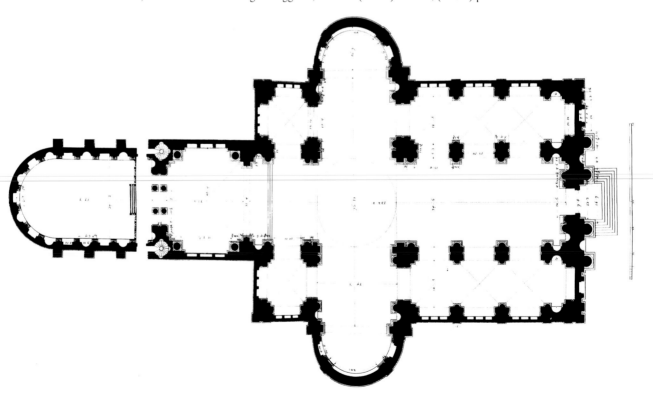

105. Il Redentore, Venice, 1576-92. View into presbytery and nave

106. S. Giorgio Maggiore. Nave

107. Palladio. Il Redentore, Venice

lights throughout the church (excepting the choir).

By virtue of the features here singled out the plan and elevation of S. Giorgio Maggiore are worlds apart from any central Italian church. Palladio's intentions become more obvious in the Redentore (Fig. 107), where he adapted all these elements to a different type of plan. The nave has three deep chapels to each side but no aisles. Like Alberti's nave of S. Andrea at Mantua, the nave of the Redentore is a re-creation of a hall in Roman thermae; it consists of a vast space unified by the impressively simple vault as well as by the contraction before the domed area: at both sides of the large arch of the crossing is a narrow bay with two niches, one above the other, repeating exactly the articulation of the entrance wall, thereby emphasizing the uniformity and isolation of the nave. The isolation of the nave is further supported by the three steps separating it from the chapels and the domed area.

This is not the place to speak of the Redentore's unparalleled solemnity which cannot fail to impress every visitor to the church. We are concerned with the fact that, with his inflexible determination to clarify fundamentals, Palladio tackled anew the old problem of the 'composite' type of church in which a centralized domed structure is joined to a longitudinal nave. We have shown in the First Part of this book that Renaissance architects attempted to solve this problem with proportional and anthropomorphic devices (Fig. 2). While they tried thus to weld together two generically different units, Palladio went the opposite way and clearly detached the longitudinal nave from the centralized area with its three semi-circular apses.[139]

To be sure, essential features of the articulation of the nave are repeated in the centralized unit, but not without significant modifications. Palladio transformed

139 It need hardly be emphasized that Palladio had recourse to a native Venetian tradition.

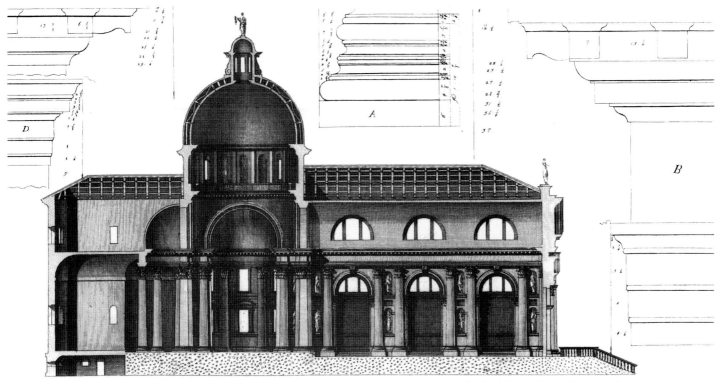

108, 109. Il Redentore: (*above*) section, (*below*) plan, with visual lines drawn in (both from Bertotti Scamozzi)

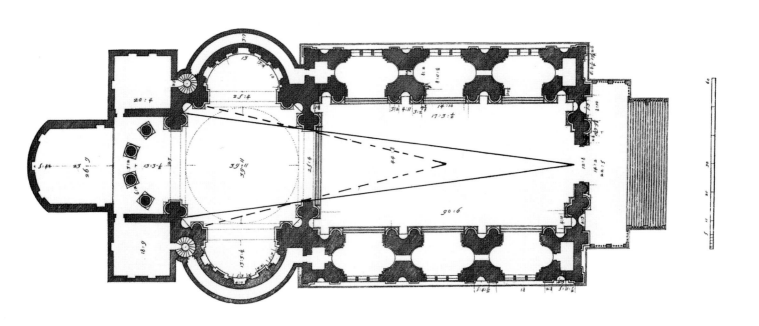

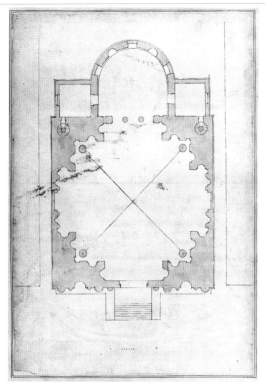
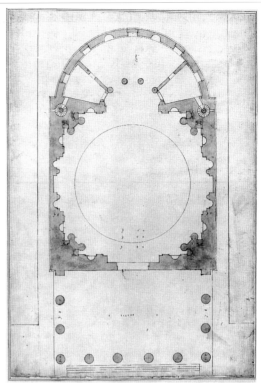

110, 111. Palladio. Plans for S. Nicola da Tolentino, Venice, 1579

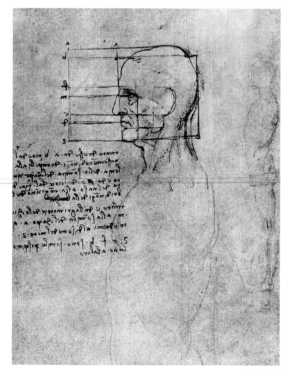

112. Leonardo da Vinci. Study in human
proportion, showing the ratios 1:3:1:2:1:2

113. Villard de Honnecourt. Page from
his sketch-book

the half-columns of the nave into pilasters in the lateral apses and into free-standing columns in the apse behind the high altar. Although he continued the main horizontal divisions of the nave in the presbytery (Figs. 105, 108), he desisted from carrying over the small order; in addition, he replaced the columned aediculae of the altars of the chapels by window frames with pilasters (otherwise identical in design), and the mullioned Roman windows of the chapels by simple rectangular windows. Thus the 'orchestration' of the nave and the presbytery differs to a considerable extent. If one looks in the direction of the nave from any point in the centralized part, one is aware of diversity in unity – or, better, of unity in spite of diversity. But looking from the nave towards the centralized part (the natural direction for the congregation) quite a different and radically new feature comes into play.

The visual lines drawn into the ground plan (Fig. 109) show that from the entrance door the visitor sees at the far end of the crossing a half-column coupled with a pilaster, a precise repetition of the same formation under the arch of the nave. Proceeding along the central axis, he views more and more of the farther dome supports, until from a point half-way along the nave a grouping of half-columns and niches closely similar to the bays at the end of the nave appears in his field of vision. By means of this repetition, Palladio created a new kind of coherence between the nave and the centralized part. The unification of separate spaces is achieved by the creation of corresponding vistas across large spaces rather than by the uniform handling of wall articulation, as was customary in central Italy. Thus optical devices, reminiscent of the effect of a stage setting, counterbalance and supersede the objective structural separation.

Another revolutionary feature is the arc of free-standing columns, derived from Roman thermae and anticipated in the less developed realization of S. Giorgio Maggiore. These columns have a triple function. First, they form a powerful finale, a crescendo near the altar, showing the half-columns of the nave freed, as it were, from their attachment to the wall. Secondly, they serve to maintain the uniformity of the centralized part, for the shape of the apse 'read' along the columns corresponds to that of the lateral apses while, at the same time, the monks' choir remains, as it must, an integral part of the church: an ingenious way of reconciling the customary requirement of the eastern prolongation with the ideal of centralized planning. Finally, the screen of columns also invites us to let the eye wander into the space beyond – a space to which the congregation is not admitted, and the utter simplicity of which is not to be measured by the standards gained in the richly articulated church. Thus these columns are an optical and psychological barrier and, simultaneously, an optical and psychological link to a world not accessible to the layman.

Palladio applied the lesson of the Redentore to the slightly later project for a centrally planned church (Figs. 110, 111).[140] In the first of the two plans he repeated the solution of S. Giorgio Maggiore, in the second (the later one) that of the Redentore. It is evident from these plans that the device of screening columns helps to preserve the integrity of the centralized space and, at the same time, to overcome its limitations. Optical and psychological conceptions of this kind were adumbrated in Palladio's earlier works, but it was the ideas realized in the Redentore that were extraordinarily fertile not only with such different Italian masters as Longhena, Bernini, Guarini, Juvarra and Vittone, but also with architects north of the Alps.

140 W. Timofiewitsch (in ARTE VENETA, XIII-XIV, 1959-60, p.79 ff.) showed rather convincingly that these drawings (which I previously related to the church at Maser) belong to Palladio's project for S. Nicola da Tolentino in Venice (1579), later executed by Scamozzi from a different design.

1 Cf. above, pp. 22 f., 31 f.

2 In addition to earlier references given above, p. 25, some mid- and late-sixteenth century authorities may be quoted. Daniele Barbaro in his comm. to Vitruvius III, i, ed. 1556, p. 63, writes: 'La natura maestra ce insegna come havemo à reggersi nelle misure e nelle proportioni delle fabbriche à i Dei consecrate, imperoche non da altro ella vuole che impariamo le ragioni delle Simmetrie, che ne i Tempi usar dovemo, che dal Sacro Tempio fatto ad imagine, et simiglianza di Dio, che è l'huomo, nella cui compositione tutte le altre meraviglie di natura contenute sono, e però con bello avvedimento tolsero gli antichi ogni ragione del misurare dalle parti del corpo humano . . . '

Cf. also Lomazzo's *Trattato dell'arte della pittura*, etc., 1584, I, chap. 30: 'Come ancora le misure delle navi, tempij, ed edifizj sono tratte dal corpo umano.' A similar chapter in the same author's *Idea del tempio delle pittura*, 1590, chap. 34, begins thus: 'il corpo umano, il quale è un opera perfetta, e bellissima fatta dal grande Iddio a simiglianza della sua Immagine, con grandissima ragione è stato chiamato mondo minore. Perchè contiene in se con più perfetta composizione, e con più sicura armonia, tutti i numeri, le misure, i pesi, i moti, ed elementi. Onde da lui principalmente, e non da altra fabbrica che uscisse dalla mano d'Iddio e dalle sue membra fu tolta la norma, ed il modello di formar i Tempij, i Teatri, e tutti gli edificj con tutte le sue parti come colonne, capitelli, canali, e simili; naviglij, machine, ed ogni sorte d'artificio.'

Michelangelo, in a letter of about 1560, wrote that 'there is no question but that architectural members reflect the members of Man' and that those who do not know the human body cannot be good architects (Milanesi, *Le lettere di Michelangelo Buonarroti*, Florence, 1875, p. 554).

Palladio (Bk. II, chap. 2) compares in a brief sentence the structure of the human body with that of a building.

Vincenzo Danti's work on proportion, planned in fifteen books of which only the first appeared, in 1567, would have contained in Book XIV: 'proporzioni dell'architettura cavata de la proporzione de la figura del huomo', and in Book XV: 'pratica di questa arte in universale'; see A. Comolli, *Bibliografia storico-critica dell'Architettura*, Rome, 1788, I., p. 16.

PART IV

THE PROBLEM OF HARMONIC PROPORTION IN ARCHITECTURE

The conviction that architecture is a science, and that each part of a building, inside as well as outside, has to be integrated into one and the same system of mathematical ratios, may be called the basic axiom of Renaissance architects. We have already seen[1] that the architect is by no means free to apply to a building a system of ratios of his own choosing, that the ratios have to comply with conceptions of a higher order and that a building should mirror the proportions of the human body; a demand which became universally accepted on Vitruvius' authority. As man is the image of God and the proportions of his body are produced by divine will, so the proportions in architecture have to embrace and express the cosmic order.[2] But what are the laws of this cosmic order, what are the mathematical ratios that determine the harmony in macrocosm and microcosm? They had been revealed by Pythagoras and Plato, whose ideas in this field had always remained alive but gained new prominence from the late fifteenth century onwards.

1. Francesco Giorgi's Platonic Programme for S. Francesco della Vigna

Hardly any more telling evidence in proof of this has survived than a document relating to S. Francesco della Vigna at Venice (Fig. 114). On the 15th of August, 1534, the Doge Andrea Gritti laid the foundation stone of the new church, and the structure was begun in accordance with Jacopo Sansovino's design. But differences of opinion soon arose about the proportions of his plan, and the Doge commissioned Francesco Giorgi, a Franciscan monk from the monastery attached to that church, to write a memorandum about Sansovino's model.

Andrea Gritti's choice of his expert is interesting. This Francesco Giorgi had made his name by a study of the problem of proportion in all its aspects. In 1525 he had published a large folio on the harmony of the universe[3] in which Christian doctrines and neo-Platonic thought were blended, and the old belief in the mysterious efficacy of certain numbers and ratios was given new impetus. The memorandum on the proportions of S. Francesco is a practical application of the theories of that book.[4]

Giorgi suggests making the width of the nave nine paces, which is the square of three: 'Numero primo e divino'. In the Pythagorean conception of numbers,

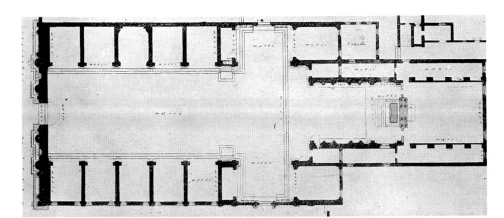

114. Plan of S. Francesco della Vigna, Venice

three is the first real number because it has beginning, middle and end.[5] It is divine as the symbol of the Trinity. The length of the nave he wants to be twenty-seven paces, i.e. three times nine. The square and cube of three, Giorgi goes on, contain the consonances of the universe as Plato has shown in the *Timaeus*; and neither Plato nor Aristotle, who knew the forces effective in nature, went beyond the number twenty-seven in their analysis of the world. However, it is not the actual numbers but their ratios that are of importance; and that the cosmic ratios are to be regarded as binding for the microcosm also, is evident from God's command to Moses to build the Tabernacle after the pattern of the world and Solomon's resolve to give the proportions of the Tabernacle to the Temple. Giorgi also expresses the suggested proportion of width to length of the nave (9:27) in musical terms; it forms, as he says, a diapason and a diapente. A diapason is an octave and a diapente a fifth. 9:27 constitutes an octave and a fifth, if seen in the progression 9:18:27; for 9:18=1:2=an octave, and 18:27= 2:3=a fifth.

To understand Giorgi's reasoning it should be recalled that it was Pythagoras who discovered that tones can be measured in space. What he had found was that musical consonances were determined by the ratios of small whole numbers. If two strings are made to vibrate under the same conditions, one being half the length of the other, the pitch of the shorter string will be one octave (diapason) above that of the longer one. If the lengths of the strings are in the relation of two to three, the difference in pitch will be a fifth (diapente), and if they are in the relation of three to four, the difference in pitch will be a fourth (diatessaron). Thus the consonances, on which the Greek musical system was based – octave, fifth and fourth – can be expressed by the progression 1:2:3:4. And this progression contains not only the simple consonances octave, fifth and fourth, but also the two composite consonances which the Greeks recognized, namely octave plus fifth (1:2:3) and two octaves (1:2:4), One can understand that this staggering discovery made people believe that they had seized upon the mysterious harmony which pervades the universe. And on this was built much of the number symbolism and mysticism, which had an immeasurable impact on human thought during the next two thousand years. In the wake of the Pythagoreans, Plato in his *Timaeus* explained that cosmic order and harmony are contained in certain numbers. Plato found this harmony in the squares and cubes of the double and triple proportion starting from unity, which led him to the two

For the unity of the cosmological and aesthetic aspect of proportion during the Renaissance as well as for related questions see the fundamental article by Panofsky, 'Die Entwicklung der Proportionslehre als Abbild der Stilentwicklung', MONATSHEFTE FUR KUNSTWISSENCHAFT, 1921, p. 208 ff. English version in *Meaning in the Visual Arts*, Doubleday, 1955, p. 89 ff. See also G. Nicco Fasola's introduction to Piero della Francesca, *De prospectiva pingendi*, Florence, 1942, particularly p. 15 ff.

3 *De Harmonia Mundi totius*, Venice, 1525. This work has hardly been noticed by modern scholars although its influence during the sixteenth century seems to have been not inconsiderable. A new edition appeared in Paris, 1545, a French translation in Paris, 1579. Panofsky, in MONATSHEFTE F. KUNSTW., 1921, p. 209, was the first to draw attention to Giorgi's work; cf. also *id.*, *The Codex Huygens*, 1940 p. 113. There are short notes on Giorgi in Thorndike, *Hist. of Magic*, 1941, VI, p. 450 ff. D. Mahnke, *Unendliche Sphäre und Allmittelpunkt*, 1937, p. 106 f., discussed some of the sources of Giorgi's book. About Giorgi's influence on French thought cf. Frances A. Yates, *The French Academies of the Sixteenth Century*, The Warburg Institute, 1947, pp. 88, 91 f. and *passim*. A recent analysis of Giorgi's ideas in D.P. Walker, *Spiritual and Demonic Magic from Ficino to Campanella*, London, 1958, p. 112 ff.

4 Though often mentioned, the memorandum was printed only by Gianantonio Moschini, *Guida per la città di Venezia*, 1815, I, i, pp. 55-61. Considering its extraordinary importance, never sufficiently realized, I have given the full text in English as Appendix I (p. 138 ff.), which should be consulted for the following paragraphs.

5 For the Pythagorean symbolism of 'three' see Aristotle, *De Coelo* I, 1 (268a) and Plutarch, *Sympos.* IX, quaest. 3. Marsilio Ficino, in his commentary to Plato's *Timaeus*, followed this definition of 'three' (*Opera*, 1576, II, p. 1459): 'Trinitas numerorum prima, principium et medium, finemque rerum continere videtur, atque solar inter numeros ratione quadam individua continere.'

6 This is not the place to describe Plato's ideas more fully than in Giorgi's own words which follow. For further explanations, cf. F.M. Cornford, *Plato's Cosmology*, London, 1937, pp. 49, 66 ff.

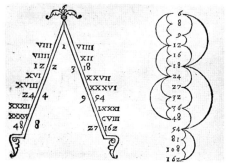

115. Diagram from F. Giorgi's *De Harmonia Mundi*, 1525

geometrical progressions, 1, 2, 3, 4, 8 and 1, 3, 9, 27.[6] Traditionally represented in the shape of a *Lambda* $\begin{smallmatrix}1\\2 \quad 3\\4 \quad \quad 9\\8 \quad \quad \quad 27\end{smallmatrix}$ the harmony of the world is expressed in the seven numbers 1, 2, 3, 4, 8, 9, 27 which embrace the secret rhythm in macrocosm and microcosm alike. For the ratios between these numbers contain not only all the musical consonances, but also the inaudible music of the heavens and the structure of the human soul.[7]

In his *Harmonia Mundi* Giorgi, closely following Ficino, gave proof of his familiarity with these ideas. His Fifth Book deals with the Pythagorean-Platonic theory of numbers. It begins with the words: 'It is absolutely evident to all Pythagoreans and Academicians that the world and the soul were defined first by Timaeus of Locri and then by Plato by certain laws and musical proportions, just as a heptachord made of seven strings (*limitibus*), beginning with unity, duplicating up to the cube of two (i.e. $2^3=8$) and trebling up to the cube of three (i.e. $3^3=27$). According to the writings of Pythagoras it was believed that in these numbers and proportions the fabric of the soul and the whole world was arranged and perfected. And from the odd as from the male, and from the even as from the female – from these powers together everything is generated. But in the cube of the one and the other, they said, the work was terminated. For one cannot proceed beyond the third dimension in length, width and depth. And also all power of activity and passivity is contained in these numbers and proportions, and all consonances are accumulated in them.'[8]

It is now clear why Giorgi does not want to go further than the number twenty-seven, and why ratios measured in space and as tones are for him synonymous. What Giorgi suggests for S. Francesco is the progression of the side of the Platonic triangle beginning with the 'perfect' three (3, 9, 27). His further recommendations fall in line with these principal ratios. The 'cappella grande' at the far end of the nave, like the head of the body, shall be nine paces long and six wide, so that its length repeats the width of the nave and its width is related to that of the nave in the ratio of 2:3, a diapente (fifth) in musical terms. At the same time the ratio of 2:3 is also valid for the width to the length in the cappella itself. The choir behind the 'cappella grande' should repeat the measures of the 'capella grande' – 6:9. The whole length of the church is therefore five times nine. He calls it a fivefold proportion or, in musical terms, a bisdiapason (*scil.* disdiapason) and diapente.[9] The transept should be six paces wide, thus corresponding to the width of the 'cappella grande'. He suggests making the chapels at each side of the nave three paces wide, which is what he calls a triple proportion to the width of the nave itself (3:9), or musically (3:6:9=) a diapason (3:6) and a diapente (6:9= 2:3). The relation of the width of the small chapels to that of the 'cappella grande' is 3:6, i.e. a diapason. And the relation of the width of the chapels of the transept to that of those of the nave should be 4:3, or a diatessaron, 'proportione celebrata.'

So far Giorgi's recommendations were carried out. Most of the actual proportions do not correspond exactly to his ratios, but the divergences are small and due to the kind of irregularities which occur in practice. The three steps leading up to the chapels and the 'cappella grande', which he suggested and which, indeed, Sansovino had already planned, were also executed. He was not followed, however, in the height of the ceiling which he wanted flat and coffered, and related to the width of the nave in the ratio 4:3.

7 Cf. *Timaeus*, 35b-36b (F.M. Cornford, *ibid.*, and A.E. Taylor, *A Commentary on Plato's Timaeus*, Oxford, 1928, p. 116 ff.).

For the 'harmony of the spheres' cf. Plato's myth of Er, *Rep.* X (616 ff.); also Aristotle's survey of Pythagoreanism in *Met.* A.5, and his explanation and refutation of this theory in *de coelo*, 290 b 12 ff.

8 *Op. cit.*, fol. 81 verso.

9 But here Giorgi seems to have committed an error which we are unable to explain without having seen the original text. 9:18:36 is two octaves, or a disdiapason, and 36:45=4:5 and not 2:3 (the diapente). Giorgi may have had in mind 36:54 which is a diapente. On the other hand, it would be most surprising to find such an error in a man for

By basing in this somewhat extraordinary way all the proportions of the building on the Pythagoreo-Platonic philosophy of harmonic numbers, Francesco Giorgi may have created a precedent. But the three men who were consulted about the memorandum seem to have shown no undue surprise; for they approved of it. They were a painter, an architect and a humanist. This fact shows that proportion in architecture was not regarded as the province of architects alone; the unity of all arts and sciences made every literato a trustworthy judge in these matters. And the eminence of the three people chosen as consultants is a clear sign of the importance attached to Giorgi's ideas. The painter was no less a man than Titian; the architect was Serlio, who was at that time in Venice preparing his work on architecture, the first part of which (Book IV) appeared in 1537, and who, already in 1534, seems to have been regarded as particularly well versed in the theory of architecture. The humanist was Fortunio Spira, who is now almost forgotten but who enjoyed a high reputation in his own day for his many accomplishments. Francesco Sansovino[10] called him 'Filosofo celeberrimo, di profonda scientia' and Aretino praised his 'maestà nella presentia, gentilezza ne'costumi, maniera nell' attioni, gratia nei gesti, bontà nella natura, felicitade nell'ingegno, fama nelle opere, e gloria nel nome' – 'regal appearance, his polite manners, promptness in action, graceful gestures, the goodness of his nature, his happy talent, the renown of his works, the glory of his name'.[11]

Giorgi demands at the end of his memorandum that the ratios of the interior should be repeated in the façade, 'che per esso si puoi comprendere la forma della fabbrica, et le sue proportioni'. It appears certain that Palladio, a generation later, knew Giorgi's memorandum and derived from it the mysterious twenty-seven moduli which he applied to the width of the central portion of his façade.[12] Titian's and Serlio's approval of the memorandum suggests not only a familiarity with these ideas among artists, but also a readiness to apply them in practice, and it can be assumed that Palladio appreciated Giorgi's Platonic speculations. His knowledge of Platonism must have been considerable. In Trissino's circle he absorbed the spirit of the Platonic Academy, his humanist friends were steeped in the study of Plato and Aristotle, and his close association with Daniele Barbaro, particularly during the preparation of the Vitruvius edition, must have deepened his insight into ancient philosophical thought.[13]

2. The Mean Proportionals and Architecture

It has been shown in the First Part that architects were dependent on Platonic speculations in recommending the circular form for churches. In view of this fact and with Giorgi's Platonic memorandum before us, it seems appropriate to inquire how far the harmonic ratios of the Greek musical scale influenced architectural proportion of the Renaissance in theory and practice. Alberti and Palladio are our main sources for an accurate estimate of Renaissance opinion on this point. Before discussing their contributions, it may be recalled that we found at least a deliberate insistence on the ratios of the small integers not only in Alberti's façade of S. Maria Novella but also in other Renaissance buildings.[14]

At a first glance Palladio's pragmatic Quattro Libri seem to yield disappointingly little, for there is hardly a word on the principles of proportion. The work abounds in definite statements about proportions without any explanation why

whom the system of harmonic ratios was of such over-riding importance.

10 Venetia . . . descritta, 1581; in the ed. of 1663, p. 154.

11 Aretino, Del primo libro de le lettere, Paris, 1609, p. 187. Spira died about 1560. A rich collection of material about him is to be found in Cicogna, Iscr. Venez., 1830, III, p. 307 ff.

12 Cf. above Part III, p. 94 f. The height from the ground to the main entablature repeats the same measure.

13 Cf. above p. 64 ff.

14 Cf. above, p. 51 and also p. 29 (S. Maria delle Carceri), p. 34 (Bramante's S. Peter's), and pp. 46 f. (S. Francesco in Rimini).

one particular ratio rather than another has been chosen. Proportion is, it need hardly be said, the whole issue in any consideration of the orders, and Palladio opens the account of his celebrated system of the orders with the laconic remark that they must be related 'con bella proportione' to the whole building.[15] Behind Palladio's matter-of-fact rules there is usually more thought and accumulated wisdom than might be apparent to the modern reader. It is obvious that his notes on proportion cannot be arbitrary, but must refer tacitly to some generally accepted mathematical rule.

One example may be given as an illustration. It is of central importance and leads right into the problem of harmonic proportion. Palladio supplies general rules for the proportions of the height of rooms to their width and length, that is for the relationship of the three dimensions which constitute the shape of a room. Before discussing this important subject he gives what he considers the most beautiful ratios of width to length of rooms, that is, he talks in terms of two dimensions. For various reasons it seems opportune to follow Palladio's plan although we shall concentrate on his ratios of three quantities. He recommends seven shapes of rooms in the following sequence: (1) circular, (2) square, (3) the diagonal of the square for the length of the room, (4) a square and a third, i.e. 3:4, (5) a square and a half, i.e. 2:3, (6) a square and two-thirds, i.e. 3:5, (7) two squares, i.e. 1:2. With the exception of the third case, all these ratios are commensurable and as simple as possible.[16] However, the diagonal of a square in relation to its side is $\sqrt{2}:1$. The shapes of the rooms recommended by Palladio show him following in the footsteps of his predecessors. Similar lists of approved shapes for rooms were given by Alberti[17] and Serlio[18] and both mention the incommensurability of the diagonal of the square while Palladio, with his usual restraint, does not make the point. As far as we can see this is the only irrational number widely propagated in the Renaissance theory of architectural proportion.[19] It came straight out of Vitruvius,[20] where its occurrence – amidst a module system, which otherwise presupposes commensurable ratios – has been thought with good reason to be a residue of the Greek architectural theory of proportion, all but forgotten in Roman times.[21] It is probably right to say that rarely did Palladio or any other Renaissance architect use irrational proportions in practice,[22] and this is an argument *per negationem* in favour of the case we are going to state. We must repeat that Palladio's conception of architecture, as indeed that of all Renaissance architects, is based on commensurability of ratios.[23] This creed he expressed in these words.[24] ' . . . . in all fabrics it is requisite that their parts should correspond together, and have such proportions, that there may be none whereby the whole cannot be measured, and likewise all the other parts.'

When we turn to the relations of three magnitudes, the theoretical position is surprisingly simple. Palladio declares three different sets of ratios for height to width and length to be good proportions for rooms.[25] For each of the three cases he gives a method of calculating the height from the length and width by a geometrical as well as by an arithmetical process. We need not follow his procedure; it will suffice to record the result. His first example: suppose a room measures six by twelve feet; its height will be nine feet. Second example : a room is four by nine feet;[26] its height will be six feet. Third example: a room is again six by twelve feet; its height will be eight feet. In his exposition Palladio sticks strictly to the practical side of the *métier* without mentioning what these proportions

15 Bk. I, chap. 11.

16 Bk. I, chap. 21. For the ratios 1:1, 1:2, 2:3, 3:4 the reader may be referred back to p. 105; the ratio 3:5 will be discussed later.

17 Cf. below, p. 111 f.

18 *Libro primo d'architettura*, in the Venetian ed. of 1560-2, p. 15.

19 For the diagonal of the square in Francesco di Giorgio's theory, cf. his *Trattato di architettura*, ed. Promis, 1841, p. 57 f.

20 VI, iii, 3.

21 Cf. Jay Hambidge, *The Parthenon and other Greek Temples*, 1924, p. 2 f. Also *id., Dynamic Symmetry*, 1920, p. 145.

22 Palladio himself asserts (Bk. II, chap. 6) that he dimensioned the atrium of the Convent of the Carità in Venice according to the diagonal of the square, following thus Vitruvius VI, 4.

23 The time for a reliable survey of Renaissance buildings has not yet come, but I feel confident that it would confirm my assumption.

24 Bk. IV, chap. 5.

25 Bk. I, chap. 23. Compare Alberti's much more complicated answer to the same problem (Bk. IX, chap. 3). Scamozzi, on the other hand, simplified Palladio still further; in the five types of perfectly shaped rooms recommended by him the height is always the arithmetic mean between width and length (*Idea dell'arch. univ.* I, p. 308 f.) This is typical of Scamozzi's academic transformation of Palladio's precepts.

26 Concerning this ratio which does not occur among Palladio's seven approved shapes of rooms, cf. below, p. 111 f.

27 Cf. Moritz Cantor, *Vorlesungen über Geschichte der Mathematik*, 1907, I, p. 166; Sir Thomas Heath, *A History of Greek Mathematics*, 1921, p. 85.

28 My definitions follow Porphyry's *Commentary on Ptolemy's Harmonics*, cf. Ivor Thomas, *Selections illustrating the History of Greek Mathematics* (Loeb Class. Libr.), 1939, I, p. 133.

29 Whenever the term harmonic appears in inverted commas, I refer to this type of proportion. Without inverted commas the term is used here in its wider meaning as commensurable ratios or proportions agreeing to musical consonances.

really signify. In actual fact, in these three examples the height of the room represents the arithmetic, geometric and 'harmonic' mean between each of the two extremes. These three types of proportion are traditionally attributed to Pythagoras[27] and without them no rational theory of proportion can be imagined.

We have to be more explicit: in the arithmetic proportion the second term exceeds the first by the same amount as the third exceeds the second[28] ($b—a=c—b$, as in 2:3:4, i.e. Palladio's first example); in the geometric proportion the first term is to the second as the second to the third ($a:b=b:c$, as in 4:6:9, i.e. Palladio's second example). The formula for the 'harmonic' proportion, Palladio's third case, is more complicated. What we now call three terms in 'harmonic' proportion is defined in the *Timaeus* (36) as 'the mean exceeding one extreme and being exceeded by the other by the same fraction of the extremes'. In other words, three terms are in 'harmonic' proportion when the distance of the two extremes from the mean is the same fraction of their own quantity (i.e. $\frac{b-a}{a} = \frac{c-b}{c}$).[29] In Palladio's example 6:8:12 the mean 8 exceeds 6 by ⅓ of 6 and is exceeded by 12 by ⅓ of 12 (i.e. $\frac{8-6}{6} = \frac{12-8}{12}$).

Ficino in his Commentary to the *Timaeus* had discussed the three means very clearly at considerable length,[30] and possibly through him they became of overwhelming importance in Renaissance aesthetics. In the Venetian circle of Palladio's time they were examined by Giorgi[31] as well as by Daniele Barbaro,[32] but it seems probable that Palladio's source was Alberti who had treated of them in terms more easily accessible to an architect.[33]

Before explaining the three types of means, Alberti discussed the correspondence of musical intervals and architectural proportions. With reference to Pythagoras he stated that 'the numbers by means of which the agreement of sounds affects our ears with delight, are the very same which please our eyes and our minds',[34] and this doctrine remains fundamental to the whole Renaissance conception of proportion. Alberti continues: 'We shall therefore borrow all our rules for harmonic relations ('finitio') from the musicians to whom this kind of numbers is extremely well known, and from those particular things wherein Nature shows herself most excellent and complete.'[35] It is probably correct to interpret this passage as meaning that, for Alberti, harmonic ratios inherent in nature are revealed in music. The architect who relies on those harmonies is not translating musical ratios into architecture, but is making use of a universal harmony apparent in music: 'Certissimum est naturam in omnibus sui esse persimilem'[36] ('It is indisputable that Nature always manifests herself consistently').

Alberti as well as later artists were, no doubt, conscious of the fact that the musical consonances are determined by the mean proportionals;[37] for that the three means constitute all the intervals of the musical scale had been shown in the *Timaeus*.[38] Classical writers on musical theory discussed this point at great length. An exhaustive exposition is to be found in Boethius' *De Musica*,[39] first printed in Venice in 1491-2, and of very great importance for the doctrine of numbers throughout the Middle Ages and during the Renaissance. Francesco Giorgi, reinterpreting the *Timaeus*, gave a summary of the position, based on the relevant chapters of Ficino's commentary.[40] In order to be able to find the 'harmonic' and arithmetic means as whole numbers between the terms of Plato's original series (1, 2, 4, 8 and 1, 3, 9, 27), he suggests using 6 as the lowest term. By multiplication with 6 we get the series 6, 12, 24, 48 and 6, 18, 54, 162. Into these geometric progressions the 'harmonic' and arithmetic means can be inserted

30 *Opera*, Basle, 1576, II, p. 1454 f.; 'Item comparationem eiusmodi esse triplicem, scilicet arithmeticam, geometricam, harmonicam. Arithmeticam in numeri paritate consistere. Sic inter tria & septem medius est quinarius, numero eodem, scilicet binario alterum terminum superans, ab altero superatus, per proportionem utrinque bipartientem. Geometricam vero in rationis aequalitate sitam esse, in qua sunt multiplex atque superparticularis: quando videlicet ita comparamus, sicut se habent tria ad novem, ita novem ad septem atque viginti, nam utrobique tripla. Item quod est novenarius iuxta senarium, idem est senarius iuxta quaternarium. Nam et hic et ibi est proportio sesquialtera. Denique proportionem harmonicam in quadam similitudine collocant, per quam tribus terminis in ordinem positis, sicut maximus terminus aspicit minimum, similiter differentia inter terminos maior minorem respicit differentiam. Sic enim ponas tria, quatuor, sex, differentia inter sex & quatuor est binarius: differentia inter quatuor & tria, unitas, sicut autem inter sex & tria dupla ratio est, ita inter duo & unum est ratio dupla. Viget hic altera quoque similitudo, scilicet portionum: Simili namque extremorum portione medius terminus excedit atque exceditur.'
31 *De Harmonia Mundi*, I, v, fol. 82.
32 Comm. to Vitruvius, Bk. III, preface.
33 *De re aed.*, Bk. IX, chap. 6.
34 *ibid.*, chap. 5: 'Certissimum est naturam in omnibus sui esse persimilem. Sic se habet res. Hi quidem numeri per quos fiat ut vocum illa concinnitas auribus gratissima reddatur, iidem ipsi numeri perficiunt, ut oculi animusque voluptate mirifica compleantur.'
35 Ed. of 1485; fol. yii verso: 'Ex musicis igitur quibus ii tales numeri exploratissimi sunt: atque ex his praeterea quibus natura aliquid de se conspicuum dignumque praestat tota finitionis ratio producetur.'
36 See also Luca Pacioli, *Summa de Arithmetica*. Venice, 1494, dist. VI, tract. 1, artic. 2: ' . . . impossibile e alcuna cosa in natura persistere: se le non e debitamente proportionata a sua necessita.'
37 However, not every proportion with a mean results in a musical consonance. Alberti was well aware of this; cf. his introductory passages to the mean proportionals in IX, chap. 6.
38 35 C, 36; cf. Cornford, *op cit.*, p. 70 f.
39 Ed. Oscar Paul, Leipzig, 1872, bk. II, chaps. 12-17.
40 Ficino, *op cit.*, II, particularly p. 1461 f., chap 36.

without fractions: 'For the means lying between 6 and 12 are 8 and 9, where 9 is exceeded and exceeds by the same quantity. But 8 exceeds and is exceeded by the same fraction of the extremes themselves. Between 12 and 24 the means are 16 and 18, between 24 and 48 they are 32 and 36. One set of means is "harmonic", the other arithmetic,' while the geometric means are contained in the progression 6, 12, 24, 48 itself.

So far Giorgi was only concerned with the mathematical definition of the means. Now follows their application to musical theory:

However, they all belong to harmony. For the ratio of the greater extreme to the smaller is a double proportion and makes the diapason (6:12). From the minor extreme to the major mean is a sesquialtera proportion and makes the diapente (6:9). But from the same extreme to the minor mean is a sesquitertia proportion and makes the diatessaron (6:8). And the same results from the ratio of the major mean to the major extreme (9:12). A diapente results from the minor mean to the major extreme (8:12). From one mean to the other results a sesquioctave, which makes a tone (8:9)[41] . . . In the same way is related the other side (*scil.* of the triangle of numbers) which is multiplied by 3, where the first extremes are 6 and 18 between which the means are 9 ('harmonic') and 12 (arithmetic). The other extremes are 18 and 54 between which lie the means 27 and 36. On the other hand, the means between 54 and 162 are 81 and 108 . . . From the mass which has been written this much may be added about what the geometric, arithmetic and harmonic means are: The arithmetic mean is the proportion of excess, the geometric mean is the proportion *par excellence* ('proportio proportionum').[42] From the two, results the harmonic mean.[43] . . . With these rules all the intervals can be filled, short of the semitones and quarter-tones . . .[44]

Thus by applying the Pythagorean theory of 'means' to the ratios of the intervals of the Greek musical scale, the latter received a mathematical *raison d'être*, for the geometric progression constitutes the octaves, and the 'harmonic' and arithmetic means determine the intervals of the fourth and fifth and the tone. The interlocking of these ratios is well shown in Giorgi's diagram (Fig. 115). Whenever one meets ratios of the series 6, 8, 9, 12, 16, 18, 24, 27, 32, 36, 48, etc., it is safe to presume that this is not casual but the result of reflections which depend directly or indirectly on the Pythagoreo-Platonic division of the musical scale. And when Palladio recommended one of the three means – and only these – for the height of his rooms, he was, no doubt, aware that 'they belong to harmony'.

A thorough investigation would certainly lead to the discovery of similar principles with other architects of the Renaissance. However, the foregoing pages prove sufficiently that the three means which determine musical consonances take up a central position in the deliberations on proportion of those architects who absorbed humanist and neo-Platonic ideas.

We may now conclude that, when Palladio wants churches to be built 'in such a manner and with such proportions, that all the parts together may convey a sweet harmony (*una soave armonia*) to the eyes of the beholders',[45] he did not think of a vague, indefinable appeal to the eye but of the spatial consonances produced by the interrelation of universally valid ratios. The memorandum which he was

41 8:9 is the interval between fourth and fifth for:

fifth   fifth

6 : 8 : 9 : 12

fourth tone fourth

and is therefore the ratio of the major tone.
42 Regarded as such in antiquity, for a geometric progression from unity to squares and cubes represents line, surface and solid. See T. L. Heath, *The Thirteen Books of Euclid's Elements*, 1908, II, p. 292 f., and *Timaeus* 31 C.

asked to write about the new design for the Cathedral of Brescia in 1567 is mainly concerned with proportion, and one sentence shows that he was thinking in the same terms as Francesco Giorgi: 'The proportions of the voices' he said, 'are harmonies for the ears; those of the measurements are harmonies for the eyes. Such harmonies usually please very much, without anyone knowing why, excepting the student of the causality of things.'[46] We may safely surmise that Palladio regarded himself as one who knew why. The parallelism of musical and spatial proportions is an oft-repeated commonplace, and yet, against the background of a mass of Renaissance material, it appears to have been more than a simile.

3. Alberti's 'Generation' of Ratios

The Renaissance identification of musical and spatial ratios was only possible on the basis of a specific interpretation of space which, as far as we can see, has not been properly understood in modern times. When Francesco Giorgi called the relation of width to length of the nave of S. Francesco della Vigna a diapason and diapente he expressed the simple ratio 1:3 (9:27) in terms of the compound ratio 1:2, 2:3 (9:18, 18:27). Is this only a theoretical proposition of applying musical ratios to space or does it imply a particular mode of space perception? If we suppose the latter it would mean that for Giorgi the length of the nave is not simply a triplication of its width, but that the length itself is charged with definite relations; for one unit (9) is seen in relation to its duplication, and the two units together (18) are visualized in relation to the whole length of three units (27). A graph of the two different approaches makes the position abundantly clear:

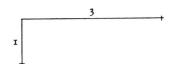 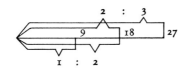

We may say Giorgi perceives the length like a monochord, on which by stopping at ½ and ⅔ of its length respectively the octave and the fifth are produced. That for Giorgi these intervals are not simply theoretical breaks is proved by the fact that they coincide with important cæsuras in the building: the first unit of 9 with the centre of the central chapel and the second unit, 18, with the end of the nave proper. With this kind of 'generation' of the compound ratio 9:27 from the simple ratios 9:18 and 18:27 Giorgi expressed himself in a language which was generally understood in his day. He expounded a method for which Alberti had laid the theoretical foundation.

*　　　*　　　*　　　*　　　*

Alberti differentiates between three types of plans: small, medium and large ones.[47] Each type can be given three different shapes. To the small plans belong the square (2:2) and the shapes of one to one and a half (2:3) and one to one and a third (3:4). These ratios comply with the simple musical consonances and need no further explanation. Medium-sized plans 'duplicate' the ratios of small plans,

43 This will be understood by comparing the three formulas (1) $b = \frac{a+c}{2}$ ('proportion of excess'), (2) $b = \sqrt{7a}\,c$ ('proportio proportionum'), (3) $b = \frac{2ac}{a+c}$ ('harmonic' proportion).

44 Giorgi, op. cit., V, iii, p. 82 f.

45 Quattro Libri, Bk. IV, preface.

46 Cf. Magrini, Memorie intorno Andrea Palladio, 1845, Appendix, p. 12:' . . . secondo che le proportioni delle voci sono armonia delle orecchie, così quelle delle misure sono armonia degli occhi nostri, la quale secondo il suo costume sommamente diletta, senza sapersi il perchè fuori che da quelli che studiano di sapere le ragioni delle cose.'

47 Bk. IX, beginning of chap. 6.

48 Cf. ed. of 1485, fol. yiii.

i.e. one to two, one to twice one and a half and one to twice one and a third. With these more complicated ratios the matter becomes very interesting. To draw a plan of one to twice one and a half, the architect puts down a unit which we may call 4, extends it up to the ratio one to one and a half, i.e. 4:6, and adds to the unit 6 another ratio of one to one and a half, i.e. 6:9; the result is a ratio of 4:9.[48] In other words, Alberti anticipates exactly Francesco Giorgi's procedure, for he breaks up the ratio 4:9 into two ratios of 2:3 in the following manner:

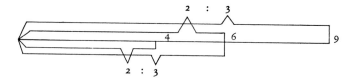

We may now say that the ratio of 4:9 is generated from the two ratios 4:6 and 6:9. In the same way the ratio of one to twice one and a third, 9:16, is generated from 9:12:16, for 9:12=1:1⅓ and 12:16=1:1⅓.

The three classes of large plans are formed first, by adding to the double square, 2:4, one half so that the proportion 1:3 is generated from 2:4:6; secondly, by adding to the double square, 3:6, one third so that the proportion 3:8 is generated from 3:6:8; and, thirdly, by doubling the double square so that the quadruple proportion 2:8 is generated from 2:4:8. Now, the double proportion 1:2 (musically an octave) is a composite of the two ratios 2:3 and 3:4 (for ½= ⅔ x ¾) so that it is generated from 2:3:4: or 3:4:6 (musically from fifth and fourth or fourth and fifth). We can now say that, for instance, the proportion of 1:4 is generated from 2:3:4:8, or 2:3:4:6:8 (i.e. from fifth and fourth, and fifth and fourth), or 3:6:9:12, or 3:4:6:9:12 (i.e. from fifth and fourth, and fifth and fourth), etc. After the foregoing pages it hardly needs pointing out that all these ratios should also be interpreted in terms of mean proportions. For Alberti the splitting up of compound proportions into the smallest harmonic ratios is not an academic matter, but a spatial experience, as is shown by his explanation of the architect's procedure when planning the proportion 4:9. Harmonic ratios like the double, the triple and the quadruple are compounds of simple consonant ratios. Alberti is very explicit that sub-ratios of a compound ratio cannot be used indiscriminately by architects; they must be exactly those ratios which belong to the compound ratio. If one wants, for instance, to build the wall of a room, the length of which is double its width, one would not use for the length the sub-ratios of the triple proportion, but those of which the double is compounded. The same is true for a room in the proportion of one to three; no other than the numerical relations of which the triple is composed should be used.[49]

*   *   *   *   *

The splitting up of ratios for the sake of making the proportions of a room harmonically intelligible appears to us very strange. And yet, this is the way the whole Renaissance conceived of proportions. A wall is seen as a unit which contains certain harmonic potentialities. The lowest sub-units, into which the whole unit can be broken up, are the consonant intervals of the musical scale, the cosmic validity of which was not doubted. In some cases only one way of

49 Ed. of 1485, fol. yiii: 'His numeris quales recensuimus utuntur architecti non confuse et promiscue: sed correspondentibus utrinque ad armoniam. Utique parietes velit attollere in area fortassis: cuius longitudo sit ad sui latitudinem dupla: is istic utatur respondentiis non quibus tripla: sed iis tantum: quibus eadem ipsa componatur dupla. Acque itidem sequetur in area tripla: nam suis quoque utetur respondentiis: utetur inquam non aliis quam suis. Itaque diffiniet diametros ternatim numeris quos recensuimus: ut accommodatiores eos venire suum ad opus intelligat.' Alberti's conception of the generation of ratios, made abundantly clear in his text, has been misunderstood by the students of his theory: cf. I. Behn, *L.B. Alberti als Kunstphilosoph*, 1911, particularly p. 104, and Paul-Henri Michel, *La pensée de L.B. Alberti*, Paris, 1930, p. 454 f.

generation is possible, but in others two or even three different generations of the same ratio can be carried through; as we have seen, the ratio 1:2, the octave, can be seen as fourth and fifth (3:4:6) or as fifth and fourth (2:3:4). But the ratios of the musical intervals are only the raw material for the combination of spatial ratios. Alberti's harmonic progressions 4:6:9 and 9:12:16 are a sequence of two fifths and two fourths respectively, i.e. musically they represent dissonances. The ratios of musical intervals are regarded as binding, and not the building up of consonant intervals into musical harmonies. Nothing shows better than this that Renaissance artists did not mean to translate music into architecture, but took the consonant intervals of the musical scale as the audible proofs for the beauty of the ratios of the small whole numbers 1:2:3:4.

In analysing the proportions of a Renaissance building one has to take the principle of generation into account. It can even be said that, without it, it is impossible fully to understand the intentions of a Renaissance architect. We are touching here on fundamentals of the style as a whole; for simple shapes, plain walls and homogeneity of articulation are necessary presuppositions for that 'polyphony of proportions' which the Renaissance mind understood and a Renaissance eye was able to see.

4. Musical Consonances and the Visual Arts

From all that has been said so far it will be realized that the Renaissance analogy of audible and visual proportions was no mere theoretical speculation; it testifies to the solemn belief in the harmonic mathematical structure of all creation. But, in addition, music had a particular attraction for Renaissance artists because it had always been ranked as a mathematical 'science'. There was an unbroken tradition coming down from antiquity[50] according to which arithmetic, the study of numbers, geometry, the study of spatial relationships, astronomy, the study of the motion of celestial bodies, and music, the study of the motions apprehended by the ear, formed the *quadrivium* of the mathematical 'arts'. By contrast to these 'liberal arts', painting, sculpture, and architecture were regarded as manual occupations. In order to raise them from the level of the mechanical to that of the liberal arts, they had to be given a firm theoretical, that is to say, mathematical foundation. This transformation was the great achievement of fifteenth-century artists. No wonder that they turned to music as the only respectable liberal art and studied musical theory for guidance in grappling with their own problems. A familiarity with musical theory became a *sine qua non* of artistic education.[51]

It comes as a confirmation of one's expectations to find that Brunelleschi, according to his biographer Manetti, studied the musical proportions of the ancients.[52] Manetti, writing after 1471 and under the influence of Alberti, may have read these ideas into the past; his remark, in any case, shows how acutely aware his generation was of the importance of the problem, and this is also illustrated by Alberti's famous warning to Matteo de' Pasti during the erection of S. Francesco at Rimini that by altering the proportions of the pilasters 'si discorda tutta quella musica' – 'all the musical relationships are destroyed'.[53] Nobody expressed his belief in the efficacy of harmonic ratios behind all visual phenomena with more conviction than Leonardo. We may recall in particular his well-known saying that music is the sister of painting. This was not meant as a

50 For the ancient tradition, cf. John Burnet, *Greek Philosophy: Thales to Plato*, London, 1932, p. 213 ff. and *passim*. For the mediaeval tradition, cf. R. Allers in *Traditio*, II, 1944, particularly p. 375 ff. For the Renaissance: R. Wittkower, *The Artist and the Liberal Arts*, London, 1952, and P.O. Kristeller, 'The Modern System of the Arts,' JOURNAL OF THE HISTORY OF IDEAS, XII, 1951 and XIII, 1952.

51 Classical antiquity showed the way, for Vitruvius (I, i, 3) requested musical training for the architect. For Palladio's musical education in Trissino's circle, cf. above, p. 62.

52 Manetti, *Filippo Brunellesco*, ed. Holtzinger, 1887, p. 16.

53 Corrado Ricci, *Il Tempo Malatestiano*, 1924, p. 587; Cecil Grayson, *An Autograph Letter from Leon Battista Alberti to Matteo de' Pasti*, New York, 1957.

vague simile but as indicating a close relationship; for both, music and painting, convey harmonies; music does it by its chords and painting by its proportions. Musical intervals and linear perspective are subject to the same numerical ratios, for objects of equal size placed so as to recede at regular intervals diminish in 'harmonic' progression.[54]

The 'exactissima harmonia' of the human body was the subject of Pomponius Gauricus' *De Sculptura*, 1503. Gauricus asks 'what geometrician, what musician must He have been who has formed man like that?' – thus apostrophizing the fundamental unity of geometry and music. The *Timaeus*, quoted more than once by Gauricus, seems also for him the book of wisdom in which the mystical harmony in the universe was revealed. These ideas remained alive throughout the sixteenth century. Lomazzo, in his scholastic *Trattato dell'arte della pittura* (1584), talked of human proportions in musical terms. He carried on a habit of thought which is first to be found in Alberti's writings. Alberti interprets, for instance, the ratio 4:9 which he analysed as the product of two ratios of 1:1½,[55] also as a double proportion (4:8) plus one *tone* (8:9),[56] and the ratio 9:16, generated from two ratios of 1:1⅓, also as a double proportion (9:18) minus a *tone* (18:16).[57] Failing an algebraic symbolism, musical terminology was ready at hand for an adequate description of proportions. In the same vein Lomazzo regarded the applicability of musical terms to the proportions of the body as so self-evident that he not only omitted a discussion of the common laws of musical and spatial proportions, but referred constantly to spatial ratios as if they were an acoustic experience. For instance, the distance from the top of the head to the nose 'resounds (*risuona*) with the distance from there to the chin in triple proportion, producing the *diapason* and *diapente*; and the said distance from the nose to the chin and that from the chin to the meeting of the collarbones resounds with a double proportion which makes the *diapason* . . . '[58]

In his later *Ideal del Tempio della Pittura* (1590) Lomazzo formulated theoretically what was implied in the quotation we have just given. Here he declared that masters like Leonardo, Michelangelo and Gaudenzio Ferrari 'have come to the knowledge of harmonic proportion by way of music';[59] the human body itself is built according to musical harmonies. This microcosm 'created by the Lord in his own image' contains 'all numbers, measures, weights, motions and elements'.[60] Therefore all the buildings in the world together with all their parts follow its norm.[61]

Lomazzo's information about the great Renaissance artists strikes a familiar note. Seventeenth-century artists, particularly those who carried on the classical tradition, shared the enthusiasm for the study of musical theory. Lucio Faberio in his commemoration speech at Agostino Carracci's funeral tells us that the latter was a student of philosophy, arithmetic and geometry, astrology, and, above all, music; arithmetic, the foundation of music, taught him the origin of the musical consonances.[62] Domenichino who made arithmetic, perspective and architecture his special study, speculated with zest about ancient musical theory;[63] and based on Zarlino, Poussin compared the different styles of painting with the modes of ancient music.[64]

The belief in the importance of 'musical proportions' for art and architecture was by no means confined to Italy. Artists and scholars in France, above all,[65] but also in England[66] and Spain were steeped in these ideas. Spain, it seems, had a long tradition regarding the application of musical proportions to architecture.

54 Cf. J.P. Richter, *The Literary Works of Leonardo da Vinci*, 1939, I, pp. 72 f., 76 ff. For an analysis of Leonardo's procedure, cf. R. Wittkower, in JOURNAL OF THE WARBURG AND COURTAULD INSTITUTES, XVI, 1953, p. 285 ff.

55 Cf. above, p. 111.

56 *De re aed.*, 1485, fol. y iii: 'Excedat igitur longitudo maxima istic brevissima ex dupla atque amplius ex duplae tono.'

57 *ibid.*: 'Ergo hic maior linea exceditur a dupla minoris uno minus tono.'

58 *Trattato*, ed. 1844, I, p. 63 f.

59 2nd ed., p. 112.

60 Reference to *Wisdom of Solomon*, XI, 20; cf. below, p. 123, note 105.

61 *ibid.*, p. 117. The whole passage is given in Italian above, p. 104, note 2. Compare this with L. Pacioli's words quoted above, Part I, p. 25.

62 Cf. Malvasia, *Felsina Pittrice*, 1678, I, p. 428.

63 *ibid.*, II, p. 339. Cf. also Domenichino's letter to Albani, December 7, 1638, Bottari, *Racc. di lettere*, 1822, V, p. 47.

64 Antony Blunt in BULL. DE LA SOC. DE L'HISTOIRE DE L'ART FRANÇAIS, 1933, p. 125 ff., Frances Yates, *The French Academies of the Sixteenth Century*, London, 1947, p. 298. On Zarlino cf. below, p. 124.

65 See pp. 115, 131 ff.

66 See p. 130.

Simón García, in his *Compendio de arquitectura y simetría de los templos conforme a la medida del cuerpo humano* of 1681,[67] was as explicit in this respect as the Venetian Francesco Giorgi had been. García's treatise was to a large extent compiled from a work by Rodrigo Gil de Hontañón (*c*.1500-77), the architect associated with the building of Segovia and Salamanca Cathedrals. Juan de Herrera, Emperor Charles V's architect, too, applied musical proportions in his design of the Cathedral of Valladolid.[68]

*   *   *   *   *

Lomazzo reports a story which shows that in his day the analogy between musical harmonies and architectural proportions was taken more literally than ever before. The architect Giacomo Soldati added to the three Greek and two Roman orders a sixth 'which he calls harmonic and which by sound he makes intelligible to the ear, but it can hardly be noticed by the eye; with this order he wanted to imitate the ancients who not less by sound than by design and building made known to the world the harmony of their five orders'.[69]

Not much is known about this Giacomo Soldati.[70] However, he must have been a man of great reputation in his own day. In 1561 he was, together with Pellegrino Pellegrini, 'architetto della Regia Camera dello Stato' at Milan and in 1570 he belonged to the court of arbitration which had to decide about the attacks by Bassi against Pellegrini. Six years later he was appointed court architect to Emanuele Filiberto of Savoy and he seems to have spent the last fifteen years of his life in that position at Turin. He made his name particularly with engineering and hydraulic works; his whole career shows that the man was a sober scientist rather than a visionary.

Palladio had contacts with Soldati's circle. He was one of the architects who had sent a report in answer to Bassi's inquiry in the above-mentioned quarrel with Pellegrini;[71] before that date he had lived and worked in Turin[72] and as an expression of his gratitude for the excellent treatment at the court he dedicated the Third and Fourth Books of the *Quattro Libri* to Emanuele Filiberto 'who alone in our era through his prudence and valour is like the ancient Roman heroes'. Under Emanuele Filiberto, Turin became perhaps the most vigorous intellectual centre in Italy and it must have been on account of no common qualities that Soldati was appointed ducal architect.

Soldati's harmonic order is unknown, but the impulse for his undertaking is not too difficult to guess. A sixth order which should embrace all the qualities of the other orders and express more clearly than they did the basic harmonies of the universe became a preoccupation of architects. This order was believed to have been originally inspired directly by God when He charged Solomon to build the Temple, and architects therefore attempted to re-create this perfect archetype from which all the other orders were thought to be derived. Thus the Temple of Jerusalem became a natural focusing point for the cosmological-aesthetic theories of proportion. Here was a test-case for the philosophical endeavour of the Renaissance to reconcile Plato and the Bible; for was it not God Himself who had enlightened Solomon to incorporate the numerical ratios of the celestial harmony into his building? While Francesco Giorgi[73] used the Bible as a lever for the recommendation of the Pythagoreo-Platonic system of musical proportion, the French architect, Philibert de l'Orme, who had contact with the

67 Ed. José Camón, Salamanca, 1941; in addition, *id.*, in ARCHIVO ESPAÑOL DE ARTE, XIV, 1940-1, p. 300 ff., and G. Kubler, in GAZ. DES BEAUX ARTS, XXVI, 1944, p. 135 ff.

68 R. C. Taylor, in ACADEMIA. ANALES Y BOLETIN DE LA REAL AC. DE SAN FERNANDO, 1952, p. 31 f.

69 *Lomazzo*, p. 30:' . . . il sesto (ordine) . . . che egli chiama armonico, e col suono facilmente lo fa sentir a l'orecchie, ma agli occhi stenta rappresentarlo, volendo in questo imitar gl'antichi che non meno sonando, che disegnando, e fabbricando fecero conoscere al mondo l'armonia dei suoi cinque ordini.'

70 Cf. Thieme-Becker, *Künstler-Lex.*, for further literature.

71 Dated July 3, 1570 and often printed; first in Martino Bassi's *Dispareri in materia d'architettura, et perspettiva*, 1572, pp. 42-5. For an analysis of this letter cf. Panofsky: 'Die Perspektive als "symbolishe Form",' *Vorträge der Bibl. Warburg*, 1924-5, p. 325 f.

72 Cf. Temanza, *Vita di Andrea Palladio*, 1762, p. 45. Magrini, *op. cit.*, pp. 112, 249, xlviii. On Palladio's relations with Emanuele Filiberto cf. also *Nozze Gioco-Antì*, Vicenza, 1928 and C. Fenoglio in TORINO (RASSEGNA MENSILE DELLA CITTÀ), III, 1928, pp. 105, 121.

73 See above, p. 105.

116. Diagram. From H. Prado and G.B. Villalpando, *In Ezechielem Explanationes*, 1596-1604

Venetian circle, proposed to apply systematically the proportions revealed in the Old Testament: 'les divines proportions venues du ciel'.[74]

Before the close of the sixteenth century Giovan Battista Villalpando developed these ideas further with an almost unbelievable amount of scholarship. His vast commentary of Ezekiel,[75] a work which had a continuous and international influence on architects, contains the most famous reconstruction of the Temple. It was, in fact, Platonic musical harmony that, according to Villalpando, had been revealed by God to Solomon. Villalpando's system is absolutely flawless. After discussing the three mean proportionals and after insisting on harmonic proportions throughout the building, he winds up with the familiar reference to music.[76] He follows explicitly Barbaro's Commentary on Vitruvius in accepting only the Pythagorean three simple and two composite consonances[77] – diatessaron, diapason, diapente, and diapason cum diapente, disdiapason – and rejecting Vitruvius' sixth consonance, diapason cum diatessaron.[78] An impressive example of the orthodox use of these five

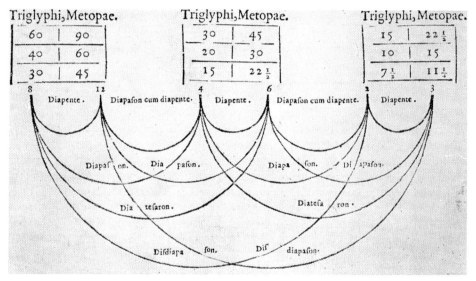

74 De l'Orme, in his *Le premier tôme de l'architecture*, published in 1567, tells the reader that his second volume would contain a full exposition of Divine proportion 'conformémant avec les mesures et proportions qui se trouvent en la sainct Bible'. Although the volume never appeared, sufficient information can be gleaned from the first volume to reconstruct de l'Orme's trend of thought. For a full discussion, cf. Anthony Blunt, *Philbert de l'Orme*, London, 1958, p. 124 ff.

75 H. Prado and G.B. Villalpando, *In Ezechielem Explanationes*, 1596-1604. The reconstruction of the Temple by Villalpando fills a large part of the second volume. On the influence of this work, cf. the author's note in the JOURNAL OF THE WARBURG AND COURTAULD INSTITUTES, VI, 1943, p. 221. Villal-pando's new order was incorporated into a number of seventeenth- and eighteenth-century treatises on architecture. For a full discussion of Villalpando's reconstruction of the Temple, see R.C. Taylor, 'El Padre Villalpando (1552-1608) y sus ideas esteticas', ACADEMIA. ANALES Y BOLETIN DE LA REAL ACADEMIA DE SAN FERNANDO, 1952.

76 *Op. cit.*, II, p. 458: 'Illud vero huius aedificij proprium est, ac maxime observandum, idque ad harmonicam proportionem spectat; quod non alia ratione visus huius aedificij partibus contemplandis delectari videatur, quam auditus vocum, aut instrumentorum suavi modulatione perfruatur.'

77 Barbaro, comm. to Bk. V, iv, 7. Cf. also Alberti, *De re aed.*, IX, chap. 5.

78 Based on Ptolemy; cf. I Düring, *Ptolemaios und Porphyrios über die Musik*, Göteborg, 1934, p. 29 (5, ii).

79 *Op. cit.*, p. 449.

80 On Villalpando cf. A. de Backer, *Bibl. des écrivains de la Compagnie de Jésus*, 1876, III, p. 1407.

consonances is the relation of the parts of the entablature and of the triglyphs to the metopes 'in domo domini', 'in atriis' and 'in domo regia' of the Temple. A glance at the diagram (Fig. 116)[79] showing the ratios between triglyphs and metopes reveals the harmonic interrelation not only inside one order, but also between the orders of the three parts of the Temple. Simple consonances were chosen for the ratios of the same order (2:3) and those between triglyphs of one order and the next, between metopes of one order and the next (1:2), and between the triglyph of a larger and the metope of a smaller order (3:4). The ratio between a metope of a larger and a triglyph of a smaller order is based on composite consonances (1:3), and so is the ratio between the largest and the smallest order (1:4). Thus, the ratios between the triglyphs and metopes of the three orders express the five musical consonances, and no other ratios than these are possible.

It may be argued that the speculation of a Counter-Reformatory theologian,[80] in which the spirit of the Middle Ages was peculiarly revived, have little in common with the work of architectural practitioners and that an unbridgeable gulf separates them from a book like Palladio's *Quattro Libri*. Admittedly, there lies a whole world between the architect of the Venetian nobility of the mid-sixteenth century and the Spanish Jesuit of the next generation. Nevertheless, Villalpando's ideas have their roots in Alberti, Francesco Giorgi, Barbaro and others, and the difference is one of emphasis rather than of fundamentals. It is not surprising that the bulkiest architectural treatise written in Italy, that of Palladio's pupil Scamozzi, produced in the familiar Venetian *ambiente* but in Villalpando's time, is heavy, dogmatic and scholastic and reads, compared with Palladio's *Quattro Libri*, like a mediaeval exposition of the subject. Scamozzi upholds the traditional system of the liberal arts with philosophy as 'nutrice di tutte le scientie' and music in its old place in the *quadrivium* 'delle Matematiche', and also reverts to the ancient division of music into 'musica theoricale' which is concerned with the harmonies of the spheres, and 'musica naturale' which is concerned with the sound of voices and instruments. Architects, Scamozzi maintains, should have a knowledge of music because they ought to be acquainted with the reasons for the consonances and dissonances of sounds. The whole circle of related ideas is revived by Scamozzi; he dwells at length on the importance of the Platonic numbers, on the anthropomorphic character of architecture, and, with reference to Aristotle, on the 'regola homogenea', the modulus, which must be effective throughout the building, inside as well as outside.[81]

Not only Palladio himself but also the other architects of his generation were less eloquent than the late Mannerist Scamozzi. Vignola's *Regole delli cinque ordini* (1562) has no text at all and only a short introduction. But here too the *topos* of the analogy of musical and architectural proportions returns. His effort at systematizing the orders was centred in the problem of finding even for the smallest members 'certa corrispondenza et proportione de'numeri insieme' ('a definite correspondence and continuous proportion of figures'). The satisfaction attained by such a system has been proved by the theory of music.[82] In spite of more than a hundred years of theoretical studies by architects, Vignola was still convinced that music had a better scientific foundation than architecture. The leading musical theorist of the period, Gioseffo Zarlino, maintained in the dedication of his *Dimostrationi harmoniche* (1571) that 'per la certezza della Dimostratione' ('owing to the certitude of proof') music without any doubt was superior to architecture. It was Vignola's aim to give architecture a 'certezza' of ratios equal to that in music.

The certainty inherent in mathematical deduction had always been the basis of musical theory. Franchino Gafurio, the famous Renaissance musical theorist, made this the subject of the frontispiece to his *De harmonia musicorum instrumentorum* of 1518 (Fig. 117). He is shown lecturing to his pupils; on the left are three organ pipes of different length, marked 3, 4, 6, illustrating the ratios of the octave divided by the harmonic mean 4 into fourth and fifth. On the right there are three lines, repeating the ratios 3, 4, 6, and a pair of dividers, thus indicating that musical harmony is geometry translated into sound. At the same time the picture propounds the old thesis that harmony results not from the consonance of two tones, but from two unequal consonances which are drawn from dissimilar proportions[83] (i.e 3:4 and 2:3, fourth and fifth which together form the octave). That is the reason why Gafurio preaches to his pupils: 'Harmonia est discordia concors' ('harmony is discord concordant') which

81 Cf. Scamozzi, *Idea dell'architettura universale*. 1615, I. pp. 3, 23, 307 f., II, pp. 4, 31 f. and *passim*.
82 From the preface to the *Regole*: Those orders are most beautiful which have 'certa corrisponden-za et proportione de' numeri insieme . . . Laonde considerando più adentro quanto ogni nostro senso si compiaccia in questa proportione et le cose spiacevoli essere fuori di quella come ben provano li Musici nella lor scienza . . . '
83 Bk. III, chap. 11: Harmony 'nempe duabus consonantiis inaequalibus constat, quae ex dissimilibus proportionibus . . . conducuntur.'
84 Philolaos defined harmony as 'the unification of the composed manifold and the accordance of the discordant' (ἁρμονία δὲ πάντως ἐξ ἐναντίων γίνεται, ἔστι γὰρ ἁρμονία πολυμιγέων ἕνωσις καὶ δίχα φρονεόντων συμφρόνησις) cf. H. Diels, *Die Fragmente der Vorsokratiker*, Berlin, 1934, I, p. 410, fragm. 10.
85 Dr. Paul Hirsch informs me that this woodcut appeared already in the first edition of 1480, while Fig. 117 was first published in Gafurio's *Angelicum* of 1508.
86 Cf. above, p. 105 f.

117. Gafurio Lecturing. From F. Gafurio, *De Harmonia musicorum Instrumentorum*, 1518

118. Tubalcain, Pythagoras, Philolaos. From
F. Gafurio, *Theorica musice*, 1492

appears written on a scroll near his mouth. Gafurio accepted Philolaos' Pythagorean definition of harmony,[84] which had such a far-reaching influence on Renaissance thought, and in a truly Platonic spirit he regarded this principle of harmony as the basis of macrocosm and microcosm, body and soul, painting, architecture and medicine.

Gafurio's earlier *Theorica musice* of 1492 had a striking frontispiece with a fuller illustration of musical consonances (Fig. 118).[85] The top left picture shows Tubalcain, the biblical founder of music, presiding over a forge where six smiths are busy hammering iron on the anvil. In the next picture Pythagoras beats bells and glasses filled with liquid to different heights. In the lower row Pythagoras is shown striking chords to which weights of different size are fixed, and in the last picture Pythagoras and Philolaos appear with flutes. In all these cases the objects which are used to produce sound bear the figures 4, 6, 8, 9, 12, 16, and the heads of the hammers, the bells, the liquid, the weights, the length of the flutes illustrate these ratios by the gradation of size. The figures comprise two octaves, the 'Greater Perfect System' of the Greeks,[86] with their fourth and fifth and the major tone (8:9). Pythagoras is shown testing the consonance of the octave 8:16; in the last picture he does it in concert with Philolaos, one blowing a flute half as long as that of the other (8 and 16), while Philolaos holds two flutes expressing a fifth (4 and 6) and Pythagoras two others expressing a fourth (9 and 12). The whole page is an illustration of the discovery of the musical consonances by Pythagoras, and the designer followed almost verbally the story as reported in Boethius' *De Musica*.[87] It is not surprising to find that Gafurio was regarded by his contemporaries as a critic in architectural matters. In 1490 he was sent to Mantua in order to discuss with the architect Luca Fancelli the construction of the *tiburio* (tower above the crossing) of Milan cathedral.

What is shown with delightful naïveté in Gafurio's somewhat barbaric woodcut was represented by Raphael on the tablet facing the figure of Pythagoras in the School of Athens. He gave here, in an ingenious diagrammatic design of the four strings of the ancient lyra, the whole system of the Pythagorean harmonic scale (Fig. 119).[88] This representation is interwoven with and expressive of Raphael's complex programme; however, it must suffice here to say that above the teacher Pythagoras appears the heroic figure of his great pupil carrying the *Timaeus* in one hand and pointing upward with the other. This is Raphael's interpretation of the harmony of the universe which Plato had described in the *Timaeus* on the basis of Pythagoras' discovery of the ratios of musical consonances.

We are back in the intellectual atmosphere which prompted Francesco Giorgi to apply the Pythagoreo-Platonic system of harmonic ratios directly to architecture. And when Raphael mentions, in a letter of 1514, that the Pope has appointed the aged Fra Giocondo as his architectural adviser so that he may learn 'whether he has some *bello secreto* in architecture',[89] it hardly seems far-fetched to believe that these secrets were more than mere technicalities.

5. Palladio's 'fugal' System of Proportion

To the minds of the men of the Renaissance musical consonances were the audible tests of a universal harmony which had a binding force for all the arts.

119. Pythagorean Musical Scale. Detail from Raphael's *School of Athens*, Vatican

87 Bk. I, chaps. 10, 11.
88 At the bottom inside the 'lyra' and in the arches connecting the first string with the second and the third, the fourth string with the third and with the second, and the first string with the last, are inscribed the words ΔΙΑΤΕΣΣΑΡΩΝ, ΔΙΑΠΕΝΤΕ, and ΔΙΑΠΑΣΩΝ: at the top are the numbers VI, VIII, VIIII, XII, which show the ratios of the intervals. There is an arch between 8 and 9 and above it stands the word ΕΠΟΓΛΟΩΝ, i.e. the tone. No more convincing diagrammatic system of the Pythagorean scale could be devised. It is worth recording that sheer logic led Zarlino in his *Istitutioni harmoniche*, 1558, p. 59, to represent the basic consonances in exactly the same manner.
Under Raphael's musical diagram is the representation of the perfect Pythagorean number 10. As can be seen in Raphael's tablet, 10 is the sum of the first four figures which constitute all musical harmonies. Moreover, the Pythagorean δεκάς (number 10), which comprises all numbers, was regarded as sacred and as the 'mother of the universe'.
For further information cf. H. Hettner, *Italienische Studien*, 1879, p. 198 ff., who was the first to decipher and interpret Raphael's Pythagorean tablet.
89 Cf. V. Golzio, *Raffaello*, 1936, p. 32.

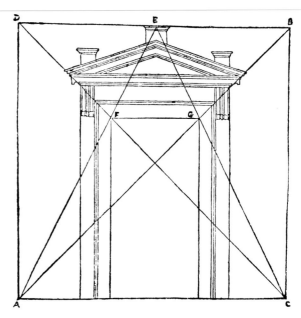

This conviction was not only deeply rooted in theory, but also – and this is now usually denied – translated into practice. It is true, that in trying to prove that a system of proportion has been deliberately applied by a painter, a sculptor or an architect, one is easily misled into finding those ratios which one sets out to find. In the scholar's hand dividers do not revolt. If we want to avoid the pitfall of useless speculation we must look for unmistakable guidance by the artists themselves. Strangely enough, no scholar has yet attempted to do this. Such guidance is not very common, but a careful survey would certainly yield considerable evidence. One must, above all, be able to decipher and interpret the artist's indications. One example may show what we mean.

At the end of his First Book Serlio illustrates a geometrical scheme as a guide for the 'right' construction of the door of a church (Fig. 120). He completes the central bay, in which the door should be placed, into a square (by drawing a line parallel to the base), draws the diagonals (AB, CD) and erects from the two corners of the base an isosceles triangle (AEC). The intersections between the diagonals and the sides of the triangle (F, G) mark the height and width of the door.[90] The drawing seems to suggest a geometrical procedure, not very different from the 'ad quadratum' method practised during the later Middle Ages. In both cases the geometric pattern leads to the arithmetically irrational focal points of the design (point F, for instance, divides the $\sqrt{2}$ diagonal CD as well as the $\sqrt{5}$ line AE into one part and two parts). But in Serlio's case the geometrical scheme is posterior rather than prior to the ratios chosen for the door. His design was evidently the result of commensurable divisions of the large square. The door itself is a double square, its width and height in the light are related to the side of the square as 1:3 and 2:3, the frame of the door and the height of the pediment are related to the width of the opening as 1:3 and 1:2 respectively, and so forth. Thus an interrelated series of ratios of small integral numbers is really at the basis of Serlio's design. 'Mediaeval' geometry here is no more than a veneer that enables practitioners to achieve commensurable ratios without much ado. But there is material at hand of a much less ambiguous nature.

90 The letters, not in Serlio's woodcut, were here added.

91 Cf. for instance O. Bertotti Scamozzi, *Les Bâtimens et les desseins de André Palladio*, 1776-83, I, p. 8, and T. Temanza, *Vita di Andrea Palladio*, 1762, pp. 15, 44.

92 Cf. above, p. 63 f.

93 Mistakes obviously occurred, as for instance when the width of the hall of Villa Saraceno at Finale is given as eighteen feet instead of twenty-eight. But apart from such slips Palladio had often very good reason for changes between building and plate. One reason was that he did not want to hand down to posterity the designs of structures which he had built a long time ago and which no longer satisfied him. The most conspicuous case is that of the Villa Godi Porto at Lonedo, begun in 1540 (i.e. thirty years before the publication of the book), the

By far the most important practical guide to a coherent system of proportion known to me is embodied in the illustrations of Palladio's *Quattro Libri*. If properly interpreted, they are no less a key to the problem of harmonic proportion than Alberti's theories. Palladio's Second Book contains his own buildings in elevation, plan, and section, and it is they that must now be considered. The many discrepancies between the plates and the actual buildings were and are usually attributed to careless publication.[91] Yet the plan of the whole work[92] reveals that Palladio did not publish his buildings merely as an autobiographical contribution. He made a statement to this effect in the preface to the *Quattro Libri* with these words: 'In the Second (Book) I shall treat of the quality of the fabricks that are suitable to the different ranks of men: first of those of a city; and then of the most convenient situation for villas . . . And as we have but very few examples from the antients, of which we can make use, I shall insert the plans and elevations of many fabricks I have erected . . .' In this light many differences between buildings and plates can be explained.[93]

The illustrations were to him a means of expounding his conceptions not only of planning but also of proportion, hence his theoretical measurements could deviate from the executed ones. If this is a right deduction, the hypothesis seems justified that Palladio wanted his inscribed measurements to convey ratios of a general character and of universal importance beyond the scope of the individual buildings.[94] In most of his plans ratios of width to length of the rooms are prominently placed and easily readable, while – with the exception of a few large-scale details – it is generally more difficult to read them in the elevations. For heights of rooms, which are given only in the relatively few sections, he often refers in his text to the method employed. These arrangements seem to reveal a definite scheme which we propose to follow by confining ourselves to an examination of some of Palladio's plans.

What kind of proportion did Palladio exemplify, with his inscribed measurements? The early Villa Godi at Lonedo (Fig. 56) contains the gist of the story in a simple form. Each of the eight small rooms – four at each side of the hall – measures sixteen by twenty-four feet, i.e. width:length=1:1½ which is one of the seven shapes of rooms recommended by Palladio.[95] The ratio of width to length is 2:3. The portico has the same size of sixteen by twenty-four, while the hall behind it measures twenty-four by thirty-six; its ratio – 1:1½ or 2:3 – is therefore equal to that of the small rooms and the portico. The use of the same ratio throughout the building is apparent. But beyond this, the equation $\frac{16}{24} = \frac{24}{36}$ shows that rooms and hall are, one might say, proportionately firmly interlocked. The series underlying the plan as a whole is the progression 16, 24, 36, which we know from Alberti's analysis of the ratio 4:9 as 4:6:9 and which can be expressed in musical terms as a sequence of two diapente. Thus, for those who understood the language of proportion, Palladio's meaning was made abundantly clear by the conspicuous inscriptions of measurements in the plans; without them the reader would be left with no key to the architect's intentions. On the other hand, the notation of the measurements as executed would have interfered with the clarity of the harmonic concept, for the depth of the portico is actually 14·9 feet instead of 16 feet and the widths of the two adjoining rooms are 15·5 and 17·3 feet.

The ratios of Palladio's later structures are somewhat more complicated as can be illustrated in the Villa Malcontenta (Fig. 121). The smallest room on either side of the cross-shaped hall measures twelve by sixteen feet, the next one sixteen

front of which was retrogressive in style. This was 'over-hauled' in the plate and the principles of the late style were grafted on to the early building. In other cases Palladio adjusted irregularities which were forced upon him by circumstances. The Palazzo Valmarana had to be planned for an irregular site. In the plate he shows a regular plan such as he would have built on an ideal site. In his text he does not even mention that he gave the plan as he would have liked to build it, and not as it was built.

94 That Palladio expected the intelligent observer to draw his own conclusions about the meaning of his measurements is clearly indicated by a sentence in his letter to Conte Giulio Capra to whom he sent his plans of the Redentore for criticism. The scale at the foot of the elevation, he remarks, replaces all explanations (Bottari. *Lett. pitt.*, 1822, p. 562).

95 Cf. above, p. 108.

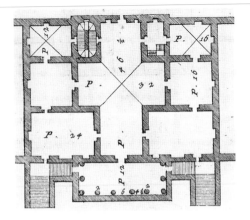

121. Villa Malcontenta on the Brenta. From Palladio's *Quattro Libri*

122. Villa Thiene at Cicogna. From Palladio's *Quattro Libri*

by sixteen and the largest sixteen by twenty-four, while the width of the hall is thirty-two feet. Thus, the consistent series 12, 16, 24, 32 is the keynote to the building. As if in an overture the first and last members of this series appear in the ratio 12:32 of the portico, which is a diapason and diatessaron (i.e. 12:24:32). The intercolumniation of the centre (6 feet) is related to the depth of the portico (12) as 1:2. The smaller inter-columniations are 4½ feet; they are related to the central one as 3:4 which, incidentally, is the ratio of the smallest rooms. Finally, the diameter of the columns, 2 feet, represents the smallest unit, the module, and by a process of multiplication beginning with two all the ratios of the building can be derived.[96]

An organic structure developed from the module, the 'regola homogenea', has no room for incommensurable quantities; however, the application of the module does not necessarily mean that the ratios throughout a whole building must be harmonic.[97] But the systematic linking of one room to the other by harmonic proportions was the fundamental novelty of Palladio's architecture, and we believe that his wish to demonstrate this innovation had a bearing on the choice and character of the plates and the inscription of measurements. Those proportional relationships which other architects had harnessed for the two dimensions of a façade[98] or the three dimensions of a single room were employed by him to integrate a whole structure.

The demand that 'the parts should correspond to the whole and to each other' was generally adhered to in churches, for the relation of nave, aisles and chapels, and here the Renaissance could build on mediaeval traditions. But for domestic buildings the decisive step was taken by Palladio.[99] He formulated his views on this point in one very important sentence which will add weight to our analysis of two of his villas: 'But the large rooms ought to be so related (*compartite*) to the

96 The only measurement in this building which is not easily intelligible is the length of the hall measuring 46½ feet, where one would have expected 48 feet. The measurement can be analysed in more than one way, for instance as 6 x 7 plus 4½ (6 and 4½ being the widths of the intercolumniations), but I cannot offer a fully satisfactory explanation.

97 Cf. below, p. 127, note 112.

98 Cf. our analysis of the façade of S. Maria Novella, above, p. 51.

99 It would not be difficult to give earlier examples which show similar tendencies. But as far as we can see, none of Palladio's predecessors developed this problem systematically. Francesco di Giorgio seems to be the only one who discussed it theoretically in his treatise on architecture; cf. Promis, *Trattato di architettura civile e militare di Francesco di Giorgio Martini*, 1841, Pls. 1, 2. See also E. Langenskiöld, *Michele Sanmicheli*, Uppsala, 1938, p. 191 and Figs. 92, 93.

100 Bk. II, chap. 2: 'Ma le stanze grandi con le mediocri, e queste con le picciole deono essere in maniera compartite, che (come ho detto altrove) una parte della fabrica corrisponda all'altra, e cosi

middle ones, and these to the small, that, as I have said elsewhere, one part of the building may correspond with the other, so that the whole body of the edifice may have in itself a certain harmony (*convenienza*) of members which may make it entirely beautiful and graceful.'[100]

A thorough acquaintance with Renaissance ideas on proportion is often necessary to understand the legitimacy of the ratios given by Palladio. In the Villa Emo (Fig. 124) rooms of 16 x 16, 12 x 16, 16 x 27 frame the portico (also 16 x 27) and the hall (27 x 27). The ratio 16:27 can only be understood by splitting it up in the way Alberti has taught us; it has to be read as 16:24:27, i.e. as a fifth and a major tone (=2:3 and 8:9) and similarly the compound ratio 12:27 can be generated from 12:24:27, i.e. an octave and a major tone (=1:2 and 8:9). Thus the figures 27, 12, 16 which, written one under the other, strike the reader's eye, are perfectly intelligible by means of the generation of ratios. Ratios of the same order are to be found in the wings; 12 is again the middle term, this time inscribed between 24 and 48. The harmonic character of this series is obvious (2:1:4, 1:4 being two octaves=1:2:4. The whole building appears now like a spatial orchestration of the consonant terms 12, 16, 24, 27, 48.[101]

The same theme was developed in other structures with different measurements. The Villa Thiene at Cicogna (Fig. 122) has 4 as module (diameter of columns) and the rooms are based on the harmonic series 12, 18, 36. In the four corners are square rooms measuring 18 x 18 feet; they flank a double square room, 18 x 36, and this ratio is repeated in the two porticos which flank the hall which is 36 x 36 feet, i.e. four times the size of the small corner rooms. The progression 18:18, 18:36, 36:36 is broken between the small squares and the porticos by rooms measuring 12 feet in width, so that the sequence 18, 12, 18 (3:2:3) is repeated four times.[102]

Progressions of 1:1, 1:2, 2:2 used in the Villa Thiene occur in other buildings. Rooms of 20 x 20, 20 x 30, 30 x 30 form the core of the Palazzo Porto-Colleoni, and ratios based on the series 12, 16, 18, 24, 27, 32, 36 are frequent.[103] All these spatial proportions have their equivalent in the consonances of the Greek musical scale. But we are far from suggesting that Palladio, while planning his buildings, was consciously translating musical into visual proportions. Francesco Giorgi, in his memorandum, did not set out to prove the applicability of musical consonances to architecture, but worked with them for the design of S. Francesco della Vigna as a matter-of-course procedure. 'The rules of arithmetic', said Daniele Barbaro, elaborating Vitruvius,[104] 'are those which unite Music and Astrology: for proportion is general and universal in all things given to measure, weight and number'.[105] We have Palladio's own word for it, that for him the proportions of sounds and in space were closely related, and he must have been convinced of the universal validity of one and the same harmonic system. These were convictions which belonged to the general intellectual make-up of the Renaissance, needing no particular sophistication to translate them into practice.

6. Palladio's Ratios and the Development of Sixteenth-Century Musical Theory

It should now be said that ratios based on the small integral numbers of the Greek musical scale (1:2:3:4) are by no means the only ones to be found in Palladio's plans. Palladio showed a predilection for rooms measuring 18 x 30 or

tutto il corpo dell'edificio habbia in se una certa convenienza di membri, che lo renda tutto bello, e gratioso.'

101 The depth of the rooms in the wings is 20; the ratios of the depth to the widths of the rooms (12, 24, 48) will be explained in the next section.

102 This description follows the inscribed numbers. One can, of course, also read 18, 12, 36 (length of the portico).

103 For instance Villa Pojana (18, 36), Villa Trissino at Meledo (12, 18, 36), Villa Sarego at Santa Sofia (12, 18, 24, 36), Villa Cornaro at Piombino (16, 24, 27, 32). In all these buildings one finds, together with this basic series, other figures which would need further explanation.

104 Commentary to Bk. I, i, 16.

105 The theological connotation is evident, cf. *Wisdom of Solomon*, XI, 20: 'But by measure and number and weight thou didst order all things.' This passage was often quoted in support of the Christian belief in the all-embracing virtue of numbers. Luca Pacioli in his *Summa de Arithmetica*, Venice, 1494, dist. VI, tract. 1, artic. 2 (2nd ed., 1523, f. 68 v.) refers to it with reference to St. Augustine.

12 x 20, i.e. for a ratio of 3:5. There are buildings with ratios of 4:5 and 5:6[106] and these and similar ratios occur not only in the proportions of one room but also in the relation of one room to another – 4:5 in the Villa Valmarana at Lisiera, 5:6 in the Villa Ghizzole, 3:5 in the design for the Palazzo Angarano, 5:9 in that for Count della Torre at Verona, and this list could be considerably extended. All these buildings present new problems which cannot be understood without considering the fundamental changes in the approach to proportion during the sixteenth century. In the course of this century ratios became perceptible which were outside the grasp of fifteenth-century artists. The development of musical theory during that period, particularly in Northern Italy, is a reliable guide. It was Ludovico Fogliano of Modena who, in his *Musica theorica* of 1529, first protested against the sole authority of the Pythagorean consonances; according to him experience teaches that, apart from the five Pythagorean consonances, minor (5:6) and major third (4:5) minor (5:8) and major sixth (3:5), and major (2:5) and minor tenth (5:12), eleventh (3:8), and minor and major sixth above the octave (5:16 and 3:10) are all consonances.[107] But it was Zarlino, the great Venetian theorist of the mid-sixteenth century who, with his rigorously scientific approach,[108] classified the entire harmonic material which had come down from antiquity. It is a phenomenon which Zarlino calls 'veramente maraviglioso' ('truly miraculous').[109] that the consonances are determined by the arithmetic as well as by the 'harmonic' mean. The arithmetic mean 3 between 2 and 4 divides the octave into fifth and fourth (2:3 and 3:4); the same result, inverted, is achieved by the 'harmonic' mean 8 between the extremes 6 and 12 (6:8=3:4 and 8:12=2:3). Zarlino could show that the same law applies to the division of the fifth, for 2:3 or 4:6 with the arithmetic mean 5 determines the ratios of major and minor third (4:5 and 5:6) and with the 'harmonic' mean – as in 10, 12, 15 – the ratios of minor and major third. A further division of the major third is possible; the insertion of the arithmetic mean between 4 and 5 leads to the ratio 8:9:10, 8:9 being the major tone and 9:10 the minor tone, while the 'harmonic' mean 80 between the extremes 72 and 90 divides the series into minor and major tone. Zarlino can now show in a diagram the '*divisione harmonica della Diapason nelle sue parti*' ('harmonic division of the octave into its parts'):[110]

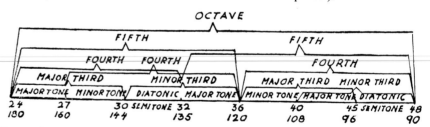

If we take this new development into consideration, most of the problematic ratios in Palladio's buildings beome intelligible. A comparatively simple example for the combination of the old with the new consonances is the Villa Pisani at Bagnolo (Fig. 123). The smallest room measures 16 x 16 feet, the middle one 16 x 24 and the largest one 18 x 30, while the cross-shaped hall is 32 x 42 feet. We have met with the sequence 16 x 16, 16 x 24 in the Villa Malcontenta. The measurement 30 of the largest room is not inscribed, but Palladio says in his text that these rooms are 'lunghe un quadro e due terzi' ('one two-thirds long', i.e. 18 plus 12). This shape, recommended by Palladio as one of

106 Such ratios occur in some of the structures which we have discussed. In fact, they are so frequent that no detailed list need here be given.
107 *Musica theorica*, Venice, 1529, II, chap. 1, fol. xi verso. Cf. H. Riemann, *Geschichte der Musiktheorie im IX.-XIX. Jahrhundert*, Leipzig, 1898, p. 326: 'haec autem quae addimus sunt consonantiae quae a *practicis* appellantur (follow the consonances mentioned in the text) . . . quae omnia intervalla esse *veras et valde delectabiles consonantias non potest negari.*'
108 *Le Istitutioni harmoniche*, Venice, 1558, p. 21: 'la Musica è scienza, che considera li Numeri, e le proportioni.' – 'Music is a science which is concerned with numbers and proportions.'
109 *ibid.*, p. 161.
110 *ibid.*, part II, chap. 39, p. 122. We have slightly altered Zarlino's diagram by translating his terms and also by quoting the arithmetic series 24, 36, 48 together with Zarlino's harmonic series 180 to 90. The diatonic semitone 15:16 is necessary, for without it one cannot proceed from the major third to the fourth.

the seven 'più belle e proportionate maniere di stanze' ('most beautiful and proportionate types of rooms'), is musically a major sixth (3:5) and it can be divided into 18:24:30, i.e. 3:4:5, a fourth and a major third. The figures 16 of the square room and 18 of the largest room express the firm proportional relationship of the major tone (8:9); in addition, 18 and 16 are linked to the 24 of the room between them by the ratios 3:4 (fourth) and 2:3 (fifth). All these affinities are suggested by the inscription of the numbers 16, 24, 18 in the right-hand side of the plan. Moreover, the length of the central room, 24, is related to the (uninscribed) length of the largest room, 30, as 4:5 (major third). The length of the hall, 42 feet, results from the addition of 18 and 24 (the lower part of the hall forms a square of 18 x 18); and the figures 18, 24, 32 (width of the hall) represent two ratios of 3:4.

In the Villa Sarego at Miega (Fig. 125) the sequence 12:16, 16:16, 16:27 recurs which we have met in a different order in the Villa Emo. But the central part of the building, between the three flanking rooms of each side, seems to follow a different system of ratios. In the portico are inscribed the numbers 10, 15 and 40, in the hall 20 and 40 and in the rooms connecting the hall with the wings 9 and 24. The numbers 10, 15, 20, 40 form a series of the order known to us (2, 3, 4, 8). 9:24 is an octave and a fifth (9:18:24), and both terms are not only linked in many ways with the adjoining rooms but also connect the series of terms in the outlying rooms with those in the centre: thus 9:12 is a fourth, 9:20 an octave and a minor tone (9:18:20); while 24 is related to 12, 16 and 27 as octave, fifth, and major tone, and to 20 and 40 of the hall as minor third (5:6) and major sixth (3:5; this proportion can also be expressed as fourth and major third, i.e. 24:32:40). All this, however, does not exhaust the relations which Renaissance men could here envisage. With the development of sixteenth-century musical theory in mind we can now grasp something of the harmonic 'cross-currents' in such a building. The ratios of 9 and 10, 10 and 12, 15 and 16, 12 and 20, although not occurring in adjoining rooms, must be understood as parts of the same theme.

Instead of carrying this analysis further, we may turn to another building, the Villa Maser (Fig. 126), in which the basic harmonic unity of all the inscribed numbers may be demonstrated in detail. The long wings behind the main building contain three groups of three rooms each – two of these groups are repeated at each side of the central group – the widths of which are inscribed as 16, 12, 16; 20, 10, 20; 9, 18, 9. It is obvious that the ratios in each set of rooms are consonant (4:3:4; 2:1:2; 1:2:1).[111] But one can go a step further. In the front of the main building are three rooms – of which the middle one is part of the cruciform hall – all 12 feet wide (together 36); in the corresponding part of the wing the three rooms reappear with the different orchestration 9, 18, 9 (together 36). Twelve is the harmonic mean between 9 and 18 and divides the octave into fourth and fifth; the two inscribed figures 12 and 18, one above the other, are indicative of Palladio's intentions. We find the figure 12 again in the outside group of rooms of the wings, while the depth of the front rooms, 20, is repeated in the width and depth of the middle group of the wings. In other words, the three groups of rooms of the long wing repeat and develop the theme of the main building. At the same time, the figures inscribed in the three groups of the wings are interrelated, the smaller class of rooms as 9:10:12 (minor tone and minor third), the larger class of rooms as 16:18:20 (major tone and minor tone). The relation between the lengths of rooms, 20 and 32 (farthest group), is 5:8 (minor sixth, or minor

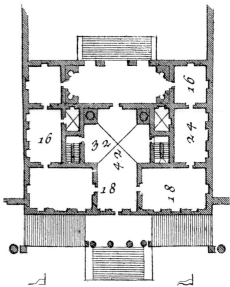

123. Villa Pisani at Bagnolo. From Palladio's *Quattro Libri*

111 The plan published by Palladio does not show that each group of rooms represents a distinct unit through the treatment of the ceilings. The central group of rooms has barrel vaults, and inside this group there is a gradation of heights: the higher room in the main axis is framed by the two smaller rooms with lower barrel vaults. In the adjoining groups of three rooms which are covered by flat ceilings the relation is reversed: the higher rooms frame a lower one. The principal structure projecting in front of the long wings has barrel vaults in the arms which intersect in the crossing. The vaults of these arms are considerably lower than the barrel vault of the room behind. Thus the gradation of heights of the rooms and the variation in the construction of the ceilings help to make Palladio's harmonic scheme a poignant visual experience. Since no measured sections of the villa exist, it is at present not possible to say at what relations (between the heights of rooms inside one group and between different groups) Palladio was aiming.

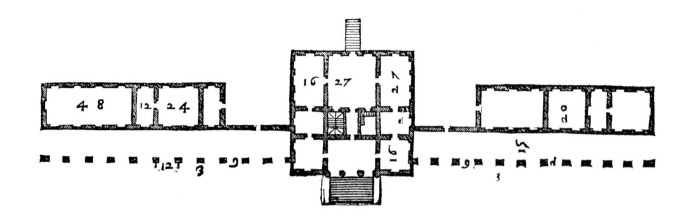

124. Villa Emo at Fanzola. From Palladio's *Quattro Libri*

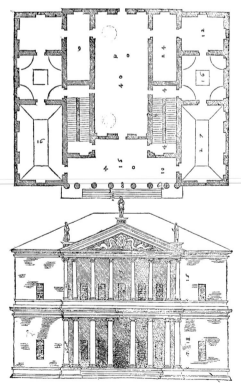

125. Villa Sarego at Miega. From Palladio's *Quattro Libri*

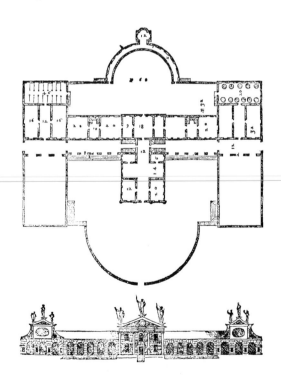

126. Villa Maser near Asolo. From Palladio's *Quattro Libri*

third and fourth – 20:24:32). The stables, the courtyard, the colonnade all form part of this building.[112] 12, the basic term of the building, returns in the width of the fountain in the main axis at the farthest end of the yard and also in the width of the colonnade. Divisions of the key number 12 (6, 3, 4) are inscribed in the smallest room of the house and in the niches and the passage of the esedra leading to the fountain. The depth of the cortile, 32, corresponds to the length of the farthest group of rooms, and the width of the esedra, 60, is a fivefold proportion of 12 or a triple proportion of the equally important term 20. As the ratios of this building are evolutions of one and the same harmonic pattern, the proportional affinities could be stated in still greater detail.

However the reader may doubt whether Palladio's inscribed figures are really so full of implications. In spite of our close adherence to his own figures we may be accused of the error, so often made by modern writers on proportion, of interpreting into a building relations which were never intended by its architect. Yet nobody can deny that Palladio's numbers were meant to be indicative of certain ratios, and it is not this fact but only the degree of interpretation which may be questioned. Now the position in architecture is exactly paralleled by that in musical theory and practice. Such a brilliant student of musical theory as Matthew Shirlaw described the art of harmonic composition in Zarlino's time with these words:

> The older art, although it was not on harmony alone that it depended for its aesthetic effect, was nevertheless capable of a very high degree of harmonic expressiveness. Composers of that time did not consider that there was any lack of harmonic material; for them a rich means of harmonic variety existed in the various consonances, and in the various ways of combining them. Not only so, but by different arrangements of these consonances it was possible to obtain a great many different tone-combinations which varied in harmonic effect and expressiveness: a delicate and subtle art which has since been to a great extent lost.[113]

Any uneasiness about Palladio's intentions can be resolved by reading the relevant chapters of the Commentary to Vitruvius by Daniele Barbaro, the very man for whom Palladio built the Villa Maser. Vitruvius' work contains no real theory of proportion.[114] Barbaro could not let this pass and so, after Vitruvius' preface to the Third Book, he inserted a circumstantial discourse on proportion.[115] He considered it of such importance that he introduced it with a formal address to the reader who is desirous to look 'più a dentro, à ritrovare la verità delle cose' ('behind the surface in order to rediscover the truth [hidden] in things').

The discourse begins with that complicated classification of numerical ratios which was in use from the times of Nicomachus' Arithmetic[116] to the seventeenth century, when the modern fractional notation was generally introduced. After this introduction, Barbaro turns to 'proportionalità' which he declares to be the essence of every work of art, exclaiming: 'The whole secret of art consists in *proportionalità*'. Following the traditional usage of the Latin words 'proportio' and 'proportionalitas', Barbaro defines 'proportione' as the ratio of two magnitudes and 'proportionalità' as 'the comparison not of one magnitude with another, but of one proportion with another'.[117] Barbaro then explains in great detail methods of subtraction, addition, multiplication and division of ratios and of finding the common denominator of two and more 'proportioni'. He winds up with compound ratios which he considers of the utmost importance and for which

112 However, two measurements occur – 14 (width of horizontal arm of hall) and 46 (length of stables) – which do not fit into the harmonic pattern. For Zarlino all harmonies are contained in the progression 1, 2, 3, 4, 5, 6, which includes even the minor sixth (5:8, generated from 5:6, minor third, and 6:8, i.e. 3:4, fourth); however, 7 forms no part of his harmonic series. And yet, both figures, 14 as well as 46, are firmly linked to the rest of Palladio's terms. This will be evident by reading the whole series from which the proportions of the building were generated: 2, 3, 4, 6, 8, 9, 10, 12, 14, 16, 18, 20, 32, 46, 60. – 14 and 46 are the arithmetic means between 12 and 16, and 32 and 60. Moreover, the distance of the mean 46 from the extremes 32 and 60 is 14.

The 'dissonant' ratio 6:7 as well as the arithmetic mean are to be found in other buildings. The Villa Zeno at Cessalto is generated from the terms 12, 14, 21½, 29; 21½ being the arithmetic mean between 14 and 29, but no two numbers correspond here to musical intervals.

113 Matthew Shirlaw, *The Theory of Harmony*, London, 1918, p. 37. – It would be illuminating and full of interesting implications if one were to find that Zarlino, Daniele Barbaro and Palladio belonged to the same circle. So far as I am aware, no documents in support of intimate contacts have been published, but it is worth noting that Zarlino in his *Supplimenti musicali* (Venice, 1588, pp. 179, 288, *passim*) quotes Barbaro's Vitruvius edition more than once and with great personal respect for the author.

114 This statement has recently been challenged by P.H. Scholfield (*The Theory of Proportion in Architecture*, Cambridge, 1958, p. 16 ff.), although he admits that Vitruvius' theory of proportion is neither full nor detailed and lacks coherence as well.

115 Ed. 1556, p. 57 ff.

116 Cf. the table of Nicomachus' terminology in Heath, *A History of Greek Mathematics*, 1921, I, p. 101 ff.

117 Barbaro, p. 58: 'si come la proportione è rispetto, & convenienza di due quantità comprese come due estremi sotto un'istesso genere, cosi la proportionalità è rispetto, & comparatione non d'una quantità all'altra, ma d'una proportione all' altra.' Compare with this definition Boethius' 'proportionalitas est duarum vel plurium proportionum similis habitudo' (*De musica*, ed. Friedlein, p. 137), which is the Greek , cf. *Timaeus* 31c and Aristotle's 'Proportion is equality of ratios' (*Eth. Nic.* V, 6, 1131 a 31). Barbaro's admiration of 'proportionalità' was firmly rooted in Renaissance thought; see Ghiberti's 'Ma la proportionalità solamente fa pulcritudine' (J. von Schlosser, *Lorenzo Ghibertis Denkwürdigkeiten*, 1912, p. 105).

he follows, as he professes himself, the system of 'Alchindo'.[118]

Barbaro's discourse contains nothing new for the theory of numbers. What is important about it is that he regarded his expositions as fully applicable to architecture; and he comes to the conclusion that 'the possibilities of using now one, now another proportion are unlimited, for instance in subdividing the bulk of buildings ('i corpi delle fabbriche'), or in *atria, tablina*, halls, loggias, basilicas, and other cases of great importance'.[119] It would be entirely wrong to interpret this sentence outside its context, as if the architect were free to handle proportion without the firm basis of science – on the contrary, the system is so complex and the definitions are so detailed that there is no room left for arbitrary proportions. Beauty results only from the right proportions: 'Divina è la forza de'numeri tra se con ragione comparati.'[120] This means that numbers have a divine power when the proportions are consonant. Other passages clearly reveal the trend of Barbaro's thought. Barbaro leaves us in no doubt: 'Every work of art must be like a very beautiful verse, which runs along according to the best consonances one followed by the other, until they come to the well-ordered end.'[121] The proportions of the human body are consonant and harmonious like the chords of a guitar. Of singers it is expected that their voices should be in tune, and the same applies to the parts in architecture. 'Questa bella maniera si nella Musica, come nell'Architettura è detta Eurithmia, madre della gratia, e del diletto . . . ' ('This beautiful manner in music as well as in architecture is called harmony, mother of grace and of delight').[122]

The theme of proportions runs through Barbaro's whole commentary like a guiding thread and he returns to it with ever renewed emphasis. Perhaps the most illuminating passage is that following the part from which we have just quoted. In commenting further on Vitruvius' notions of 'symmetria' and 'eurythmia' Barbaro says:

> Symmetry is the beauty of order as 'eurythmia' is the beauty of disposition. It is not enough to order the measurements singly one after the other, but it is necessary that those measurements be related to each other, that is to say that there must be some proportion between them.

This sentence seems to imply a recommendation of Palladio's 'symphonic' principle of proportion. To be sure, the conclusion drawn by Barbaro in the next sentence reveals his sympathy with Palladio's practice:

> Thus, where there is proportion there can be nothing superfluous. And as nature's instinct is the ruler of natural proportion, so the rule of art is master of artificial proportion. From this it results that proportion belongs to form and not to matter, and where there are no parts there cannot be proportion.

Here Barbaro touches on the manner in which proportion was perceived during the Renaissance.[123] Falling back on Aristotle's notions of matter and form, he regards it as the prerequisite of 'formed matter' that it should consist of parts which are proportionately related to each other.

> For proportion originates from composite parts and their relationship to each other; and, as has been shown, there must be at least two terms in each relation.

He ends with a panegyric on proportion, and throws light on the ideas which guided him when he inserted, in the Third Book, his discourse on proportion:

> One cannot sufficiently praise the effect of proportion, on which is

---

118 Al-Kindi's *Libellum sex quantitatum* (9th century) was already referred to by Ghiberti (cf. Julius von Schlosser, *Leben und Meinungen des flor. Bildhauers Lorenzo Ghiberti*, Basel, 1941, p. 185) and probably used by Leonardo, cf. Richter, *op. cit.*, I, p. 243. For Al-Kindi cf. G. Sarton, *Introduction to the History of Science*, 1927, I, p. 559 f.

119 Barbaro, *op. cit.*, p. 101. I cannot agree with the conclusions of a valuable paper by V.P. Zoubov ('Vitruve et ses commentateurs du XVIe siècle', *La science au seizième siècle*, Colloque international de Royaumont, Paris, 1957, p. 79 ff.), according to whom Barbaro differentiated between an abstract system of mathematical rules and the concrete problem of architectural practice. For the latter, Zoubov maintains, Barbaro advocated artistic liberty. In my view (see the text above), Barbaro's postulate of the variability in the application of proportions is a far cry from their abrogation.

120 *ibid.*, p. 57. Barbaro continues: 'One can say that neither in the structure of this world nor in the microcosm is there anything more extensive and full of dignity than propriety of weight, number and measure from which time, space, movement, virtue, speech, art, nature, knowledge, in short everything divine and human is composed, has grown, and has been perfected.' Once again, the reference to *Wisdom of Solomon*, xi, 20, is evident.

121 Barbaro, p. 24, ad Vitruvium I, ii, 3.

122 *ibidem*.

123 Cf. above, p. 111 ff.

based the glory of architecture, the beauty of the work and the miracle of the profession. This will become apparent when we talk about proportion and explain the secrets of this art demonstrating the innate quality of proportion, its terms, use and effect and by what power it determines the appearance of things.[124]

Those who work through Barbaro's chapter on proportion – not an easy task nowadays – will put it aside with the conviction that this man expected and saw in a building proportional relationships which are outside our range of perception. The reader, we hope, will agree that Palladio, like Barbaro, firmly believed that proportion contained 'all the secrets of art'. Moreover, the analysis of some of Palladio's buildings may have convinced him that this architect was a master in the application of 'proportionalità'. Considering Palladio's friendship with Barbaro and their community of interests,[125] one is tempted to say that the former was pre-destined to realize in Barbaro's own villa those subtle harmonic relationships in which patron and architect equally believed.

After all the foregoing, it can hardly be doubted that Palladio controlled and corrected his innate sense of proportion by a rational theory.[126] There exists, moreover, an interesting proof of this. In the letter to Martino Bassi in which he stated his reasons for supporting Bassi's case against Pellegrino Pellegrini,[127] Palladio mentions that he wanted to hear the opinion of 'huomini intendenti' ('men of competence'). He had therefore shown Bassi's suggestions to the painter Giuseppe Salviati, a specialist on perspective, and to Silvio Belli, 'the most excellent geometrician whom we have here'. This Silvio Belli, in whose judgment Palladio had such confidence, was the author of a work on proportion, entitled *Della Proportione, et Proportionalità*, which appeared in 1573 and which covered much the same ground as Barbaro's discourse. The lucidity and simplicity of Belli's presentation is congenial to Palladio's conception of architecture. Belli was not only a mathematician, he was above all a practical man. He had won laurels as an engineer; and as a co-founder of the Olympic Academy he must have been in close contact with Palladio for many years.[128]

A contemporary scholar coupled the names of Palladio and Belli in a remarkable passage at a time when the two men were still alive. It appears to us a strange and unexpected tribute when he says in their praise: 'Certainly everybody knows how much talent and nature means even without learning; or if he does not know it, let him turn to Andrea Palladio and Silvio Belli. For these with a minimum of erudition, but a maximum of meditation and skill bring back into use the measurements, forms and works according to the rules of Archimedes, Euclid and Vitruvius and embellish our age with very beautiful buildings.'[129] Measured by our standards Palladio's considerable learning was closely tied up with his whole approach to architecture. But to absorb Euclid and Vitruvius and other classical knowledge was for the mid-sixteenth-century architect no more than what in our time would be a young architect's university training. It was the foundation upon which talent could build.

The case of Palladio, it would appear, has typical significance. The theory and practice of Renaissance proportion were not divorced from each other, nor should proportion in Renaissance buildings be regarded in isolation as a purely aesthetic phenomenon. Under a Renaissance dome a Barbaro could experience a faint echo of the inaudible music of the spheres.

124 The whole passage (p. 24) runs as follows: 'La Simmetria è la bellezza dell'Ordine, come la Eurithmia della Dispositione. Non è assai ordinare le misure una dopo l'altra, ma necessario è, che quelle misure habbiano convenienza tra loro, cioè sieno in qualche proportione, & però dove sarà proportione, quivi non può essere cosa superflua; & si come il maestro della natural proportione è lo instinto della natura, cosi il maestro dell'artificiale è l'habito dell'arte, di qui nasce che la proportione piu presto della forma, che della materia procede (later edition: è propria della forma, & non della materia), e dove non sono parti, non può essere proportione: perchè essa nasce dalle parti composte, & dalla relatione di esse, & in ogni relatione è forza, che ci sieno almeno due termini (come s'è detto) ne si può lodare abastanza l'effetto della proportione, nella quale è posta la gloria dell'Architetto, la fermezza (later ed: bellezza) dell'opera, & la maraviglia dell'Artificio, come si vedrà chiaramente, quando ragioneremo delle proportioni, & apriremo i secreti di questa Arte, dimostrando qual rispetto s'intende essere nella proportione, quali termini siani i suoi, qual' uso & quanti effetti, & di che forza essa faccia le cose parere.'

125 Cf. above, Part III, p. 64 ff.

126 But Palladio reserved for himself the right to break the rules. This is an important ingredient of his art and theory. He concludes his survey of rules for the proportion of rooms with the words: 'There are still other heights for rooms which fall under no rule, and the architect has to use them according to his judgment and need' (Bk. I, p. 50). Similarly, the next chapter on 'The Measurements of Doors and Windows' begins with the statement that 'one cannot give a certain and absolute rule about their height and width'. Such unorthodox statements punctuate Palladio's treatise, and in the stress laid on individual judgment and practical experience, reflected also in his work (cf. above p. 122, note 96 and p. 127, note 112), one might see the typically North Italian Aristotelian accretion (cf. above, p. 66) to the Platonic substance with which the foregoing pages were concerned.

127 Cf. above, p. 115.

128 On Belli cf. Angiolgabriello di Santa Maria [Calvi], *Biblioteca, e storia di . . . scrittori . . . di Vicenza*, 1772-82, Vol. IV, pp. 103-107.

129 Sebastiano Montecchio, *De Inventario haeredis*, Venice, 1574, p. 163 (quoted after Magrini, *op. cit.*, p. 2): 'Nemo quippe ignorat quantum valeat ingenium et natura etiam sine disciplina; vel si ignorat, respiciat in Andream Palladium et Sylvium Bellum. Hi enim ut minimum eruditioni, ita plurimum meditationi artificioque attendentes, Archimedis, Euclidis, Vitruvii regulis, dimensiones, figuras, opificia in usum revocant, nostramque aetatem pulcherrimis exornant substructionibus.'

7. The Break-away from the Laws of Harmonic Proportion in Architecture

It need hardly be recalled that the doctrine of a mathematical universe which, with all its emanations, was subject to harmonic ratios, was triumphantly reasserted by a number of great thinkers in the seventeenth and eighteenth centuries. We find this conception of the world fully expounded in Kepler's *Harmonia Mundi* (1619), we find it in Galileo,[130] and later in Shaftesbury, for whom, truly Platonic, the laws of musical harmony are effective also in human nature: '*Virtue* has the same fix'd Standard. The same *Numbers, Harmony*, and *Proportion* will have place in Morals; and are discoverable in the *Characters* and *Affections* of Mankind.'[131]

The poets echo these ideas.[132] Dryden thinks in terms of the Greek musical scale in 'A Song for St. Cecilia's Day':

> From harmony, from heav'nly harmony
> This universal frame began;
> From harmony to harmony
> Thro' all the compass of the notes it ran,
> The diapason closing full in man.

But long before this was written, the voice of doubt was to be heard. John Donne[133] had sung in 1611:

> And new Philosophy calls all in doubt,
> The Element of fire is quite put out;
>
> . . .
>
> 'Tis all in peeces, all cohaerence gone;
> All just supply, and all Relation.

With the rise of the new science the synthesis which had held microcosm and macrocosm together, that all-pervading order and harmony in which thinkers had believed from Pythagoras' days to the sixteenth and seventeenth centuries, began to disintegrate.[134] This process of 'atomization' led, of course, to a re-orientation in the field of aesthetics and, implicitly, of proportion.

But before discussing the new ideas which slowly emerged, it should be pointed out that a knowledge of the old belief in a universal harmony is to be found in seventeenth- and eighteenth-century writers on architecture. In England, Inigo Jones, a true descendent of the humanist tradition, founded his theoretical deliberations on the metaphysical belief in the universal efficacy and beauty of numbers.[135] This also accounts for his famous blunder about Stonehenge. To him it was the ruin of a Roman temple, because after taking careful measurements he had found that 'betwixt this Island of Great Britain and Rome itself there's no one Structure to be seen, wherein more clearly shines those harmonical Proportions of which only the best Times could vaunt, than in this Stone-Heng'. To Inigo's circle belonged Sir Henry Wotton, who was partial to the same ideas and in his *Elements of Architecture*, 1624, gave full expression to the importance he attached to harmonic proportions. As a student of Vitruvius, Alberti, Palladio and French theorists such as Philibert de l'Orme, he could write: 'In truth, a sound piece of good Art, where the *Materials* being but ordinary Stone, without any garnishment of Sculpture, do yet ravish the beholder (and he knows not how)[136] by a secret *Harmony* in the *Proportions*.' In his chapter on doors and windows he is more explicit, reminding the reader that Vitruvius himself wishes the architect 'to be no superficial, and floating *Artificer*; but a *Diver* into *Causes*, and into the *Mysteries of Proportion*.' And following Alberti's

130 Cf. E. Cassirer, *Das Erkenntnisproblem*, 1911, I, p. 383 ff.

131 In 'Advice to an Author', *Characteristicks*, ed. 1737, I, p. 353. See also the hymn on harmony in nature in 'The Moralists', *ibid.*, II, p. 284 ff.

132 For Shakespeare and Milton, cf. L. Spitzer, 'Classical and Christian Ideas of World Harmony', *Traditio*, III, 1945, p. 333 ff.

133 In *An Anatomie of the World*. However, Donne's view of the world was still firmly grounded in the Platonic tradition. The image of the circle as a symbol of God (cf. Part I) constantly recurs in his poetry, see Milton Allan Rugoff, *Donne's Imagery*, New York, 1939, p. 64 ff.

134 Cf. R. Allers, 'Microcosm', *Traditio*, II, 1944, p. 393 ff. Frances Yates has shown how the universality of the sixteenth-century encyclopedia in France, based on the traditions of the Florentine Platonic Academy, began to dissolve into specialized disciplines in the course of the seventeenth century (*The French Academies of the Sixteenth Century*, London, The Warburg Insitute, 1947. p. 290 ff.)

135 Wittkower, 'Inigo Jones, Architect and Man of Letters', JOURNAL OF THE ROYAL INSTITUTE OF BRITISH ARCHITECTS, LX, 1953, p. 83 ff.

136 See Palladio's wording of the same idea, above p. 110.

interpretation of Pythagoras he explains how to reduce 'Symmetry to *Symphony*, and the *Harmony of Sound*, to a kind of *Harmony in Sight*'.[137] One hundred-and-fifty years later, Reynolds, steeped in classical art theory, still advocated the basic unity of all the arts and the validity of the same proportions in music and architecture, though one might argue that the following remark in the Thirteenth Discourse lacks conviction: 'To pass over the effect produced by that general symmetry and proportion by which the eye is delighted, as the ear is with music, architecture certainly possesses many principles in common with poetry and painting.'

It was Palladio's work which remained canonical for those academic architects who abided by the conception of harmonic ratios. But this conception, whenever and wherever adhered to in architecture, tended to lose its universal application, and soon, moreover, Renaissance ideas on proportion were completely reversed. There was an important French classicist current, the representatives of which kept alive the Platonic conception of numbers in a doctrinal and didactic sense. François Blondel was perhaps the first architect who gave this academic turn to the old Italian ideas on proportion. Almost a whole book of his *Cours d'architecture*, 1675-83,[138] deals with musical proportions in architecture. His approach to the problem is historical and apologetic, for, in contrast to his Renaissance predecessors, he has to prove a case of which many of his contemporaries were ignorant. Alberti's theory and Palladio's buildings were, as one would expect, used as test-cases for his theory; a whole chapter is devoted to an analysis of façades by Palladio, for the proportions of which Blondel found the key in the simple consonances 9, 6, 4; 6, 4, 3; 4, 2, 1, etc.[139] The answer to Blondel was given by Claude Perrault in his *Ordonnance des cinq espèces de colonnes*, 1683. He broke decisively with the conception that certain ratios were *a priori* beautiful and declared that proportions which follow 'the rules of architecture' were agreeable for no other reason than that we are used to them. Consequently, he advocates the relativity of our aesthetic judgment and, quite logically, maintains that musical consonances cannot be translated into visual proportions.

Blondel's treatise was the result of his teachings at the 'Académie royale de l'architecture', to which he was appointed the first director in 1671. Eighty years later Briseux wrote his *Traité du Beau essentiel dans les arts*, 1752, in defence of Blondel's principles, against Perrault. The author is well versed in Platonism, and he even harnesses Newton's theory of colour in support of the ancient truth. Much of his material was based on Blondel whom he follows entirely in the choice and interpretation of the Palladian examples. But in spite of Briseux's claim to the universality of harmonic ratios, he is largely concerned with the demonstration that 'les mêmes proportions produisent les mêmes effets', thus revealing a shift of emphasis from universally valid to psychologically conditioned standards.

In his work Briseux tried to revive a tradition which was in danger of being forgotten. In fact, the chain was broken and proportion in architecture was regarded as a mystery the knowledge of which had to be rediscovered. William Gilpin, in his *Three Essays on Picturesque Beauty*,[140] mourned: 'The secret is lost. The ancients had it . . . If we could only discover their principles of proportion . . . ' Half a century before him Robert Morris, an architect associated with the Burlington group, believed, in his *Lectures on Architecture*, 1734-36, that he had found the secret 'which was by the Antients found out, and but by a few Moderns known and practis'd'.[141] For this classicist, Palladio was, of course, the

137 Sir Henry Wotton discourses here at length on the nature of the fifth and the octave, 'the two principall *Consonances*, that most ravish the eare'. Ed. of 1624, p. 53 f.
138 Vth Part, Fifth Book, p. 727 ff.
139 Blondel's exposition culminates in a summary of Ouvrard's *Architecture Harmonique, ou l'Application de la doctrine des proportions de la Musique à l'Architecture*, a book which I was unable to see. Ouvrard was a musician, and his work was undoubtedly an important link in the revival of what Blondel calls the 'ancienne doctrine'. This is also shown by Ouvrard's attempt – possibly based on Soldati (cf. above, p. 115 f.) – to create a sixth harmonic architectural order, see A. Comolli, *Bibliografia storico-critica dell'architettura*, Rome, 1790, III, p. 228 ff.
140 First ed. 1792, 2nd ed. 1794, p. 32.
141 Preface.

chief reviver of ancient wisdom[142] and, guided by his works, he developed a system of hard and fast rules of harmonic proportions based on the 'only seven distinct notes in music' the ratios of which 'produce all the Harmonick Proportions of Rooms'. From ready-made tables the reader or architect can pick out the shape of rooms, façades, doors and chimneys with the correct harmonic proportions.

*   *   *   *   *

The break with the great tradition of the sixteenth century and the isolation of the problem of proportion is also to be observed on Italian soil. The architect Octavio Bertotti Scamozzi, undoubtedly the most penetrating student of Palladio, asserted to have found that Palladio used musical ratios; but he made this discovery only after his work *Les Bâtimens et les desseins de André Palladio* (1776-83) was well on the way. In the preface to his third volume he submits his ideas on that point to the judgment of the critics. After having carefully studied the proportions of Palladio's buildings, he declares to have come to the conclusion that they depend on 'des principes beaucoup plus solides que ce qu'on appelle bon goût dans le sens vulgaire'. These 'principes solides', the musical ratios, are discretely pointed out by him in the descriptions of Palladio's buildings.[143] It is apparent that Bertotti Scamozzi had no idea of the general principles which directed a Renaissance mind. Though his results are often convincing, because they are obvious to those who are familiar with Palladio's methods, he developed his thesis entirely in a void. Briseux's book had come to his knowledge just before his work was finished, and he notes with satisfaction the similarity of their conclusions. What he did not know, however, was that discussions on harmonic proportions had been going on all the time and that in the neighbouring Treviso they were even translated into practice in his own days.

In 1762 appeared Tommaso Temanza's *Vita di Andrea Palladio*, which is still one of the most important sources for Palladio's life. Temanza states that in the ratios of length, width and height of his rooms Palladio made clever use of the arithmetic, geometric and 'harmonic' means 'as is clearly manifest in his works'.[144] On this matter ensued a controversy with the Trevisan architect Francesco Maria Preti, which is worth recording because it throws light on the ideas about proportion in architecture and music during the late eighteenth century. Preti, apparently still dependent on Zarlino,[145] advocates 'a firm and stable law' which is alone guaranteed by the musical progression 1, 2, 3, 4, 5, 6 (octave, fifth, fourth, major and minor third).[146] He concludes dogmatically that there is no beauty outside these proportions, for – and here we find the old pattern – the same consonances 'che dilettano l'orecchio dilettano anche la visione' ('which please the ear also please the eye').[147] Temanza, in his long-winded answer,[148] agreed that in the widest sense numbers regulate buildings as well as music. He still insists on commensurability throughout a structure; but apart from that, he maintains, proportion in music and architecture are widely different.[149] His criticism of the general applicability of musical consonances in architecture boils down to two objections which reveal an entirely new standpoint. The one objection is that the eye is not capable of perceiving simultaneously the ratios of length, width and height of a room;[150] the other that architectural proportions must be judged from the angle of vision under which

142 p. 52.
143 Roberto Pane, the author of a biography of Palladio, is singularly insensitive to the humanist mode of thinking. He calls Bertotti Scamozzi's 'discovery' 'questa novella alchimia'. (*Andrea Palladio*, Turin, 1948, p.15).
144 p. 81. – Cf. above, p. 108 f.
145 Cf. above, p. 127, note 112.
146 Bottari, *Lett. Pitt.*, 1822, VIII, p. 277. Preti's letter dates from May 1, 1762 (Publ. by Bottari with the wrong date 1760).
147 Preti also maintains that these consonances are universal. But his wording is interesting: 'Per le osservazioni da *me* fatte entra la musica non sola in architettura, ma nel sistema universale del mondo' (p. 280).
148 Dated June 29, 1762, cf. Bottari, *op. cit.*, V, pp. 462-80.
149 *ibid.*, pp. 470, 472, 473.
150 *ibid.*, p. 465: 'quel piacere che dal giudizioso accozzamento delle consonanze musicali risulta, convenebbe che l'uomo avesse l'organo della vista accomodato in modo di vedere nello stesso tempo, ed in un'occhiata sola, tutte e tre le dimensioni...'

the building is viewed.[151] In other words, architectural proportions cannot be absolute but must be relative. The emphasis has shifted from the objective truth of the building to the subjective truth of the perceiving individual. It is for this reason that Temanza regards the use of the mean proportionals as 'più misterioso che ragionevole' ('mysterious rather than rational').[152] It will be noticed that Temanza's theoretical position is not quite clear; for in spite of his introducing revolutionary factors into the problem of proportion, he still cannot get away from traditional notions. In a later letter addressed to Bottari in which Temanza again states his case, he insists that the use of harmonic proportions in architecture would lead to sterility.[153] For an eighteenth-century classicist this was a very sound observation.

F.M. Preti, Temanza's opponent, had grown up in Treviso in a stubbornly academic tradition according to which only the 'harmonic' mean should be used to determine the height of a room. Giovanni Rizzetto (b. 1675), mathematician and architect, had worked out the theory. His son Luigi Rizzetto, Ottavio Scotti, Andrea Zorzi, Jacopo Riccati and the latter's sons Vicenzo, Giordano and Francesco and, last but not least, Francesco Maria Preti, all of them interested in mathematics and music, had consolidated their restricted system of proportion, convinced that musical consonances had to be applied to architecture. Preti (d. 1774) was perhaps the most prolific theorist and practitioner of the school which left a number of buildings in Treviso and the province, erected according to the rule of the 'harmonic' mean.[154] His narrow dogmatism was no more than a late and provincial survival of the Renaissance tradition. He lacked Alberti's and Palladio's 'symphonic' approach to proportion as well as that cosmic vision which had given it breadth and universality. This fact is amply illustrated by the dry, neo-classical imitation of Palladio in that school (Fig. 102).

In the same part of the country the learned Alessandro Barca, Professor in Padua, advocated a theory of musical proportions in lectures delivered before the Accademia delle Scienze of his city between 1793 and 1798 which were published as late as 1806.[155] Barca was well acquainted with the research of the Treviso architects as well as with the entire history of proportion in architecture. But he was not simply a revivalist, for he introduced a new note by focusing on the principle of the repetition of ratios.

It is true that the speculations about the applicability of musical proportions to art and architecture had a stronger appeal during the middle and second half of the eighteenth century than is generally realized. Girolamo Francesco Cristiani, engineer and mathematician, advertised the conclusions of the school of Treviso at Brescia;[156] and some men of reputation wrote treatises on the subject which – and this seems characteristic – remained unpublished: foremost amongst them were a *Dissertazione metafisica del bello* by the celebrated translator and commentator of Vitruvius, Marchese Galiani,[157] and works by the Roman painter Niccolò Ricciolini and the architect Antoine Derizet. They made, according to Galiani,[158] 'profondi studi, ricerche, esami, e scoperte sopra l'applicazione delle proporzioni musiche all'Architettura' ('profound studies, researches, examinations, and discoveries regarding the application of musical proportion to architecture').

Derizet was a friend of Anton Raphael Mengs, and from that fact we may perhaps derive an idea of the trend of his thought. Mengs' friend and the editor of his writings, Giuseppe Niccola D'Azara, reports how he found the painter

151 *ibid.*, p. 474.

152 *ibid.*, p. 478.

153 Letter dated March 19, 1768. *Ibid.*, VIII, pp. 293-306, particularly p. 302.

154 For detailed information cf. P. Federici, *Memorie Trevigiane*, 1803, II, pp. 144 ff., 173 ff; Comolli, *op.cit.*, IV, 1792, p. 36 ff. See now also Favaro-Fabris, *L'architetto Francesco Maria Preti*, Treviso, 1954, with a full discussion of his works. A late advocate of the validity of the harmonic mean in architecture was Leopoldo Cicognara in his work *Del Bello*, Milan, 1834, p. 77 ff.

155 Alessandro Barca, *Saggio sopra il bello di proporzione in architettura*, Bassano, 1806. For a discussion of Barca's ideas, see P.H. Scholfield, *The Theory of Proportion in Architecture*, Cambridge, 1958, p. 80 and *passim*.

156 *Della media armonica proporzionale da applicarsi nell'architettura civile. Due dissertazioni epistolari a M.G. Bottari*, Brescia, 1767. About Cristiani's life and work, cf. Comolli, *op. cit.*, III, p. 133 ff.

157 *ibid.*, p. 234 ff. with short indications of content.

158 Cf. Galiani's translation of Vitruvius, 1758, quoted by A. Prandi in *Roma*, XXI, 1943, p. 18 ff. – Comolli (*op. cit.*, p. 232) possessed a MS. by Derizet with an extract from Ouvrard's work (see p. 131, note 139). Ricciolini's book went to press in 1773, but never appeared.

For further material on music and architecture, cf. Comolli's notes, Vol. III, pp. 228-35.

whistling and singing while painting the Annunciation, his last picture. When asked for the reason, Mengs explained that what he was singing was a sonata by Corelli, for he wanted his picture to be in Corelli's musical style.[159] This 'materialistic' eighteenth-century approach to the translation of music into painting throws a clear light on the change which had come about since the days of the Renaissance, when the conception of one universal harmony bound together both music and the visual arts.

But another almost anachronistic architectural author and practitioner deserves mention, namely Bernardo Antonio Vittone from Turin, whose *Istruzioni elementari* of 1760 and *Istruzioni diverse* of 1766 are in a class of their own. The dedication of the *Istruzioni elementari* – probably unique of its kind – is addressed to God, 'the archetype of perfection' who has revealed harmony and beauty to mankind. Like Briseux, Vittone uses Newton's discoveries in support of the universal applicability of the law of numbers,[160] and he is deeply convinced that a knowledge of musical theory is essential for an understanding of proportion in architecture.[161] He therefore includes a chapter[162] on the 'Generation and Nature of Musical Proportion' which is still dependent on Zarlino, and his *Istruzioni diverse* contains an extensive and cumbersome treatise on music. It is idle to speculate on the fact that for Vittone, perhaps the most creative architect Italy had at that period, the great Renaissance tradition was still a living force.

The relation in the academic camp between Perrault and Briseux finds an interesting parallel in the Baroque atmosphere of Turin. For eighty years before Vittone's publication, Guarino Guarini – for whom Vittone had a great veneration and whose treatise on architecture he even published posthumously – had broken with the Renaissance tradition.[163] Guarini's line of argument differs from Perrault's and is, in a way, more radical. The eye of the beholder is for him the only judge of proportion – 'per compiacere agli occhi, si dee levare, o aggiungere alle Simmetrie, essendo che altro un'oggetto appare sotto l'occhio, altro appare in alto, altro in un luogo chiuso, altro in aperto'[164] ('to please the eye one must take away from, or add to, the proportions because one object is placed under eye level, another at great height, another in an enclosed space, and yet another in the open air') – and he does not even discuss the possibility of objective truth on which Renaissance aesthetics was founded. In the same vein, a hundred years later, Milizia, the foremost Italian theorist of the late eighteenth century, subordinated the rules of proportion to the laws of perspective, since buildings are seen at different distances and in different situations. He goes a decisive step further on the path shown by Temanza twenty years before; his theory of proportion depends on sensation and, like Guarini's, is based on the impression which a building makes on the eye. Logically he refutes the efficacy of the three mean proportionals, and even the necessity of commensurable dimensions. Proportion for him is a matter of experiment and experience.[165] The modern approach of the architect to the problem of proportion is taking shape.

*　　*　　*　　*　　*

It was, however, in England, that the whole structure of classical aesthetics was overthrown from the bottom. Hogarth was only the mouthpiece of the new tendencies when he rejected any congruity between mathematics and beauty.[166] Without an idea of the universality of the classical conception of proportion, he

159 Cf. *Opere di Antonio Raffaello Mengs*, Bassano, 1783, I, pp. lxvi, lxxi. Mengs' belief in the possibility of influencing one art by another through sympathetic magic may be compared with Canova's method of having Homer read to him while working with the chisel.

160 B. A. Vittone, *Istruzioni elementari*, p. 88 f. See R. Wittkower, *Art and Architecture in Italy 1600-1750*, Pelican History of Art, 1958, p. 282 ff.

161 *ibid.*, p. 242.

162 *ibid.*, p. 245 ff.

163 For Guarini, see Wittkower, *op. cit.*, p. 268 ff.

164 *Architettura civile*, Turin, 1737, p. 6. Many similar quotations could be given. Guarini died in 1683. The roots of the ideas here elaborated can be traced back to Alberti and Leonardo. Similar ideas had also been advocated by Bernini.

165 *Memorie degli Arch. ant. e mod.*, 1785, I, p. xli ff. It is exceedingly important to find such views

comments on the 'strange notion' that because 'certain uniform and consonant divisions upon one string produce harmony to the ear', 'similar distances in lines belonging to form, would, in like manner, delight the eye. The very reverse of which has been shown to be true . . . yet these sort of *notions* have so far prevail'd by time, that the words, *harmony of parts*, seem applicable to form, as to music.'

The man in whom the new ideas found the most marked expression was Hume. Just as he declared that 'all probable reasoning is nothing but a species of sensation', so he turned objective aesthetic into subjective sensibility. Already in his earliest work, *A Treatise of Human Nature*, published in 1739,[167] he propounded that the distinguishing character of beauty consisted in giving 'pleasure and satisfaction to the soul'. In his essay *Of the Standard of Taste*, first published in 1757, he continued this trend of thought and broke with unprecedented boldness with the basic axiom of all classical art-theory, according to which beauty is inherent in the object provided the latter is in tune with universal harmony. He now explained that 'beauty and deformity, more than sweet and bitter, are not qualities in objects, but belong entirely to the sentiment . . . ' But although he seems to hold the opinion that 'each mind perceives a different beauty . . . To seek the real beauty, or real deformity, is as fruitless an inquiry, as to pretend to ascertain the real sweet or real bitter,' he modifies this radical view by advocating general rules of art derived from experience and 'the common sentiments of human nature'.[168] Like Perrault before him, he is manifestly convinced of aesthetic relativity.

In the same year 1757 appeared Burke's *Enquiry into the Origin of our Ideas of the Sublime and Beautiful*. With his sensual and emotional approach and his exaltation of sublimity he subjected the classical conception of proportion to a detailed analysis and tore it to shreds. He denied that beauty had 'anything to do with calculation and geometry'. Proportion is, according to him, solely 'the measure of relative quantity', a matter of mathematical inquiry and 'indifferent to the mind'. His further analysis shows again that his generation had lost the faculty of understanding even the most general principles of the classical conception. He does not see that the Beauty of the classical theory has its roots in the idea of an all-pervading harmony, which was regarded as an absolute and mathematical truth, and he is therefore unable to grasp that, for instance, ratios of parts of a body remote from each other may be compared. Nor can he understand the relation between the human body and architecture which was, as will be remembered, at the basis of Renaissance thought on proportion. What he says on this point reveals most clearly the complete break with the past which, also for the perception of proportion, the age of empiricism and emotionalism had brought about. 'I know that is has been said long since, and echoed backward and forward from one writer to another a thousand times, that the proportions of building have been taken from those of the human body. To make this forced analogy complete, they represent a man with his arms raised and extended at full length, and then describe a sort of square, as it is formed by passing lines along the extremities of this strange figure.[169] But it appears very clearly to me, that the human figure never supplied the architect with any of his ideas. For in the first place, men are very rarely seen in this strained posture . . . ' Burke winds up with the following remark: 'And certainly nothing could be more unaccountably whimsical, than for an architect to model his performance by the human figure,

expressed by a dogmatic neo-classicist like Milizia.

166 *Analysis of Beauty*, 1753, p. 76 f.

167 Book II, part I, section 8: 'Of Beauty and Deformity'.

168 David Hume, *Essays Moral, Political, and Literary*, ed. Green and Grose, 1889, I, p. 268 ff., 273. See also T. Brunius, 'D. Hume on Criticism', in *Figura*, II, 1952.

169 This refers, of course, to Vitruvius' famous and often illustrated description in Bk. III, chap. 1. Cf. above, p. 25 f.

170 For the passages here quoted cf. the 9th ed., 1782, pp. 175 ff., 181 ff.

171 Cf. the 8th ed., 1807, II, pp. 460 f., 463 and *passim*.

172 Archibald Alison, *Essays on the Nature and Principles of Taste*, Edinburgh, 1790, 5th ed., 1817, I, pp. 13 ff., 317, also II, pp. 20 ff., 33 f.

173 p. 169.

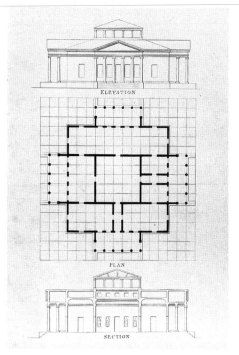

127. Page from J. Gwilt, *Rudiments of Architecture*, 1826

174 However, mathematical ratios survived in a degenerated form as a teaching expedient for architectural students and without any connection with their original meaning. Cf. Fig. 127 which is taken from Joseph Gwilt's *Rudiments of Architecture*, London, 1826. Gwilt's plate is based on J. N. L. Durand, *Précis des leçons d'architecture données à l'Ecole Royale Polytechnique*, 1819-21, a book which contains a large number of similar designs. Durand, in his turn, seems to derive from Vittone's *Istruzioni elementari*, 1760, who claimed to have invented this method, which for him was still more than a purely didactic device.

175 *The Seven Lamps of Architecture*, 1849, in 'The Lamp of Beauty'.

176 Four Vols. First ed. 1901-4, 4th ed. 1915, I, p. 138 f. Cf. also F. Hoeber, *Orientierende Vorstudien zur Systematik der Architekturproportionen*, Frankfurt, 1906, who declares that proportion in architecture as the result of an unconscious process should be the object of study of an aesthetic psychology. For a modern view of an English practitioner cf. T.W. Simpson, *Essays and Memorials*, 1923, p. 54 ff., according to whom 'proportion cannot be reduced to any mathematical or geometrical formula'.

177 I have left the text of the first edition unchanged, although the problem of proportion in art and architecture appears somewhat different today from what it did more than a decade ago. In my paper in DAEDALUS, Winter 1960, I have attempted to give an account of the present position.

since no two things can have less resemblance or analogy, than a man, and a house or temple.'[170]

Lord Kames, in his *Elements of Criticism*, 1761, is perhaps 'reactionary' as compared with Burke, and yet he launched a frontal attack against the translation of musical consonances into architecture. He begins his discussion with the words: 'By many writers it is taken for granted, that in buildings there are certain proportions that please the eye, as in sounds there are certain proportions that please the ear; and that in both equally the slightest deviation from the precise proportion is disagreeable.' From this it is evident that he too was unaware of the deeper bond that for a Renaissance mind united ratios in music and visible objects. He argued, in fact, against the doctrinal Blondel-Briseux-Morris-Preti position. It is therefore only logical when he carries on: 'To refute the notion of a resemblance between musical proportions and those of architecture, it might be sufficient to observe in general, that the one is addressed to the ear, the other to the eye; and that objects of different senses have no resemblance, nor indeed any relation to each other.' In support of this he refers to the octave which is the most perfect musical concord; but a proportion of one to two, he asserts, is very disagreeable in any two parts of a building. Here his eighteenth-century taste contrasts with that of the Renaissance when, as we have seen, a ratio of 1:2 in architecture was regarded as flawless. His main line of attack is not dissimilar to that of the Italian critics. Judgment of proportion rests with the percipient. As we move about in a room the proportions of length to breadth vary continuously, and if the eye were an absolute judge of proportion one 'should not be happy but in one precise spot, where the proportion appears agreeable'. Therefore we can congratulate ourselves that the eye is not 'as delicate with respect to proportion as the ear is with respect to concord'; if it were, this 'would not only be an useless quality, but be the source of continual pain and uneasiness'. Thus, apart from the subjective approach to proportion, Lord Kames introduced as a new element the limitations of human sight – an idea utterly foreign to Renaissance theory.[171]

Alison's theory of association, anticipated by Burke, exposes perhaps most clearly the significance of the revolution which had occurred in the course of the eighteenth century. He maintains that any abstract or ideal standard destroys the function of a work of art. It is the 'trains of thought that are produced by objects of taste', the spontaneous stimulus to the imagination which make a work beautiful and sublime. 'The sublimity or Beauty of Forms arises altogether from the Associations we connect with them, or the Qualities of which they are expressive to us.'[172] In Alison's footsteps Richard Payne Knight in his *Analytical Inquiry into the Principles of Taste*, 1805, declared that proportion 'depends entirely upon the association of ideas, and not at all upon either abstract reason or organic sensation; otherwise, like harmony in sound or colour, it would result equally from the same comparative relations in all objects; which is so far from being the case, that the same relative dimensions, which make one animal beautiful, make another absolutely ugly . . . but the same proportionate combinations of sound, which produce harmony in a fiddle, produce it also in a flute or a harp.'[173] Thus, a pseudo-logical proof was found to show that musical harmony and spatial proportions cannot have anything in common.

Within the terms of a new conception of the world the whole structure of classical aesthetics was systematically broken up, and in this process man's vision underwent a decisive change. Proportion became a matter of individual sensibility and in this respect the architect acquired complete freedom from the bondage of mathematical ratios.[174] This is the attitude to which most architects as well as the public unconsciously subscribed right down to our own days. It is hardly necessary to support this statement with a great many quotations; but brief reference may be made to two authors who interpreted the general feeling on this point. Ruskin declared that possible proportions are as infinite as possible airs in music and it must be left to the inspiration of the artist to invent beautiful proportions.[175] Julien Guadet, in the *Eléments et théorie de l'architecture*, the often re-printed handbook of the students of the 'Ecole des Beaux-Arts' in Paris,[176] explains that in order to establish a dogma of proportions, authors of the past had invoked science. But 'elle n'a rien à voir ici; on a cherché des combinaisons en quelque sorte cabalistiques, je ne sais quelles propriétés mystérieuses des nombres ou, encore, des rapports comme la musique en trouve entre les nombres de vibrations qui déterminent les accords. Pures chimères . . . Laissons là ces chimères ou ces superstitions . . . Il m'est impossible, vous le concevez bien, de vous donner des regles à cet égard. Les proportions, c'est l'infini.'

'Les proportions, c'est l'infini' – this terse statement is still indicative of our approach. That is the reason why we view researches into the theory of proportion with suspicion and awe. But the subject is again very much alive in the minds of young architects today, and they may well evolve new and unexpected solutions to this ancient problem.[177]

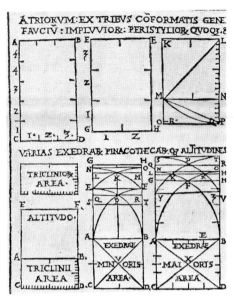

128. Page from Cesariano's *Vitruvius*, Como, 1521

APPENDIX I

Francesco Giorgi's Memorandum for S. Francesco della Vigna

(Translated from Gianantonio Moschini, *Guida per la Città di Venezia*, 1815, I, i, pp. 55-61).

April 1, 1535. In order to build the fabric of the church with those fitting and very harmonious proportions which one can do without altering anything that has been done, I should proceed in the following manner. I should like the width of the nave to be nine paces (1 pace=ca. 1.8 m.) which is the square of three, the first and divine number. The length of the nave, which will be twenty-seven, will have a triple proportion which makes a diapason and a diapente. And this mysterious harmony is such that when Plato in the *Timaeus* wished to describe the wonderful consonance of the parts and fabric of the world, he took this as the first foundation of his description, multiplying as far as necessary these same proportions and figures according to the fitting rules and consonances until he had included the whole world and each of its members and parts. We, being desirous of building the church, have thought it necessary, and most appropriate to follow that order of which God, the greatest architect, is the master and author. When God wished to instruct Moses concerning the form and proportion of the tabernacle which he had to build, He gave him as model the fabric of the world and said (as is written in Exodus 25) 'And look that thou make them after their pattern, which was shewed thee in the mount.' By this pattern was meant, according to all the interpreters, the fabric of the world. And rightly so, because it was necessary that the particular place should resemble His universe, not in size, of which He has no need, nor in delight, but in proportion, which He wills should be not only in the material places, in which He dwells, but particularly in us of whom Paul says, writing to the Corinthians: 'Ye are the Temple of God'. Pondering on this mystery, Solomon the Wise gave the same proportions as those of the Mosaic tabernacle to the famous Temple which he erected. If we, then, follow the same proportions, we shall content ourselves for the length of the nave of the Church with the number twenty-seven, which is three times that of the width, and the cube of the ternary number; beyond which [number twenty-seven] Plato, in the description of the world, would not go, nor would Aristotle in his First Book of 'De Caelo' – having command of the measurements and forces of nature – allow this number to be transgressed in any one body. The truth is that one can increase the measures and numbers, but they should always remain in the same ratios. And whosoever should presume to transgress this rule would create a monster, he would break and violate the natural laws. To this perfect and complete body, we shall now give the head, which is the 'cappella grande'.

As for the length, it should be of the same proportion, or rather symmetry which one finds in each of the three squares of the nave, that is nine paces. I consider it advisable that it should be of the same width as the nave (which as we have said should not be longer than twenty-seven); but [I prefer] that its width be six paces, like a head, joined to the body proportionately and well balanced. And to the width of the nave it will be in the ratio of 2:3 (sesquialtera) which constitutes the diapente, one of the celebrated harmonies. And, as the architects usually approve of the symmetry between the chancel and the transept, we want to make these 'wings' six paces wide, in conformity with the cappella grande. And returning to the length: adding the length of the said cappella to the nave, it forms a quadruple proportion in relation to the width, which forms a bisdiapason, a most consonant harmony. From this symmetry the choir will not be excluded. It will be another nine paces in length and will form a quintuple proportion in relation to the width: which gives it the most beautiful harmony of a bisdiapason and diapente. The width of the chapels will be three paces in triple proportion to the nave of the church which is a diapason and diapente; and with the width of the cappella grande it will be double, which results in a diapason. The chapels will not fail to be proportionate to the other chapels which will be near and adjoining [placed against: *scontri*] the cappella grande; they will be four paces in the sesquitertial ratio, which forms the diatessaron, a celebrated proportion. Thus all the measurements of the plan, lengths as well as widths, will be in perfect consonance, and will necessarily delight those who contemplate them, unless their sight be dense and disproportionate. Now for the altars of the chapels. I recommend that they be outside the square of the chapels, separated from the latter by balusters or railings like a sanctum sanctorum, into which none but the priest with his acolyte can enter. And this will be the case in all the chapels except the two false ones, for which one cannot adhere to this order. I recommend that the church should be kept above the street, and even more so the chapels, where there will be three steps, by which one will ascend to them. This has always been the opinion of everybody, and has already been begun at the cappella grande and the choir. I recommend to have all the chapels and the choir vaulted, because the word or song of the minister echoes better from the vault than it would from rafters. But in the nave of the church, where there will be sermons, I recommend a ceiling (so that the voice of the preacher may not escape nor re-echo from the vaults). I should like to have it coffered with as many squares as possible, with their appropriate measurements and proportions; which squares should be treated in a workmanlike manner with grey paint, a colour which we deem agreeable, and more impressive and durable than others. And these coffers, I recommend, amongst other reasons, because they will be very convenient for preaching: this the experts know and experience will prove it. Turning now to the height, I commend the same as that which M. Giacomo Sansovino has given to his model, namely sixty feet or twelve paces, in the sesquitertial proportion to the width, which results in a diatessaron, a celebrated and melodious harmony. And finding in that model all the other heights of the cappella grande, the medium, and the small chapels thus proportionate, I shall not enlarge on these by going into particulars. Similarly, I recommend the orders of the columns and pilasters to be designed according to the rules of the Doric art, of which I approve in this building as being proper to the Saint to whom the church is dedicated and to the brethren who have to officiate in it. Lastly it remains to speak of the front, which I wish should be in no way a square, but it should correspond to the inside of the building, and from it one should be able to grasp the form of the building and all its proportions. So that inside and outside, all should be proportionate. And this is our final intention, in which there agree with us the generals [of the Order] and the undersigned fathers, i.e. the most reverend 'padre ministro' and the 'Diffinitori.' So that nobody will be able to dare, nor be any more at liberty, to change anything.

Given in our place S. Francesco a Vigna, Venice, April 1st: authenticated in our place S. Lodovico a Ripa, the 25th of the same month, A.D. 1535.

I, F (rate) Francesco Georgio, at the request of the most serene P(adre) have made the above description so that everybody may understand that what one undertakes in this church, is done in accordance with good principles and proportions and so I commend and pray that it may be done.

APPENDIX II

The Problem of the Commensurability of Ratios in the Renaissance

In the text of this book I have returned again and again to the central issue of the Renaissance approach to proportion, namely the commensurability of ratios. Some recent learned publications tend to obscure this question by insisting on the theoretical and practical advocacy of incommensurable, i.e., geometrical proportions by Renaissance architects.[1] I cannot but disagree, not so much with the individual observations made by these scholars as with the more general implications. In an article published in *Architects' Year Book*, V, London, 1953, I stated my assessment of the Renaissance position concisely and since I am still and even more than ever convinced of its correctness, I wish to quote from this paper.[2]

It seems almost self-evident that irrational proportions would have confronted Renaissance artists with a perplexing dilemma, for the Renaissance attitude to proportion was determined by a new organic approach to nature which involved the empirical procedure of measuring and was aimed at demonstrating that everything was related to everything by number. I think it is not going too far to regard commensurability of measure as the nodal point of Renaissance aesthetics. Measuring means for Alberti 'a reliable and uniform [*scil.* commensurable] annotation of quantities, by which as much knowledge is gained about the relation of single parts of a body to each other as about their relation to the whole of a body'.[3] This principle may be checked by surveying Leonardo's many studies in human proportion. In all his studies he used exclusively numerical proportions. He measured and compared the proportions of one part of the body with another and established relationships of small integers such as 1:2 and 1:3 (Fig. 112). By contrast the thirteenth-century sketch-book of Villard de Honnecourt shows studies of figures and animals the proportions of which are determined by a framework of Pythagorean geometry such as equilateral triangles and pentagrams (Fig. 113).

While to the organic, metrical Renaissance view of the world rational measure was a *sine qua non*, for the logical, predominantly Aristotelian Middle Ages the problem of metrical measure could hardly be of similar urgency. Although the Pythagoreo-Platonic concept of the numerical ratios of the musical scale never

1 V. Zoubov, 'Quelques aspects de la théorie des proportions esthétiques de L.-B. Alberti', *Bibliothèque d'Humanisme et Renaissance*, XXII, 1960, p. 54 ff., stresses Alberti's recommendations of incommensurable ratios, but is rather cautious in his conclusions; while Howard Saalman, 'Early Renaissance Architectural Theory and Practice in Antonio Filarete's *Trattato di Architettura*', ART BULLETIN, XLI, 1959, p. 89 ff., who accumulates a mass of valuable information, tends – in my view – to distort the main issues. Completely wayward are such studies as Cesare Bairati, *La simmetria dinamica. Scienza ed arte nell'architettura classica*, Milan, 1952, and George Jouven, *Rythme et architecture: Les traces harmoniques*, Paris, 1951. These authors assume that Hambidge's incommensurable root rectangles ('dynamic symmetry') formed the basis of Italian and French proportion in architecture during the sixteenth and seventeenth, and the seventeenth and eighteenth centuries respectively. On these books as well as on the old myth of the effectiveness of the incommensurable Golden Section, see my paper 'The Changing Concept of Proportion', DAEDALUS, Winter 1960, p. 199 ff.

2 The following three paragraphs, here somewhat revised, essentially correspond to the text in ARCHITECTS' YEAR BOOK.

3 H. Janitschek, *L.B. Albertis kleinere kunsttheoretische Schriften*, Vienna, 1877, p. 179 f. The whole passage in *De Statua* reads as follows: 'Et enim dimensio quantitatum certa et constans adnotatio, qua partium alterius ad alteram inter sese atque singularum ad totam corporis longitudinem habitudo et correspondentia percipitur ad numerumque redigitur.'

4 Otto von Simson, *The Gothic Cathedral*, New York, 1956, p. XX, note 3, maintained that I had overlooked 'that the idea of reproducing in the sanctuary the harmony of the cosmos by means of proportions corresponding to the musical consonances' . . . 'prevailed in the theory and practice of medieval architecture'. I was always well aware of the survival throughout the Middle Ages of the Pythagoreo-Platonic concept of musical propor-

disappeared from mediaeval theological, philosophical, and æsthetic thought, there was no over-riding need to apply them to art and architecture. On the contrary, the mediaeval quest for ultimate truth behind appearances was perfectly answered by geometrical configurations of a decisively fundamental nature; that is, by geometrical forms which were irreconcilable with the organic structure of figure and building. The contrast between Villard de Honnecourt's and Leonardo's proportioning of figures is a typical one: the mediaeval artist tends to project a pre-established geometrical norm into his imagery, while the Renaissance artist tends to extract a metrical norm from the natural phenomena that surround him.

Of course, metrical proportions were used during the Middle Ages[5] – indeed, no building is possible without them – and geometry played a considerable part in Renaissance aesthetics and Renaissance thought. I have only to remind the reader of the importance attached to the circle.[6] On the other hand, it must be asked whether the same numerical and geometrical proportions also had the same meaning in the Middle Ages and the Renaissance. The answer seems to be in the negative. It would appear that during the Middle Ages metrical proportions were not often used as an integrated principle to which all the parts conform. Thus the height of a pier may have a metrical relationship to its diameter, but its height and width are metrically speaking arbitrary within the over-all geometrical pattern of the building.[7] During the Renaissance, by contrast, metrical proportion was the guiding principle of order and reveals the harmony between all the parts, and the parts and the whole. It is for this reason too that Renaissance rather than mediaeval architects embraced Vitruvius' module system, which contained the only guarantee of constant rational relationships throughout a whole building. Turning to geometry, we may choose the square as an example because the square played an exceptional part in mediaeval as well as Renaissance proportion. The late-mediaeval 'just measure' with its squares set into one another consists of an incommensurable geometrical configuration.[8] During the Renaissance artists became aware of the simple numerical ratios of the sides of a square, and in the ratio 1:1 (unison in music) a Renaissance mind found beauty and perfect harmony. It appears that such a simple geometrical figure as the square was used in a metrical and rational as well as in a geometrical and irrational context; it had different functions as a proportional device and may have elicited different reactions.

Support for my interpretation, in addition to the mass of material adduced in the pages of this book, may be gleaned from hundreds of references, left unrecorded. It may be argued, however, that history is never black or white. To be sure, nobody in his senses will deny that mediaeval geometrical concepts survived and were still being used in the Quattrocento. Nevertheless such a statement should not obscure a recognition of the new and characteristic pattern of the Renaissance position. It is even possible to point out precise moments of transition from a primarily goemetrical to an arithmetical approach to proportion. Where Francesco di Giorgio suggests using a mediaeval, incommensurable geometrical scheme for the design of a church, it actually serves to lead him to a rational module.[9] Where Alberti talks about his own (apparently geometrically determined) designs of buildings, he is sadly aware of his errors and of the necessity to adjust them by correct numbers.[10] And where he discusses proportions 'which are not derived from numbers, but from their roots and

tions (see above, pp. 38f, p. 110, etc.), but even von Simson does not convince me that they played an overwhelming part in mediaeval architecture. He does not seem to be convinced himself, for how can he reconcile with the above statement such well-considered conslusions as 'For all we know, the Platonists of Chartres never formulated a system of aesthetics, let alone a program for the arts' (p. 55); 'the Middle Ages . . . actually built with no theoretical science at all' (p. 97); 'the High Middle Ages . . . defined and practised architecture as applied geometry' (p. 33); 'The geometrical formulae used on the west front of Chartres . . .' (p. 155); 'The use of the pentagon by the master of Chartres . . .' (p. 208), etc.? Thus an apparent dichotomy pervades von Simson's book that on many other counts is well worth while studying.
5 P. Frankl, in particular, has dwelled on the employment of a basic measure (yardstick) in mediaeval architecture, see ART BULLETIN, XXVII, 1945, p. 46 ff., and *The Gothic*, Princeton, 1960, p. 66 f.
6 See now also Gerda Soergel's chapter 'Proportionale Kreise', in *Untersuchungen über den theoretischen Architekturentwurf*, Munich, 1958, p. 69 ff.
7 See the very pertinent passages of James Ackerman in ART BULLETIN, XXXI, 1949, p. 105 f., where I find one of the most concise statements on late-mediaeval theory I have come across.
8 See, above all, W. Ueberwasser, 'Nach rechtem Mass', JAHRBUCH DER PREUSS. KUNSTSAMMLUNGEN, LVI, 1935, and Maria Velte, *Die Anwendung der Quadratur und Triangulatur bei der Grund-und Aufrissgestaltung der gotischen Kirchen*, Basle, 1951.
9 H. Millon, 'The Architectural Theory of Francaesco di Giorgio', ART BULLETIN, XL, 1958, p. 257 ff., with a full statement on Francesco di Giorgio's professed methods of obtaining modules. See also Saalman, *ibid.*, 1959, p. 92.
10 *De re aed.*, Bk. IX, chap 10.
11 *ibid.*, Bk. IX, chap. 6.
12 In his Vitruvius commentary of 1521 (see above, p. 22), fol. 98r.

powers',[11] he immediately translates his examples into rational figures, with the only exception of the diagonal of the square ($\sqrt{2}$) 'which cannot be expressed by numbers'. But Cesariano shows on one of his plates (Fig. 128)[12] how even this incommensurable magnitude can be incorporated into a rational system.

ADDENDUM

J.S. Ackerman, 'Ars Sine Scientia nihil est. Gothic Theory of Architecture at the Cathedral of Milan', in ART BULLETIN, XXXI, p. 84 ff.

G.D. Birkhoff, *Aesthetic Measure*, 1933.

Ch.E. Briseux, *Traité du Beau dans les arts*, 1752.

A. Coan, *The Great Modules*, 1914.

S. Colman & A. Coan, *Nature's Harmonic Unity*, 1912.

S. Colman & A. Coan, *Proportional Form*, 1920.

Felix Durach, *Mittelalterliche Bauhütten und Geometrie*, 1929.

C.A. Von Drach, *Das Hüttengeheimnis von gerechten Steinmetzengrund*, 1897.

Silvio Ferri, 'Nuovi contributi esegetici al "canone" della scultura greca', RIVISTA DEL R. IST. D'ARCHEOLOGIA E STORIA DELL'ARTE, VII, 1940, p. 117 ff.

Funck-Hellet, 'L'equerre des maitres d'oeuvre et la proportion', LES CAHIERS TECHNIQUES DE L'ART, 1949, p. 37 ff. .

Funck-Hellet, *Les oeuvres peintes de la Renaissance italienne et le nombre d'or*, 1932.

Matila Ghyka, *The Geometry of Art and Life*, 1946.

G. Giovannoni, 'Tradizione architettonica italiana', *Architetture di Pensiero e Pensieri sull'Architettura*, 1945.

F. Von Juraschek, 'Weiterleben antiker Bauformen an Bauten des achten Jahrhunderts', ZEITSCHRIFT FÜR SCHWEIZERISCHE ARCHAEOLOGIE UND KUNSTGESCHICHTE, XI, 1950 p. 129 ff.

Peter Legh, *The Music of the Eye; or Essays on the Principles of the Beauty and Perfection of Architecture*, 1831.

G. Marchelli, *Trattato d. Proporzioni*, 1759.

V. Monneret de Villard, *La teoria delle proportioni*, 1908.

Robert Morris, *Lectures on architecture consisting of rules formed upon Harmony and Arithmetical Proportion*, 1734.

Ouvrard, *Architecture harmonique, ou l'application de la doctrine des proportions de la musique à l'architecture*, 1639.

John Pennethorne, *The Geometry and Optics of Ancient Architecture*, 1878.

W. Thomae, 'Das Proportionswesen', *Heidelberger Kunstgeschichtl. Abhandlugen*, 1933.

Walter Ueberwasser, *Von Mass und Macht der alten Kunst*, 1933.

Karl Witzel, *Untersuchungen über gotische Proportionsgesetze*, 1911.

John Wood, *Dissertation upon the Orders*, 1750.

H. Wotton, *The Elements of Architecture*, 1624.

A. Zeising, *Neue Lehre von den Proportionen des menschlichen Körpers*, 1854.

APPENDIX III

The Bibliographical Notes on the Theory of Proportion

While the harmonic mathematical conception of architecture was philosophically overthrown in the age of 'nature and feeling' and disappeared from the practical handling of proportion, scholars began investigating a subject which had become historical. With unlimited patience and resourcefulness a great number of contradictory systems, often with a claim to exclusive validity, were worked out which were meant to lead to an understanding of proportion in antiquity, the Middle Ages and the Renaissance.

This literature has been extensive during the last hundred years. The purpose of the following synopsis is to give the reader a few general bibliographical hints. Many of the systems which apply a mathematical formula or a geometric configuration to historical buildings are mutually exclusive. There is no bridge

1 John Pennethorne, *The Geometry and Optics of Ancient Architecture*, 1878.

2 Jay Hambidge, *The Parthenon and other Greek Temples. Their Dynamic Symmetry*, New Haven, 1924. Percy E. Nobbs, *Design. A Treatise on the Discovery of Form*, Oxford Univ. Press, 1937, particularly p. 123 ff., ('Precept in Proportion') calls Hambidge the latest 'architectural astrologer' and deals with proportion entirely under the aspect 'of more recent knowledge of the mechanism of perception'.

3 A. Zeising, *Neue Lehre von den Proportionen des menschlichen Körpers*, Leipzig, 1854. Zeising's 'historic survey of the previous systems' is very useful as an introduction. Zeising had a large following, see F.X. Pfeifer, *Der goldene Schnitt und dessen Erscheinungsformen in Mathematik, Natur und Kunst*, 1885. Interesting bibliographical material is to be found in R.C. Archibald, 'Notes on the Logarithmic Spiral, Golden Section and the Fibonacci Series' in Hambidge's *Dynamic Symmetry*, p. 152 ff.

4 Odilio Wolff, *Tempelmaasse*, Vienna, 1912.

5 F.M. Lund, *Ad Quadratum*, London, 1921. Cf. Theodore A. Cook's criticism of the theories of Lund, Hambidge and Samuel Colman: 'A New Disease in Architecture', *The Nineteenth Century*, 1922, pp. 521-32.

6 Ernest Moessel, *Die Proportion in Antike und Mittelalter*, Munich, 1926; id., *Urformen des Raumes als Grundlagen der Formgestaltung*, Munich, 1931.

7 Viollet-le-Duc, *Dict. rais. de l'architecture*, article 'symmétrie' and *Entretiens sur l'architecture*, Paris, 1863, Vol. I.

For further studies written in French on proportion see E. Henszlmann, *Théorie des proportions*, Paris, 1860; E. Lagoût, *Esthétique nombrée*, Paris, 1863; A. Aurés, *Nouvelle théorie du module, déduite du texte de Vitruve*, Nimes, 1862; L. Cloquet, *Traité d'architecture*, 1901, Vol. V, pp. 49 ff., 165 ff., with further literature; M. Borissavliévitch, *La science de l'harmonie architecturale*, 1925. Marcel-André Texier, *Géométrie de l'Architecte. Essai de géométrie relationnelle*, Paris, 1934, tries to combine hypotheses of various authors.

8 Georg Dehio, *Untersuchungen über das gleichseitige Dreieck als Norm gotischer Bauproportionen*, Stuttgart, 1894, and enlarged in scope: *Ein Proportionsgesetz der antiken Baukunst und sein Nachleben in Mittelalter und in der Renaissance*, Strasbourg, 1895.

9 D.R. Hay, *The Science of Beauty, as developed in Nature and applied in Art*, 1856, contains a summary of the author's previous detailed elaboration of his thesis in several volumes. Of these see particularly: *The Natural Principles and Analogy of the Harmony of Form*, London, 1842. Cf. also

between Pennethorne's[1] findings of harmonic ratios in Greek architecture and Hambidge's 'dynamic symmetry',[2] derived from the root two, three and five rectangles. Zeising believed he had discovered the golden section as the central principle of proportion in macrocosm and microcosm;[3] Odilio Wolff found the solution of the secret in the hexagon,[4] Lund in the pentagon;[5] and Moessel in the 'geometry of the circle'.[6] Viollet-le-Duc's triangulation[7] was modified by Dehio[8] whose results stimulated a younger generation. Hay developed a comprehensive system based on a revival of the Pythagorean law of numbers[9] to which later authors returned, sometimes without a knowledge of Hay's work; recently the Pythagorean conception re-emerged in an American 'Primer of Proportion' for practical use of architects.[10] Claude Bragdon[11] tried, from a theosophical point of view, to translate architectural compositions into musical scores. Thiersch's conclusion,[12] that harmonic proportion results from a repetition throughout essential parts of a building of the same geometric pattern, was accepted by men like Burckhardt,[13] Woefflin[14] and Giovannoni;[15] Thiersch's discovery was certainly of the greatest importance for the history of proportion during the Renaissance, but what was in fact a result was here taken as a cause. In spite of the great variety of purpose and the diversity of systems the combined effort of the last hundred years has put at our disposal a rich and comprehensive material which has helped to clear the way for an understanding of what the builders of the temples, cathedrals and Renaissance palaces thought about proportion. More recent studies by men like Thomae,[16] Ueberwasser,[17] Ghyka,[18] Hautecoeur,[19] and Frankl,[20] have this much in common, that they aim at historically correct interpretations of visual and documentary material rather than at the advocacy of an exclusive system.

In the years after the second war publications on the problem of proportion have increased to such an extent that it has become virtually impossible to keep a check on them. The bibliography by Hermann Graf (*Bibliographie zum Problem der Proportionen*, Speyer, 1958) lists almost two hundred items for the years 1945 to 1958, but is far from complete. Most of the following entries are not listed by Graf. They have been chosen because they are either pertinent to the theme of this book or because of their intrinsic interest, positively or negatively. They are quoted in chronological sequence.

1945: Eva Tea, *La proporzione nelle arti figurative*, Milan.

1946: G. Francesco Malipiero, *L'armonioso labirinto. Da Zarlino a Padre Martini* (1558-1774), Milan.

1948: Joseph Schillinger, *The mathematical Basis of the Arts*, New York (a complicated mathematical treatise).

1949: J.S. Ackerman, 'Gothic Theory of Architecture at the Cathedral of Milan', ART BULLETIN, XXXI, p. 84 ff. (a model investigation).

1950: Paul-Henri Michel, *De Pythagore a Euclide. Contribution à l'histoire des mathématiques préeuclidiennes*, Paris (documentary history of exemplary clarity). Giuliana Traverso, *Il numero in Piero della Francesca*, Milan. Le Corbusier, *Le Modulor*, Boulogne (contains spirited excursions into history). F. Von Juraschek, 'Weiterleben antiker Bauformen an Bauten des achten Jahrhunderts', ZEITSCHRIFT F. SCHWEIZERISCHE ARCHAEOLOGIE UND KUNSTGESCHICHTE, XI, p. 129 ff.

1951: *Nona Triennale di Milano. Studi sulle proporzioni. Mostra bibliografica*, Milan (Catalogue of the Exhibition which accompanied the Milanese Congress on Proportion). Maria Velte, *Die Anwendung der Quadratur und Triangulatur bei der Grund-und Aufrissgestaltung der Gotischen Kirchen*, Basel (see Ackerman's review in ART BULLETIN, XXXV, 1953, p. 155 ff.). P. Sanpaolesi, 'Ipotesi sulle conoscenze matematiche statiche e meccaniche del Brunelleschi', *Belle Arti*, pp. 25-54. C. Funck-Hellet, *De la proportion. L'équerre des maîtres d'oeuvre*, Paris (the most comprehensive of the author's many publications expounding the mysterious qualities of the Golden Section). George Jouven, *Rythme et architecture. Les tracés harmoniques*, Paris (attempt to apply Hambidge's dynamic rectangles to French architecture of the seventeenth and eighteenth centuries).

William Pettit Griffith, *The Natural System of Architecture*, London, 1845.

10 R.W. Gardner, *A Primer of Proportion in the Arts of Form and Music*, New York, 1945. The notion 'area scale' is here introduced as the visual counterpart to the musical scale.

11 Claude Bragdon, *The Beautiful Necessity*, Rochester, N.Y., 1910.

12 August Thiersch in *Handbuch der Architektur*, IV, I, 1883, p. 39 ff. Cf. also John Beverley-Robinson in *Architectural Record*, 1898, p. 297-311. Against Thiersch cf., above all, M. Borissavliévitch, *Les théories de l'architecture*, Paris, 1926 (p. 188 ff.) who denies the objective geometrical foundation of architectural harmony and regards it as a subjective optical phenomenon.

13 Jacob Burckhardt, *Geschichte der Renaissance in Italien*, 6th ed., 1920, p. 98 ff.

14 Heinrich Wölfflin, *Renaissance und Barock*, Munich, 1888, pp. 53-7.

15 Gustavo Giovannoni, *Saggi sulla architettura del Rinascimento*, Milan, 1931, p. 12 ff., and *Architettura di pensiero e pensieri sull'architettura*, Rome, 1945, p. 242 ff.

16 Walter Thomae, *Das Proportionswesen in der Geschichte der gotischen Baukunst und die Frage der Triangulation*, Heidelberg, 1933; see O. Kletzl's excellent review with a wealth of material on Gothic theory and practice, in ZEITSCHR. F. KUNSTGESCHICHTE, IV, 1935, p. 56 ff.

17 Of Ueberwasser's writings cf. particularly 'Nach rechtem Masz', JAHRBUCH DER PREUSS. KUNSTSAMMLUNGEN, 1935, pp. 250-72; also 'Beiträge zur Wiedererkenntnis gotischer Baugesetzmässigkeiten', ZEITSCHRIFT F. KUNSTGESCHICHTE, VIII, 1939, p. 303 ff., with an important review of current research.

18 Matila C. Ghyka's books (*Esthétique des proportions dans la nature et dans les arts*, Paris, 1927, and *Le Nombre d'or. Rites et rythmes pythagoriciens . . .* Paris, 1931), though difficult to digest, contain much valuable material; see particularly his lecture delivered during the International Congress of Art History at Stockholm, 1933: 'Influence de la mystique pythagoricienne des Nombres sur le développement de l'architecture occidentale', summary in *Résumés des communications présentées au congrès*, Stockholm, 1933, p. 263 ff., which has much in common with the theme of the present study. See also his work *The Geometry of Art and Life*, New York, 1946.

19 L. Hautecoeur, 'Les proportions mathématiques et l'architecture', GAZETTE DES BEAUX ARTS, XVIII, 1937, p. 263 ff. Id., *De l'architecture*, Paris, 1938, p. 198 ff. 'Les Proportions'. These two works contain a brilliant summary of the problem.

20 Paul Frankl, 'The Secret of the mediaeval Masons', ART BULLETIN, XXVII, 1945, pp. 46-60.

1952: Matila Ghyka, *A Practical Handbook of Geometrical Composition and Design*, London. Cesare Bairati, *La simmetria dinamica. Scienza ed arte nell'architettura classica*, Milan (attempt to trace root rectangles in the Italian architecture of the sixteenth and seventeenth centuries). C. Bairati, A. Cavallari-Murat, G. Levi-Montalcini, C.Mollino, various studies on proportion in antiquity, in Renaissance and Baroque, on the relativity of proportions, on rhetoric and poetry in proportion; in addition, a full report of the Milan Congress on Proportion, in *Atti e Rassegna tecnica della Società degli Ingegneri e degli Architetti in Torino*, VI, pp. 105-35.

1953: E. Camps Cazorla, *Módulo, proporciones y composición en la arquitectura califal cordobesa*, Madrid. W. Stechow, 'Problems of Structure in some Relations between the Visual Arts and Music', JOURNAL OF AESTHETICS AND ART CRITICISM, XI, p. 324 ff. In addition, my own studies, mentioned in the Preface.

1954: J. Csemegi, 'Die Konstruktionsmethoden der mittelalterlichen Baukunst', *Acta Historiae Artium* (Budapest), II, p. 15 ff. Knud Millich, 'Die Architekturästhetik der italienischen Renaissance', SCHWEIZ. TECHNISCHE ZEITSCHRIFT, LI, p. 385 ff. (discussion of the present book).

1955: R. Arnheim 'A Review of Proportion', JOURNAL OF AESTHETICS AND ART CRITICISM, XIV, pp. 44-57 (mainly concerned with Le Corbusier's modulor and psychological problems of proportion).

1956: Otto von Simson, *The Gothic Cathedral. Origins of Gothic Architecture and the Medieval Concept of Order*, New York (important study, see reference in Appendix II). Paul Booz, *Der Baumeister der Gotik*, Munich-Berlin (see review by R. Branner in ART BULLETIN, XL, 1958, p. 265 ff.). Theodor Fischer, *Zwei Vorträge über Proportionen*, Munich-Berlin (first edition, 1934; a remarkably sober and illuminating little work, although the author accepts some of the antiquated research).

1957: George Lesser, *Gothic Cathedrals and Sacred Geometry*, London (a return to the old 'folklore' on proportion; see R. Branner's review in JOURNAL OF THE SOCIETY OF ARCHITECTURAL HISTORIANS, XVII, 1958, p. 34). 'Report of a Debate on the Motion "that systems of proportion make good design easier and bad design more difficult"', JOURNAL OF THE R. INSTITUTE OF BRITISH ARCHITECTS, LXIV, pp. 456-63.

1958: P.H. Scholfield, *The Theory of Proportion in Architecture*, Cambridge (admirable study, partly derived from the present volume). Gerda Soergel, *Untersuchungen über den theoretischen Architektur-entwurf von 1450-1550 in Italien* (Munich, dissertation; contains valuable research into Alberti's and Leonardo's proportions). Guido Fiorini, *Saggi sui tracciati armonici. Metodo di controllo per via geometrica del rapporto euritmico dei volumi nell'architettura*, Rome (fanciful). M. Borissavliévitch, *Golden Number and the Scientific Aesthetics of Architecture*, London (attempts to establish the beauty of the Golden Section on grounds of a purported aesthetic law). Henry Millon, 'The Architectural Theory of Francesco di Giorgio', ART BULLETIN, XL, p. 257 ff.

1959: Howard Saalman, 'Early Renaissance Architectural Theory and Practice in Antonio Filarete's Trattato di Architettura', ART BULLETIN, XLI, pp. 89-106 (see above, Appendix II). Elizabeth Read Sunderland, 'Symbolic Numbers and Romanesque Church Plans', JOURNAL OF THE SOC. OF ARCH. HISTORIANS, XVIII, pp. 94-103. Rowland J. Mainstone, 'Structural Theory and Design', ARCHITECTURE & BUILDING, XXXIV, pp. 106 ff., 186 ff., 214 ff. (a fresh approach; theories of proportion discussed in terms of guarantors of structural stability).

1960: V. Zoubov, 'Quelques aspects de la théorie des proportions esthétiques de L.-B. Alberti', *Bibliothéque d'Humanisme et Renaissance*, XXII, p. 54 ff. (see above Appendix II). R. Wittkower, 'The Changing Concept of Proportion', DAEDALUS (Winter 1960), pp. 199-215 (concerned mainly with the 'myth' of the Golden Section). Paul Frankl, *The Gothic. Literary Sources and Interpretations through Eight Centuries*, Princeton, p. 702 ff. (a valuable survey of the older literature on proportion as far as the Gothic style is concerned).

APPENDIX IV

Proportion in Art and Architecture

The following essay in five parts is a combination of four previously unpublished lectures and essays written by Professor Wittkower in the early 1950's, shortly after the original publication of *Architectural Principles in the Age of Humanism*. Their titles are as follows:

Lecture: *Proportion in Art and Architecture*; April 19th, 1951, Yorkshire Architectural Society (PAA)

Essay: *Some Observations on Mediaeval and Renaissance Proportions*; Festschrift Essay in honour of Johannes Wilde, 1951 (MRP)

Lecture: *The Search for Proportion*; York, March 14th, 1953 (SP)

Inaugural Address to the *Convegno Internazionale su le Proporzioni nelle Arti*;
Milan, September 27-29th, 1951 (CIPA)
They have been edited into an essay meant to give an overview of Wittkower's
thoughts on proportion. It is hoped that this additional appendix, made possible
by Mrs Margot Wittkower, will provide a broad yet concise explication of the
history and relevance of proportion in the arts. Because sections were taken from
the different works, the source of each paragraph will be noted in footnotes
according to the abbreviations given above in brackets.

Part I: The Need for Order

A 'Convegno Internazionale su le Proporzioni nelle Arti' (International
Convention on Proportion in the Arts) is an historical occasion; never before
have artists and scholars met to discuss their views on this subject and I feel sure
that this opportunity of free discussion will be extremely valuable to all of us.
Although I expect much divergence of opinion, I must stress that all the speakers
have this much in common – they are convinced of the importance of the
problem. There will therefore be no question as to whether such a thing as
systematic proportion in the arts exists or has existed in the past, or is necessary
now and in the future. Some of us – to name only Ghyka and Kayser – have been
writing and talking in public about proportion for almost a generation, and artists
like Le Corbusier have devoted much of their life's work to instilling into
architecture a new, strictly mathematical order.

Compared with these men, I feel rather like a novice, for any interest in these
problems became serious only about ten years ago when I talked to a group of
architectural students on Leon Battista Alberti's opinions about proportion.
Since my talk was purely historical, I was surprised to find that it had an
electrifying effect on the students, and further discussion revealed that the
problem of proportion had a particular urgency for them. It appeared that during
their five years' study there was not a word on proportion under the pretext that
proportion was something to be felt; a sense of order which one has or has not,
but which cannot be taught. And it was for that reason that Alberti's rational
approach to the problem fascinated them.

Since those days many young artists and architects have been my pupils; and it has
struck me time and again that this question of order is uppermost in their minds.
Because this old problem seems to have a greater urgency nowadays than at any
time during the last one-hundred-and-fifty years, I regard it as an event of great
importance that we join forces for a public discussion of proportion in the arts.[1]

Let me begin with a few general observations. Our psycho-physical make-up
demands the concept of order and, in particular, of a mathematical order. The
human body itself is based on symmetry; its two halves equal each other. The
more perfectly it is proportioned, the more beautiful it appears to us. We express
the laws governing all phenomena – those which surround us as well as those of
the universe – in mathematical terms. To give an example: when Galileo studied
the laws of motion, he measured the rate of increase in motion of a falling body
and said, 'It is requisite to know according to what proportion such an acceleration is
made'. Despite the many properties one could note about falling objects, such as
their size or weight, Galileo points out that the over-riding common law of nature
is in the form of the abstract mathematical proportion of acceleration.[2]

If we agree, as I think we must, that we approach nature mathematically, then a large sector of human activity, the arts, cannot be excluded. In fact, it would not be difficult to show that all higher civilizations believed in an order based on numbers; that they sought and established a harmony – perhaps a fanciful and mystical one – between universal and cosmic concepts and the life of man, and that art was expressive of this order and harmony.[3]

The alliance between art and mathematics, then, can be traced back to the oldest civilizations. If it is true that most intellectual activities are concerned with bringing order into the chaos that surrounds us, then the two most radical processes by which this is achieved are surely those of pure science (mathematics) and artistic intuition. Such is the peculiar make-up of the human mind that the one cannot thrive without the other. I may perhaps quote Einstein who told us (and he should know) that there is no logical way to discover elementary laws; there is only the way of intuition which is helped by a feeling for the order lying behind appearance, and this order, inherent in the world of perception, is that of a pre-established harmony. Conversely, the artist's inspiration always leaned upon the unassailable truth of numbers and their relationships because they eemed to reveal something of that pre-established harmony.[4]

Viewed in this light, the procedure of nineteenth- and twentieth-century artists would seem almost contrary to nature. In any case, never before in history has there been a constellation in the arts when proportion – or the principle of order – was left exclusively to the discretion of the individual artist. Once we realize this, our position appears quite extraordinary.[5]

If a quest for a basic order and harmony does in fact lie deep in human nature, can we call it an instinct, like hunger or thirst, or is it due to an intellectual urge? It was my initial contention that the desire for order is inborn. On the other hand, mathematics is the most abstract intellectual occupation. By way of synthesis, I would say that order and proportion in the arts means giving a conscious and intellectual direction to a subconscious impulse.[6]

I want to discuss here the conscious and deliberate use of proportion, not our innate tendency to select, in the act of seeing, simple, regular and symmetrical forms and shapes. It is clear that the artist in his work automatically creates a visual order, often of simple relationships; an order we can check with a pair of dividers. Take the example of Constable's *Lane Near East Bogholt* (1809), a case in which we may be certain that the artist did not apply a premeditated scheme of proportions. One can draw other lines, see other relationships, but this game, to which quite a number of people devote considerable time, is entirely futile. It only teaches us what we know already: that by his selection and arrangement the artist creates a visual order to which we spontaneously respond. Thus artists who, during the last one-hundred-and-fifty or two hundred years, believed that they were following only their intuition, were often dependent on the past, using scraps from old ideas on proportion such as the Golden Section, which I discuss later.[7]

If, however, the desire for order is inborn, is it then the same order for which man has tried to find mathematical equivalents; in other words, is there one and only one system of proportion that is true, right and satisfactory? Most certainly not. I am not being illogical. The fact that there are many true, right, and satisfactory proportions does not prejudice the problem. To make the position clearer, take an instinct like hunger, to which I compared the quest for basic order above: people in different countries and at different periods produced and produce different food to satisfy their hunger. They have different tastes, and this means neither that hunger does not exist nor that one people is right and all the others are wrong. But these are precisely the sort of erroneous attitudes held towards proportion in the nineteenth century. The whole question was either brushed aside (mainly by artists), or treated by historians as if there was only one unassailable truth. However, each of these historians advocated a different truth as fundamental and universally valid. One saw the secret of perfect proportion in the Golden Section, another in the hexagon, a third in the pentagon, a fourth in the circle. In spite of these well-meaning efforts, the artists remained aloof.[8]

Part II: Origins of Western Proportioning Systems

It is in Egypt and Babylon in the third millenium B.C. that we find for the first time a strict mathematical order. How can we explain the fact that artists and architects created rigidly geometrical pyramids, temples and tomb chambers? Surely they were tied to a prescribed order which had been carefully worked out, and which they were neither allowed nor willing to break. Such a situation could only arise in a highly developed and complex social structure, in town civilizations based on a strictly organized hierarchy. The intellectual leadership was in the hands of the priests. It was they who regulated the rites, rituals and ceremonies, and sacred buildings had to conform to the rules laid down by them. Since all great art of the time was sacred art, it reflected or echoed that cosmic order of which the priests were interpreters and custodians.

But when we turn to Greece we are faced with a new situation. In the rising town civilizations of the Greek city-states – and particularly in Athens – we find a new class of free citizens who began a rational inquiry into the nature of the universe. In their hands, mathematics became a theoretical science, and it was they who first attempted to interpret nature mathematically. This unique achievement was never forgotten and, indeed, made our Western civilization possible.[9]

By 550 B.C., in the hands of Pythagoras, geometry had become a theoretical science. He laid the foundation for Euclid who, in about 300 B.C., summarized and systematized the work of the previous two-hundred-and-fifty years; and I need hardly remind you that until not very long ago our geometry was still purely Euclidean. Probably continuing Egyptian usage, Pythagoras applied his theoretical findings to natural phenomena and discovered wonderful and unexpected regularities and relationships. His observations led him to believe that certain ratios and proportions embodied the absolute truth about the harmonic structure of the world. He found support for this belief in the observation that musical consonances depended on invariably fixed relations of the strings of the musical instrument. This was of the greatest importance for the history of proportion in Europe and I must therefore explain it more fully.

If you strike two strings under precisely the same condition, one being half as long as the other, then the pitch of the shorter one is exactly an octave above that of the longer one – that is to say, in arithmetic terms, the ratio 1:2 is necessary to produce an octave. If you halve the shorter string again, this new ratio of 1:2 will produce the same result. The operation has resulted in two octaves which we can express arithmetically as 1:2:4. Now take a string three-quarters the length of the original string: in this case the difference in length is a fourth, which can be expressed by the arithmetical ratio 3:4. Finally, if you take a string two-thirds the length of the original one, the difference in pitch will be a fifth, so that the fifth is expressed by the ratio 2:3.[10]

The Greek musical scale consisted only of three simple consonances, namely the octave, the fifth and the fourth, and two compound consonances, the double octave and the octave plus a fifth, so that the whole harmonic system known to the Greeks was expressed by the ratios 1:2:3:4 (to repeat: 1:2 being the octave, 2:3 the fifth, 3:4 the fourth, 1:4 the double octave and 1:3 the octave plus fifth).

The discovery that all musical consonances are arithmetically expressible by the ratios of the first four integers; the discovery of the close interrelation of sound, space (length of string) and numbers, must have left Pythagoras and his associates bewildered and fascinated, for they seemed to hold the key which opened a door into the unexplored regions of universal harmony. Consequently these Pythagoreans extended their solid findings, and tried to show that the simple ratios of the musical scales are the generating mathematical principle in microcosm and macrocosm. They thought, for instance, that the planets moving in their orbits produced a mighty (though inaudible) orchestra of all the consonances. This was quite logical: they knew that a fast moving body emits a sound (another interrelation between space and music) and consequently that this must be true of the planets. Since their speed varies with their distance from the earth, they were held to produce different tones – tones in accordance with the consonances of the musical scale. This may sound rather fantastic and somewhat removed from the arts, but it is actually closely connected. The concept of the harmony of the spheres was part of the attempt to find a fundamental law (a law of numerical ratios) for all phenomena.[11]

In the wake of Pythagoras and his school, Plato, in his *Timaeus*, attempted the most coherent and imaginative explanation of the world (of course a purely mathematical world) before the rise of modern science, and the influence of the *Timaeus* remained vital for more than two thousand years. In fact, the Pythagoreo-Platonic tradition informed all European systems of proportion. Plato's *Timaeus* was always known, at least in abbreviated versions. Moreover, the essence of that tradition found its way into the most important mediaeval and Renaissance textbooks. The mathematical conceptions of the *Timaeus* were handed on until they re-emerged with the powerful Platonic revival of the fifteenth century.[12]

At this point I must clarify what is meant by the term proportion. Proportion must not be confused with ratio. Ratio is a relation between two quantities, while proportion is the equality of ratios between two pairs of quantities. That is to say, in a true proportion there must be at least three magnitudes: two extremes and a middle term, normally called mean. It was the Greeks, once again, who gave us a system of proportion that was accepted during long periods of the history of mathematics. And it is significant that the three most important types of proportion (the properties of which were clearly recognized by Pythagoras) determine the consonances of the musical scale; indeed, they are essential for the rational arithmetical understanding of musical ratios (our previous demonstration was geometrical).

The first of these proportions is the *geometric* proportion in which the first term is to the second as the second is to the third, for instance, 1:2:4. You will notice that it is this geometric proportion that determines the octave. The second proportion is called *arithmetic* proportion. Here the second term exceeds the first by the same amount as the third exceeds the second, for instance in the proportion 2:3:4 the mean 3 exceeds the first extreme by 1 and is exceeded by 1 by the second extreme. You will notice that the arithmetic proportion determines the division of the octave into fifth and fourth.[13]

The third proportion (a little more difficult to explain) is called *harmonic* proportion. Three terms are in harmonic proportion when the distance of the two extremes from the mean is the same fraction of their own quantity. Take 6:8:12 – the mean 8 exceeds 6 by one-third of 6 and is exceeded by one-third of 12. Now the proportion 6:8:12 divides the octave into fourth and fifth (while, you will remember, the arithmetic proportion divides it into fifth and fourth). Thus you see that these three types of proportion and the musical consonances are closely interlocked; we meet them constantly in Renaissance theory and practice.

We now have a rough impression of the ideas about proportion with which artists of the Renaissance were concerned and which fill the treatises of the fifteenth and sixteenth centuries. We have seen that these conceptions form part of a cultural tradition which came down almost directly from the Greeks; but the Greek heritage had still another aspect which I will try to sketch briefly.[14]

In his *Timaeus* Plato gives us a fascinating kind of atom theory which has some bearing on our problem. He imagined all matter as being built up of the five regular bodies (no more than five solids with equal sides, equal faces and equal angles are possible): tetrahedron, octohedron, cube, icosahedron, and dodecahedron. Plato assigns one of the primary bodies to each of the four elements: the cube to the earth, the tetrahedron to fire, the octohedron to air, the icosahedron to water, and the fifth regular body, the dodecahedron, was taken by him as a symbol of the enclosing sky. I can refrain from further details; the reasons for Plato's procedure are admirably explained in Cornford's work, *Plato's Cosmology*.[16]

The faces of three of these regular bodies consist of equilateral triangles, the simplest shapes from which regular solids can be constructed. The cube may be broken down into triangles by the diagonal which divides each face into two right-angled isosceles triangles. Finally, the dodecahedron consists of twelve pentagons, and the pentagon is built up of isosceles triangles in which the vertical angle is 36° and the base angles are each double that, or 72°.[17]

The construction of the pentagon – as demonstrated in Euclid's elements – is derived from the division of the long sides of the isosceles triangle into extreme and mean ratio. What Euclid called 'to cut a line into extreme and mean ratio', what Plato before him simply called the section, is today called the Golden Section, in which the smaller part is related to the larger as the larger part is to the whole. The beauty of this particular proportion had always been acknowledged because instead of four terms, as in the proportion a:b=c:d, or three terms, as in the proportion a:b=b:c, the proportion of the Golden Section consists of only two terms, namely a:b=b:a+b.[18]

Consider for a moment what we have found: the equilateral triangle, the square or cube, the right angle isosceles triangle (the diagonal of a square), the pentagon – all these figures were charged by Plato with deep and even mystic significance. I think it is due to the emotional importance attached to them by the Greek mind that these geometrical forms had an extraordinary influence on the European conception of proportion.[19]

Part III: Geometry and Mediaeval Proportions

Now Plato, in the *Timaeus*, employed two kinds of Pythagorean mathematics. His explanation and division of the world soul is based on the numerical ratios derived from the harmonic intervals of the Greek musical scale. But when dealing with what might be called his atom theory – the ordering of chaos – Plato reverts to the most simple and (as it appeared to him) the most geometrical figures.[20]

No lengthy demonstration is necessary to prove that in the history of European art two classes of proportion are used, namely proportions of aliquot numbers, and proportions which – as we shall see – cannot be expressed arithmetically, but are based on fundamental geometrical figures, such as triangles and pentagons. The first type of proportion, the arithmetical one, was favoured during the Renaissance, while the second type, the geometrical one, was preferred during the Middle Ages. I am convinced that both approaches to proportion ultimately derived from the *Timaeus*. It is not difficult to follow through the ages the transmission of Pythagoreo-Platonic mathematics. In fact, the *Timaeus* remained the only Platonic work known at all times, and there was, as Kablinsky maintains, 'hardly a mediaeval library of any standing which had not a copy of Chalcidius' version' of it. Moreover, such mediaeval and Renaissance textbooks as Boetius' *De Musica* and *De Arithmetica,* Macrobius' *In Somnium Scipionis* and, last but not least, Vitruvius' *De Architectura* (used during the Middle Ages in abbreviated versions) handed on – directly or indirectly – mathematical conceptions of the *Timaeus*.

Generally speaking, equilateral triangle, square and pentagon formed the basis of mediaeval aesthetics. It is unlikely that, as a rule, mediaeval builders were conscious of the cosmic implications found in the *Timaeus,* and yet they could visualize their work only in relation to one of these basic geometrical forms. I will give two examples of this.[21]

The first instance is that of Milan Cathedral. The Milanese, not having an able architect amongst them, called in a Frenchman and a German in succession. At the decisive meeting in 1391, the question was discussed as to whether 'this church ought to rise according to the square or the triangle. It was stated that it should rise up to the triangular figure and not farther.' The basis for the design was, in other words, the equilateral triangle. In 1392 the decision was reversed and the new plan was placed into a grid of squares. However, building had meanwhile been started according to triangulation and was continued up to the height of the piers of the aisles. But the elevation of the nave appeared too high and it was decided to switch over to another geometrical pattern. The interesting thing is that one would not just lower the nave in order to achieve the desired effect, but that it was felt that, if the nave had to be lowered, it must be done in accordance with an established geometrical concept. This was found in the celebrated Pythagorean triangle, a triangle which I have not mentioned before, but which had always been given a place of honour since its sides are related as 3:4:5 – the only 90° triangle in which the sides are in an arithmetical progression. (The particular qualities of this triangle were described in Vitruvius' Ninth Book, which regarded it as a Pythagorean invention).[22]

The second example is the interesting case of S. Petronio at Bologna, a church which had been started on a vast scale in 1399. Building progressed slowly and dragged on into the sixteenth century, when a considerable reduction not only of extension but also of height appeared necessary. An engraving dated 1592 was published as a protest against reduction of height. The critic suggests that by abandoning the mediaeval triangulation the church would lose proportion and coherence.[23]

To return to the square: we have seen that a grid system was at one time applied to the plans of Milan Cathedral. But the grid system was not the only use that was made of the square. There exists a small number of printed books dating from the end of the fifteenth and the beginning of the sixteenth centuries in which the mediaeval building tradition is fully explained. The author of such a book (entitled *On Pinnacles*) writes: 'If you want to make a plan of a pinnacle according to the mason's tradition, and geometrically correct, begin with the square.' Next he inscribes a square whose corners meet at the centre points of the sides of the original square. The surface of this inscribed square is precisely half of that of the original square. Into this square he inscribes yet another square using the same method (and so on). Turning the second square by 45° we have gained three squares with sides parallel to each other, and these squares give us the diminishing tiers of the pinnacle. This method had a very wide application, and we can trace it back to the earliest surviving notebook of an architect, dating from the thirteenth century. Again when we open Vitruvius we find the principle of the method explained, this time given as an invention of Plato. The use of the method was not confined to architecture; we also find it in painting and as late as the sixteenth century.[24]

Consider the geometric patterns in the work of Edward Schoen, a German artist and follower of Dürer. If we had only the finished engravings, it would be difficult to make a correct guess as to the geometrical basis of design. But that does not mean that the geometrical framework is arbitrary. Artists of the past attached such importance to it that they never did without it, even when they designed objects for use.

A case in point is a peculiar instrument invented by Dürer. It is what he called 'a pair of serpent compasses', with which one could, he maintained, construct serpent lines. I mention it not for the improbable performance of this strange instrument, but because Dürer published a geometrical design according to which it should be built – a purely aesthetic consideration which has nothing to do with the usefulness of the compasses. It is significant that the discs, and lengths and diameters of the arms are all based on the division of the square which we have just studied. Dürer says in his text that the relation of one part to the other should be according to the just measure. It is not idle to speculate for a moment on the fact that useful objects of past ages appear so satisfactory and even beautiful when we see them in museums – it is due to the stringent laws of proportion to which they were submitted.[25]

I may perhaps quote here Robert Grosseteste, Bishop of Lincoln, contemporary of Villard de Honnecourt, commentator of Aristotle and Boethius, and one of the greatest mediaeval theologians and philosophers. He pronounced that 'it is impossible to know nature without geometry. The principles of geometry have absolute value throughout the universe and for each of its parts. It is by lines, angles, and geometrical figures that all natural phenomena must be understood.' And we may amplify this statement by the mediaeval conception of the relation between the pre-established form and its man-made image: 'Form (and we may now say pre-established geometrical form) is the model which the artist has in his mind (forma est exemplar ad quod respicit artifex), so that he can make his work an imitation which resembles it (ut ad eius imitationem et similitudinem formet suum artificium).'[26]

This may sound Platonic, but it tells us something typically mediaeval about the artist and his work; namely that the mediaeval artist tends to project a pre-established geometrical norm onto his imagery, while the Renaissance artist tends to extract, as we have seen, a metrical norm from the natural phenomena that surround him. Dürer, after his early Gothic and implicitly geometrical beginnings, declared when returning from Italy: 'The lines determining a figure can be constructed neither with compasses nor ruler', implying, of course, that they can only be expressed by numerical ratios.[27]

Part IV: Renaissance Proportions and Commensurability

Once we have agreed that the ultimate source for both mediaeval and Renaissance proportion is to be found in the Pythagoreo-Platonic world of mathematical concepts, the question arises why it happened that the geometrical side of this tradition prevailed during the Middle Ages and the arithmetical side triumphed during the Renaissance. For an answer we must first inquire a little further into the properties of both kinds of proportion. The arithmetic proportions, as epitomized in the ratios of the Greek musical scale, consist of integral numbers or simple fractions; they consist, in a word, of commensurable ratios. By contrast, many of the proportions based on the geometry of the *Timaeus* cannot be expressed by integral numbers or simple fractions, and thus they are incommensurable. In the equilateral triangle, for instance, the height (that is the perpendicular) is incommensurable to the length of the sides, and if we want to explain this relation arithmetically we have to turn to the square root for help, in this case to $\sqrt{3}$. The hypotenuse of the right-angled isosceles triangle, that is the diagonal of the square, is related to the shorter sides which contain the right angle $1:\sqrt{2}$. All of this is by no means mysterious, and can easily be demonstrated by applying Pythagoras' theorum.[28]

It seems self-evident that irrational proportions would have confronted Renaissance artists with a perplexing dilemma, for the Renaissance attitude to proportion was determined by a new organic mathematical approach to nature in which everything was related to everything by number (i.e. arithmetic versus geometry). I think it is not going too far to regard the commensurability of measure as the nodal point of Renaissance art. Measuring means for Alberti (*De Pictura*) 'a reliable and *definite* (*viz* commensurable) annotation of dimensions, by which as much knowledge is gained about the relation of single parts of a body to each other as about their relation to the whole of a body.' Indeed, the concept of commensurability lies behind the emergence of the metrical, rational space of Renaissance perspective. (For a further discussion of commensurable ratios in the Renaissance see Appendix II).[29]

If this analysis is right, we may explode the old and continuously repeated myth of the predominant role of the Golden Section in the age of the Renaissance. It is true that Luca Pacioli published his *De Divina Proportione* in 1609; it is also true that his friend Leonardo designed the illustrations of the regular solids for this work; finally, it is true that the five Platonic bodies – and amongst them the dodecahedron with its close relation to the Golden Section – had a particular fascination for the artists of the Renaissance. To that extent they also absorbed the geometry of the *Timaeus*. But they studied these problems qua problems of space and not of proportion. Most art theorists of the Renaissance, in fact, carefully avoided discussing the Golden Section. To my mind, they omitted it because its irrational properties could not be reconciled with 'a reliable and definite annotation of dimensions'. Moreover the Golden Section was only of secondary importance in practice. In the most important group of Renaissance studies in proportion, those by Leonardo, we never find – in accordance with our expectations – a deliberate use of irrational magnitudes. [30]

In the case of the human figure, much studied by Leonardo, an absolute metrical relationship of part to part and of the parts to the whole can only be expressed by postulating a standard of measurement, such as the head or the face. Then we can say that the total height of an ideally proportioned figure should be eight heads or ten faces, that the length of the hand should equal that of the face, and so on. The greatest artists of the fifteenth and sixteenth centuries devoted endless labour to the working out of these metrical relationships. This work was not only theoretical, but was of great importance in practice. Even sitters were made to comply with ideal proportions, as in the case of the thick-set Charles V painted by Titian. [31]

Moreover, ideal proportions (in the sense of metrical relationships) were found in classical statues such as the Apollo Belvedere. The proportions and even the pose of such figures were applied by classically-minded artists to their sitters, as seen in some of the works of Sir Joshua Reynolds.

Turning from the human figure to architecture, we find the same method employed. If you study a detail of the basis of a column, by Piero della Francesca, you will see that every part is related to the other by, and only by, commensurable numbers. The diameter of the column was the unit of measurement, following Vitruvius. [32]

Architects like Palladio strictly applied numerical ratios to their buildings. I refer to the plan of his Villa Thiene; the inscribed dimensions make his intentions quite clear. The rooms are based on the harmonic series 12:18:36, 12:36 representing the ratio 1:3; 12:18, the ratio 2:3; and 18:36 the ratio 1:2. The principle of Palladio's procedure is, I think, perfectly clear. I do not suggest that Palladio or any other Renaissance architect or artist translated musical into visual proportions, but they regarded the consonant intervals of the musical scale as the audible proof for beauty and perfection. You find a full statement of this in the writings of Renaissance artists and critics. Alberti, in his *Ten Books on Architecture* (written about 1450) referred to Pythagoras and said that 'the numbers by means of which the agreement of sounds affects our ears with delight are the very same which please our eyes and mind'. And Alberti submits an arithmetical theory of proportion which is derived from the harmonic intervals of the musical scale. [33]

Renaissance artists and architects believed in an all-embracing numerical harmony in terms of the Pythagoreo-Platonic tradition. A visual demonstration is supplied in Raphael's *School of Athens* (Fig. 119), where he shows Pythagoras and before him a young man holding up to him a tablet on which the consonances of the Greek musical scale (with their Greek names) are represented in diagrammatical form (expressed by the ratios 6:8:9:12).

In Raphael's time the Pythagoreo-Platonic tradition was hardly less important than the truth of revealed religion. In fact, the philosophical work of the Renaissance was focused on the attempt to reconcile Plato and Christianity. One tried to interpret the great harmony created by God in terms of Platonic numerical order. Artists were convinced that their work should echo this universal harmony. If not, it was discordant and out of tune with universal principles.

Numerical ratios are, as it were, the hard core of Renaissance proportion. They can only be achieved in the arts and in architecture if part to part – down to the minutest details – and part to the whole are related to a common unit. A particular mode of measuring had to be devised in order to make it possible to apply a coherent numerical system of relationships throughout a figure, a picture or a building, and this unit had to be adaptable from case to case.[34]

I want to end my purely historical survey at this point. The past can, I think, teach us a lesson concerning our problems today. Our interpretation of nature is basically mathematical, and in this respect European civilization stands and always will stand on the shoulders of the Greek achievement; yet important shifts in the cultural setting have led, and are bound to lead in the future, to a revision of the principles of order in the arts.[35]

Part V: Post-Renaissance Proportioning – Dilemmas and Possibilities

We have seen that the two systems of proportion widely current in European art – the geometrical and the metrical – both stem from the same Pythagoreo-Platonic tradition. It was only in the eighteenth century that this tradition began to break down. Until then it was never doubted that objective standards of proportion are a basic requirement in a work of art (even though nobody was so naïve as to think that absolute measure can be perceived).[36]

In the new era, beauty and proportion were no longer regarded as being universal, but were turned into psychological phenomena originating and existing in the mind of the artist. Burke for instance refuted categorically the Pythagoreo-Platonic notion that beauty resides in certain fundamental and universally valid proportions and he maintained that 'proportion is a matter solely of mathematical inquiry and indifferent to the mind'.[37]

Thus beauty and proportion became dependent on what was believed to be an irrational creative urge. This was the artist's answer to the new conception of the universe which emerged from the seventeenth century onwards – a universe of mechanical laws, of iron necessity with no ulterior plan – where in contrast to the older civilizations and for the first time in history, man had lost his unique and privileged place. Never before in history (at least in the history of higher civilizations) had circumstances led to a situation in the arts where the principle of order was left exclusively to the discretion of the individual artist.[38]

Whether we are fully conscious of our place in history or not, we are tied to the prevailing trends of our time as much as the builders of the pyramids, of the Greek temples, or the Renaissance churches. However, history is never static and there are signs everywhere of a desire for a new integration of all the activities of the mind. In fact, a reversal of the artist's approach to proportion began as early as the first decade of this century with the work of the Cubists, who cast conventional forms to the wind, endeavouring to return to basic geometrical shapes. But since they thought in terms of the dynamic space-time relationships of modern mathematics, they found salvation in incommensurable ratios focused on the Golden Section.[39]

A serious new departure belongs to the recent past. I mean Le Corbusier's Modulor. In the light of history it appears as a fascinating attempt to co-ordinate tradition with our non-Euclidean world. By taking, instead of universals, man in his environment as his starting point, Le Corbusier accepted the shift from absolute to relative standards. But on this level he accepts a new consolidation. The older systems of proportion were what I might call one-track systems, in so far as they were coherent developments of basic geometrical or numerical concepts. This is not true for Le Corbusier's Modulor. Its elements are extremely simple: square and double square. These basic geometrical shapes are blended with two divergent series of irrational numbers derived from the Golden Section[40]

At the same time the Modulor testifies to the coherence of our cultural heritage. Like the proportions of plane geometry used in the Middle Ages and like the arithmetical musical proportions of the Renaissance, Le Corbusier's dual system of irrational magnitudes is still dependent on the conceptions which Pythagoreo-Platonic thought opened up for Western man. Other examples of a renewed quest for order lie outside the realm of art. Various disciplines such as philosophy, physics, natural science, mathematics and psychology are approaching the same fundamental question from different angles. Physiologists, for example, enquire how sense stimuli are ordered in the brain; how it happens that orderly patterns are created from a chaotic multitude of impressions. Similarly, *Gestalt*-psychologists are concerned with the organizing force of the human brain which tends to extricate simple and regular forms from a maze of complex sensations. Biologists, histologists and crystallographers are studying the geometry of animal and plant life and of crystals, and mathematicians and physicists of the calibre of Whitehead and Einstein re-asserted the essentially Platonic concept of pre-established harmony.[41]

All this has only strengthened our conviction that the quest for a basic order and harmony lies deep in human nature. But isn't such an assertion – aren't all the findings of modern research – an implicit support of the nineteenth-century position that the artist should be guided only by his intuition to create order out of chaos? Such a conclusion would be a fallacy. It is a truism to say that the artist is a sounding board of the civilization in which he lives.

And here I have come at last to the problems that lie before us today. What is the pattern of our civilization? We all know that when, at the end of the last century and the beginning of this one, non-Euclidian geometry became the basis of the modern view of the universe, the break with the past was as fundamental – or even more fundamental – than the break between the scholastic hierarchy of the Middle Ages and the Euclidean mathematical universe of Leonardo, Copernicus, and Newton. What bearing on proportion in the arts will the replacement of absolute measures of space and time with the new dynamic space-time relationship have? Such and similar questions will loom for years to come. By attacking these problems from various angles – historical, mathematical, physical, technical – we can try to clarify our own position according to our own approach. Inevitably, the artist will always be faced with the problem of balance between intuition and law, freedom and necessity. Surely there is no correct way, no safe way, and no single way to good proportion in the arts.[42]

The abbreviations refer to the four unpublished lectures and essays listed at the beginning of this appendix, and the page numbers are those of the original manuscripts.

1 CIPA, pp 1-2

2 PAA, p. 1.	22 PAA, p 13.
3 PAA, p. 2.	23 PAA, pp. 14-15.
4 SP, p. 1.	24 PAA, pp. 15-16.
5 PAA, p. 2.	25 PAA, p. 16.
6 PAA, p. 3.	26 CIPA, pp. 13-14.
7 SP, p. 2.	27 CIPA, p. 14.
8 PAA, pp. 3-4.	28 MRP, pp. 6-7.
9 CIPA, p. 3.	30 MRP, p. 7.
10 SP, p. 4.	31 SP, p. 11.
11 SP, P. 5.	32 PAA, p. 18.
12 SP, P. 6.	33 SP, p. 9.
13 PAA, p 10.	34 SP, p. 10.
14 PAA, P 11.	35 CIPA, p 16.
15 PAA, P. 12.	36 SP, p 17.
16 MRP, P 2.	37 SP, p. 18.
17 PAA, p 11.	38 CIPA, p. 5.
18 PAA, p 12.	39 PAA, p. 20.
19 PAA, P. 13.	40 PAA, pp 18-19.
20 SP, pp. 6-7.	41 CIPA, p. 5.
21 PAA, p. 13.	42 CIPA, p. 6.

Index

Figures in italics refer to pages containing illustrations

Academies, della Crusca, 60; Olympic, Vicenza, 66, 129; Platonic, Florence, 62, 130; royale de l'architecture, Paris, 131; Trissiniana, Vicenza, 62, 63, 107; Vitruvian, 22.
Ackerman, James, 40, 141, 142, 143.
Al-kindi, 128.
Albanese, Francesco, 64.
Albani, Francesco, 114.
Alberti, Leon Battista, 22, 26-31, 34, 38, 39, 41ff., 70, 76, 82, 89, 91, 95-100, 107-109, 111ff., 113, 114, 117, 121, 123, 130, 131, 133, 134, 140, 141; and Michelozzo, 17; and Palladio, 31, 34, 64, 70, 75, 108, 109; programme of ideal churches, 16-19; proportion of rooms, 108, 111ff.; views on arches, 18, 42f.; on basilicas, 18, on beauty, 18, 41; on columns, 41ff., 46, 51, 53; on entablature, 42, 55; on pilasters, 42; Ten Books on Architecture, 16ff., 26, 41, 42, 51, 89, *16*, 145.
Alchindo or Al-Kindi, 128.
Alessi, Galeazzo, 82.
Alison, Archibald, 135, 136.
Allers, Rudolf, 25, 113.
Alpharani, Tiberio, 91.
Ammanati, Bartolomeo, 34, 82.
Ancona, Arch of Trajan, 56, *57*.
Angaranno, Count Giacomo, 63.
Anthropomorphism and architecture, see: Harmony.
Appianus, Alessandrinus, 63.
Archimedes, 129.
Archibald, R.C., 142.
Architecture associated with *virtus*, 63f., 65f.; as applied mathematics, 39, 66, 117, 142; Palladio's universal precepts of, 67; see also: cosmic order; dome; harmony; musical theory.
Ardizoni, Pellegrino, 53f.

Aretino, Pietro, 64, 107.
Aristotle, 39, 60, 64-66, 105, 106, 107, 117, 127, 128, 129, 138, 151.
Arithmetic mean, see: Means.
Arnheim, R., 144.
Asolo, Villa Maser, 64, 65, 73, 103, 125f., church at, 34.
Atrium, see: Roman house.
Augustine, 38, 123.
D'Azara, Giuseppe Niccola, 133.

Bagnolo, Villa Pisani, *69*, 124, *125*.
Bairati, Cesare, 140, 143.
Baptistery, nr. Lateran, 17.
Barbaro, Daniele, 64ff., 80, 116, 127, 128, 129; Vitruvius ed., 64ff., 70, 76, 80, 116, 127ff.
Barca, Allessandro, 133.
Baron, 38.
Basilica at Fano, 91, *92*, 93, 94.
Bassano, 133, 134.
Bassi, Martino, 115.
Battista, Giovan, 116.
Baum, 50.
Beauty, definition of, 31, 41, 128.
Behn, 1, 112.
Belli, Silvio, 129.
Beltrami, L., 26, 91.
Belvedere, Apollo, 153.
Bembo, 60, 64.
Bernardo, Gio. Battista, 86.
Bernini, 76, 103, 134.
di Bertino, Giovanni, 49.
Beverley-Robinson, John, 143.
Billing, R., 29.
Biondo, 63.
Birkhoff, G.D., 142.
Blondel, François, 131.
Blunt, Anthony, 32, 40, 88, 114, 116.

Boethius, 109, 119, 127, 150, 151.
Bologna, S. Petronio, 97, 150.
Borissavliévitch, 142, 143, 144.
Borromeo, Carlo, 40.
Bottari, 47, 114, 129, 133.
Bragdon, Claude, 143.
Braghirolli, 17, 52, 53.
Bramante, Donato, 22, 25, 26, 29, 32, *33*, 34, *36*, 37, 42, 56, *74*, 75, 82, 91, *92*, 97, 107.
Bramantino, 29.
Brandi, Cesare, 43.
Branner, R., 144.
Brescia, Cathedral, 97, 111; Palazzo del Comune, 75; S. Maria de' Miracoli, 29.
Briseux, 131, 132, 134, 142.
Brunelleschi, 17, 29, 42, 45, 55, 113.
Bruyne, Edgar de, 26.
Burckhardt, Jacob, 15, 39, 143.
Burger, 68, 73.
Burke, 135, 136, 154.
Burnet, John, 113.

Caesar, 63.
Calvi, Fabio, 22.
di Cambio, Arnolfo, 49.
Campanella, Tommaso, 40.
Camps Cazorla, E., 144.
Canova, 134.
Cantaneo, Pietro, 40.
Cantor, Moritz, 100.
Caradosso, 34.
Capra, Conte Giulio, 121.
delle Carceri, Madonna, 34.
Carpi, Cathedral, 96.
Cassirer, E., 38, 130.
Cassius, Dio, 19.
Castiglione, 22.
Castelfranco, Cathedral, 96.

Cavalari-Murat, 144.

Centrally planned church, 15ff.; and classical structures, 17; and cult of the virgin, 40; and liturgy, 15, 22; religious symbolism of, 38ff.; see also: Leonardo.

Cerrati, M., 40, 91.

Cesariano, 22, *24*, 25, 91, *92, 137*.

Cessalto, Villa Zeno, 68, *69*, 127.

Chalcidius, 150.

Charles V, 60, 115, 153.

Churches, altars in, 17; basilical plan of, 18; composite plan of, 20, 100; Early Christian, 17; façade problems of, 45, 47, 55, 59, 89ff., 95, 97; Greek Cross plan of, 26, 29, 31, 34, 39, 52; Latin Cross plan of, 15, 34, 39, 40, 97; oval plan of, 26; see also: Centrally planned church.

Cicero, 19.

Cicogna, Villa Thiene, 68, *69, 122*, 123.

Cicognara, Leopoldo, 133.

Circle, symbolism of, 17ff., 20, 22-26, 31f., 34-39, 40, 107, 162, see also: Centrally planned church.

Civita Castellana, Cathedral, nr. Rome, 55.

Clark, Sir Kenneth, 26.

Coan, A., 142.

Cola da Capravola, 26.

Colman, S., 142.

Comolli, A., 131.

Constable, 146.

Contarini, Giacomo, 64.

Cook, Theodore A., 142.

Copernicus, 155.

Corelli, 134.

Cornaro, Luigi, 63.

Cornford, F.M., 105, 106, 109.

Cortona, S. Maria Nuova, 37.

Cosmic order, expressed in architecture, 18, 19, 32, 38, 104; and harmony, 105.

Crema, S. Maria della Croce, 29.

Cristiani, Girolamo Francesco, 133.

della croce, Angelo, 29.

Csemegi, J., 144.

de Cusa, Nicholas, 19, 38.

Cusanus, 38.

Dalla Pozza, A.M., 60, 63, 75, 76.

Danti, Vincenzo, 104.

Davari, 52.

Dehio, Georg, 142, 143.

Derizet, Antoine, 133.

Diedo, Vincenzo, 88, 89.

Diels, H., 117.

Dinsmoor, 22, 26.

Dionysius, Areopagite, see: Pseudo-Dionysius.

Dionysius of Halicarnassus, 63.

Dome, cosmic significance of, 19, 29, 37.

Donato, Bernardino, 61.

Doni, A.F., 22.

Donne, 130.

Dosio, 82, 93.

Von Drach, C.A., 142.

van Drival, 40.

Dryden, 130.

Durach, Felix, 142.

Durand, J.N.L., 38, 136.

Dürer, 64, 151, 152.

Egger, H., 29, 93.

Einstein, 146, 155.

Eisler, Robert, 19.

Emperor Constantine, 17.

Ermers, M., 29.

Etruscan temple, 16, 56.

Euclid, 129, 147, 149.

Eurythmia, 51.

Eurythmy, 128.

Eutropius, 63.

Ezekiel, 116.

Falconetto, 82.

Fancelli, Luca, 53, 56, 119.

Fanzolo, Villa Emo, *69, 72*, 126.

Fasolo, G., 68, 86.

Fauno, 63.

Favaro, Giuseppe, 25.

Federici, P., 133.

Fenoglio, 115.

Ferrara, S. Giovanni Battista, 29, S. Spirito, 29.

Ferri, Silvio, 142.

Ficino, Marsilio, 25, 38, 105, 106, 109.

Filarete, Antonio, 19, 67, 144.

Filiberto, Emanuele, 115.

Finale, Villa Saracenco, 120.

Fiocco, 60, 80.

Fiorini, Guido, 144.

Fischer, Theodor, 144.

Florence, Baptistery, 17, 26, 49; Cathedral, 20, 49; Loggia degli Innocenti, 43; SS Annunziata, 17, 19, 29; S. Maria degli Angeli, 29; S. Maria Novella, 43, 46f., *48*, 49f., *51*, 51f., 52, *59*, 97, 122; S. Miniato, 42, 49; Orti Oricellari, 62; Cappella Pazzi, 45, 55; Palazzo Rucellai, 82; Pandolfini, 82; Ricetto, 86; Uffizi, drawings, 55, 93; see: Manuscripts.

Fogliano, Ludovico, 124.

Fontana, C., 93.

Fra Giocondo, 22, *24*, 25.

della Francesca, Piero, 105, 153.

Frankl, P., 15, 56, 141, 143, 144.

Fratta, Polesine, Villa Badoer, 68, *69*.

Frey, D., 15, 20, 22.

Frommel, C.L., 91.

Fulvio, 63.

Funck-Hellet, 142, 143.

Gafurio, 117, *118*, 119.

Galiani, 133.

Galileo, 130, 145.

Gallo, R., 89.

García, Simón, 115.

Gardner, R.W., 143.

Gaye, 17, 19.

Genova, S. Maria di Carignano, 37.

Georgi, Francesco, 119, 104, 105, 106, *106*, 107, 109, 110, 111, 112, 115, 117, 138, 140.

von Geymüller, 11, 22, 26, 29, 31, 45, 59.

Ghiberti, 127, 128.

Ghizzole, Villa Ragona, 124.

Ghyka, Matila C., 143, 144.

Gilpin, William, 131.

Giocondo, Fra, 119.

di Giorgio, Francesco, 20, *21*, 22, *24*, 25, 26, 67, 108, 122, 141.

Giovannoni, Gustavo, 26, 82, 142, 143.

Golzio, V., *24*, 119.

Gombrich, E., 38, 82.

Gonzaga, Lodovico, 52, 53, 56.

Gotti, Aurelio, 22.

Grabar, A., 19.

Graf, Hermann, 143.

Grand Duke of Tuscany, 63.

Grayson, Cecil, 16, 46, 47, 113.

Greek architectural theory, 107; house, 76, 80; musical theory, 105, 106, 110, 119, 124, 130.

Griffith, William Pettit, 143.

Grosseteste, Robert, 151.

Guadet, Julien, 137.

Gualdi, Girolamo, 60, 64.

Gualdo, Giuseppe, 62.

Guarini, 103, 134.

Gwilt, J., 136, *136*.

Hambidge, Jay, 108, 140, 142, 143.

Harmonic mean, see: Means.

Harmony, expressed in architecture, 18, 41, 50, 68, 104, 108f., 110, 115f., 119, 122, 127, 139, 142f.; of the human body, 18, 22-25, 104, 114, 128; of the universe, 25, 38, 105, 106, 109, 113, 119, 130, 139; See also: Proportion, Ratios.

Hautecoeur, Louis, 19, 143.

Hay, D.R., 142, 143.

Heath, Sir Thomas, 108, 110.

Heemskerk, 93.

Henry III of France, 88.

Henszlmann, E., 142.

de Herrera, Juan, 115.

Hettner, H., 119.

Heydenreich, L.H., 20, 26.

Hirsch, Dr. Paul, 117.

Hoeber, F., 136.

Hofmann, T., 34.

Hogarth, 134.

Homer, 134.

de Honnecourt, Villard, *102*, 140, 141, 151.

de Hontañon, Rodrigo Gil, 115.

Hülsen, C., 29.

Hume, David, 135.

Intuition, theory of, 38.

Janitscheck, H., 140.

Jones, Inigo, 64, 130.

Jouven, George, 140, 143.

Von Jurascheck, 142, 143.

Juvarra, 103.

Kablinsky, 150.

Kepler, 130.

Kimball, Fiske, 29.

Kletzl, O., 143.

Kraus, F.X., 16.

Krautheimer, R., 39, 40, 59.

Kristeller, 38.

Labacco, 55.

Lampertico, F., 60.

Lang, S., 17.

Laspeyres, P., 29.

Le Corbusier, 145, 155.

Legnano, S. Magno, 29.

Lehmann, Karl, 19.

Leonardo, 20, *21*, 22, *23*, 25, 26, 27, 39, *102*, 113, 114, 128, 134, 141, 144, 153, 155; studies for centralised churches, 25f.

Leoni, James, 41.

Lepanto, 88.

Lesser, George, 144.

Levi-Montalcini, G., 144.

Lisiera, Villa Valmarana, 124.

Liturgy, see: Centrally planned church.

Livy, 63.

Lockwood, 38.

Loggia del Capitanio, 89, 94.

Lomazzo, 104, 115.

London, British Museum, drawings, 88; Royal Institute of British Architects, drawings by

Palladio, 64, 76, 84, 94, 103; Soane Museum, sketchbook, 43.

Lonedo, Villa Godi Porto, 67, *67*, 121.

Longhana, 103.

Lord Burlington, 64, 93.

Lord Kames, 136.

Loreto, Chiesa della Casa Santa, 20.

Lotz, Prof. Wolfgang, 29, 59, 86.

Lund, F.M., 142.

Macerata, S. Maria della Vergine, 37.

Macrocosm – Microcosm, 25, 32, 38, 39, 104, 106, 114, 119, 130, 143; see also: Harmony of the universe.

Maggiore, Giorgio, 97.

Magrini, 84, 86, 111, 115, 129.

Mahnke, D., 38.

da Maiano, Giuliano, 31.

Mainstone, Rowland J., 144.

Malaguzzi, F., 52.

Malatesta, Sigismondo, 43.

Mâle, Emile, 40.

Malcontenta, Villa, *71*, 121, *122*, 124.

Malipiero, C., 144.

Malvasia, 114.

Mancini, 47, 49, 52.

Manetti, 113.

Mannerist architecture, 56, 82, 84, 86, 89, 93.

Mantua, S. Andrea, 43, *52*, 55, 56, *56*, *58*, 59, 89, 95, 100; S. Sebastiano, 29, 43, 51, 52, *52*, 53, *53*, 55, 55, 56, 59.

Manuscripts, Escorial, Cod. Escurialensis, 29, 93; Florence, Bibl. Laurenziana, Cod. Ashburnham, 361, 20, 25, 26; Bibl. Naz., Cod. Magliab., 20; Paris, Bibl. Nat. 2037, 26; Inst. de France MS.B., 20, 26.

Marchelli, G., 142.

Marchini, Giuseppe, 31.

Marconi, Piero, 84.

Marliani, 63.

Maser, Church, *34*, *35*.

Mazzotti, Giuseppe, 68.

Means (Arithmetical, Geometric, Harmonic), 107, 108ff., 124, 127, 133.

Medici, Piero de', 19.

Meledo, Villa Trissino, 123.

Memmo, Tribuno, 94.

Mengs, Anton Raphael, 133, 134.

Michel, Paul-Henri, 17, 18, 112, 143.

Michelangelo, 34, 82, 84, 86, 89, 93, 104.

Michelozzo, 17, 29.

Miega, Villa Sarego, 68, *69*, 125, *126*.

Milan, Brera, drawings, 61; Cathedral, 119, 144; Palazzo Marino, 82; S. Maria della Pas-

sione, 29; S. Satiro, 91, *92*.

Milanesi, 50.

Milizia, 47, 134.

Millich, Knud, 144.

Millon, H., 20, 130, 144.

Milton, 130.

Mira, Villa Malcontenta, *69*.

Mitchell, Charles, 29.

Moessel, Ernest, 142.

Mollino, C., 144.

Mongiovino, Chiesa della Madonna, 29, 37.

Monneret de Villard, V., 142.

Montano, G.B., 29.

Montagnana, Villa Pisani, *69*.

Montepulciano, Madonna di S. Biagio, 29.

Montecchio, Sebastiano, 129.

Morris, Robert, 131, 142.

Morsolin, Bernardo, 60, 61.

Mosca, F.U., 86.

Moschini, Gianantonio, 89, 138.

Musical Theory, 19, 105, 106, 108, 109ff., 111ff., 123, 125, 128, 132.

Neo-Platonism, see: Plato.

New York, Pierpont Morgan Library, 46.

Newton, 134, 155.

Nicolas of Cusa, see: Cusanus.

Nicomachus, 127.

Nobbs, Percy E., 142.

Orciano near Urbino, S. Maria Maggiore, 29.

de l'Orme, Philibert, 115, 116, 130.

Ornament, Definition of, 41ff.

Orphic poets, 38.

Ouvrard, 133, 142.

Pacioli, Luca, 25, 26, 38, 109, 123, 152.

Padua, Palazzo della Ragione, 75.

Palazzo Porto, 80, 82.

Palazzo Valmarana, 121.

Palladio, 22, 34, *34*, 39, 42, 59, 61, *67*, 68ff., 74, 77ff., *90*, *93*, *94*, 95, 97, *98*, *100*, *102*, 103, 104, 108ff., 117, 122ff., 132, 133, 153; and Alberti, 31, 64, 107; Birthplace, 60; and Bramante, 32; and Emanuele Filiberto, 115; edition of Caesar, 62, 63; guidebooks to Rome, 62f.; Quattro libri, 62, 63ff., 65, 66, 67, 75, 76, 80-82, 93, 107, 117, 121ff., and Vitruvius, 64f.; adaption of classical elements, 70, 75-89, 91, 94, 100; influence of, 97, 131; Palladio's Villas, see: Asolo, Bagnolo, Bassano, Cessalto, Cicogna, Fanzola, Finale, Fratta Polesine, Ghizzole, Lisiera, Lonedo, Malcontenta, Meledo, Miega, Montagnana, Poiana Maggiore, Piombino,

Quinto, Santa Sofia, Vicenza.
Pane, Roberto, 68, 88, 132.
Panofsky, Erwin, 47, 115.
Papini, Roberto, 20.
Paris, Louvre, 76; see: Manuscripts.
Parma, Madonna della Steccata, 29.
Partenio, Bernardino, 61.
de' Pasti, Matteo, 43, 45, *45*, 46, 47, 113.
Pastor, L.V., 16.
Pavia, Cathedral, 20; S. Maria di Canepanova, 29.
Payne Knight, Richard, 136.
Pée, Herbert, 75.
Pellegrini, Pellegrino, 115, 129.
Perrault, Claude, 131, 134, 135.
Peruzzi, 22, 26, 37, *66*, 97,
Pevsner, N., 16.
Philolaos, 117, *118*, 119.
Piacenza, Madonna di Campagna, 29, 37.
da Pietrasanta, Giacomo, *54*.
Piombino Dese, Villa Cornaro, 68, *69*, 123.
Pistoia, S. Maria dell' Umiltà, 29.
Plato, 19, 32, 38, 65, 104ff., 109, 115, 129, 138, 148ff., 154.
Pliny, 63.
Plotinus, 25, 38.
Plutarch, 63, 105.
Poiana Maggiore, Villa Poiana, *69*.
Poleni, Giovanni, 65.
Polybius, 63.
Ponzio, Flaminio, 37.
Porphyry, 65, 108.
Prado, H., 116, *116*.
Prato, S. Maria delle Carceri, 29, *30*, *31*, *32*, 97.
Preti, Francesco Maria, *96*, 132, 133.
Promis, C., 20.
Proportion, theory of, 18, 25, 38, 50f., 56, 62, 95, 104, 108, 113ff., 119ff., 130ff., 138ff.; see also: Harmony; Ratios.
Pseudo-Dionysius, 19, 38.
Ptolemy, 116.
Pythagoras, 41, 47, 97, 104, 109, *118*, 119, 130, 131, 147, 148, 153.

de Quincy, Quatremère, 47.
Quinto, Villa Thiene, *72*, *73*, 80.

Raphael, 22, 37, *37*, 63, *74*, 75, 119, *119*, 154.
Ratios, 104, 105, 107, 111ff., 121, 123ff., 131ff.; incommensurability of, 108, 120, 122, 140ff.; see also: Harmony, Proportion.
Read Sunderland, Elizabeth, 144.
Reggio, Madonna della Ghiara, 37.
Reynolds, Sir Joshua, 153.

Riccati, Jacopo, 133.
Ricci, Corrado, 43, 45, 113.
Ricciolini, Niccolò, 133.
Richter, J.P., 20, 25.
Rimini, Arch of Augustus, 43; S. Francesco, 20, 29, 43, *44*, 45ff., *48*, 49ff., 55, 56, 59, *59*, 107, 113.
Rivoira, 52.
Rizzetto, Giovanni, 133.
Rizzetto, Luigi, 133.
Roman House, 77, 80.
Romano, Guilio, 82, 84.
Rome, Arch of Constantine, 43, 46; of Septimius Severus, 86ff., of Titus, 56; Augustus' wall, 82; Baptistery of Constantine, 32; Basilica of Constantine, 56, 94; Cancelleria, 82; Capitol, 82, 84, 86; Casa di Raffaello, 75, 76; Colosseum, 42, 80, 82; Farresina, *66*; Minerva Medica, 17, 32; Palazza Bresciano, 75; Ossoli, 75; di S. Biagio, 82; Vidoni-Caffarelli, 75; Pantheon, 19, 50, 93, *93*, 94; peripteral temple, 17; Porta Maggiore, 82; S. Agostino, *54*, 55; S. Carlo ai Catinari, 37; S. Costanza, 17, 32; S. Eligio degli Orefici, 29, 37, *37*; S. Maria di Loreto, 29; S. Maria de Popolo, 55; S. Peter's, 34, *36*; S. Pietro in Montorio, 29; S. Rocco, *96*; S. Stefano Rotondo, 17; Tempietto, 29, 32, 37, 82; Temple of Claudius, 82; Temple of Jupiter, 97; Temple of Romulus, 32; Thermae, 56, 80, 93, 100; Tomb of Annia Regilla, 52; Vatican, 56, 64; Vesta Temple, 18, 32; Villa Madama, 63.
Röthlisberger, M., 43.
Rucellai Archives, 50.
Rughesi, Fausto, 89.
Rumor, S., 76.
Rusconi, Gio. Antonio, 25.
Ruskin, 15.

Saalman, Howard, 140, 144.
Salmi, Mario, 43, 46.
Saluzzo, Cesare, 20.
da Sangallo, Antonio, 22.
da Sangallo, Guiliano, 29, *30*, 31, 34, *55*, 67, 70.
Sanmicheli, 75, 82.
Sansovino, Francesco, 107.
Sansovino, Jacopo, 76, 82, 89, 104, 106.
Sansovino, M. Giacomo, 139.
Santa Sofia, Villa Sarego, 123.
Santa Sophia, church of, at Edessa, 19.
Sarton, G., 128.
Sauer, J., 16, 39.
Scamozzi, Bertotti, *34*, *35*, 64, 67, *78*, 80, 89, *90*, *94*, 108, 117, 120, 132.

Schillinger, Joseph, 143.
Von Schlosser, J., 22, 128.
Schoen, Edward, 151.
Scholfield, P.H., 127, 133, 144.
Schumacher, 56.
Scott, Geoffrey, 15.
Scotti, Ottario, 133.
Serlio, 26, *28*, 29, *36*, 37, 63, *74*, 75, 86, 93, 107, 108, 120, *120*.
I Sforza, Francesco, 19.
Shaftesbury, 130.
Shakespeare, 130.
Shirlaw, Matthew, 127.
Siena, Cathedral, 20.
Siena, Chiesa degli Innocenti, 29.
Simpson, T.W., 136.
von Simson, Otto, 140.
Smeraldi, Francesco, 89.
Soergel, Gerda, 47, 141, 144.
Soldati, Giacomo, 115.
Solomon, 115, 116, 138.
Sophocles, 66.
Sorella, Simone, 89.
Speroni, 60, 64.
Spira, Fortunio, 107.
Spitzer, L., 130.
Spencer, John R., 19.
Spoleto, Chiesa della Manna d'Oro, 29.
Sta. Costanza, 17.
Stechow, W., 144.
Sto. Stefano Rotondo, 17.
Strack, H., 29.
Stuart Weller, Allen, 22.

Taylor, A.E., 106.
Taylor, R.C., 115, 116.
Tea, Eva, 143.
Temanza, Tommaso, 84, 115, 120, 132, 133, 134.
Texier, Marcel-André, 142.
Theuer, Max, 16, 18.
Thiersch, August, 143.
Thomae, W., 142, 143.
Thomas, Ivor, 108.
Thorndike, 38.
Timaeus of Locri, 106.
Timofiewitsch, W., 103.
Tirali, Andrea, *96*.
Titian, 107, 153.
Tivoli, Vesta temple, 32.
Todi, S. Maria della Consolazione, 26, *27*, 29.
Toffanin, G., 60.
Tolomei, Claudio, 22.
della Torre, Count, 124.
Traverso, Giuliana, 143.

Trissino, Giangiorgio, 60, 61, 62, *62*, 64, 66, 76, 107.
Tubalcain, *118*.
Turin, Cathedral, 55.

Udine, Palazzo Antonini, 80, *80*.
Ueberwasser, W., 141, 142, 143.

Valadier, Giuseppe, *96*.
Valeri, Malaguzzi, 22.
Valerius Maximus, 63.
Valladolid, Cathedral, 115.
Varchi, 60, 64.
Vasari, Giorgio, 22, 47, 80, 89, 91.
Venice, Convent of the Carità, *79*; Il Redentore, *94*, *95*, *99*, 100, *100*, 101, 103; Libreria, 76; Palazzo Ducale, *88*; S. Francesco della Vigna, 89, *90*, 91, 94, 95, 104, *105*, 106, 111; S. Giorgio Maggiore, 89, *90*, 94, *98*, 99, 100, 103; S. Giovanni Crisostomo, 29; S. Nicola da Tolentino, *102*, 103; S. Pietro di Castello, 88; S. Vitale, *96*; (near Venice) Villa Ricci, Ca' Brusa, 68.
Venturi, 26, 34.
Verona, Palazzo Count della Torre, 124; Palazzo Pompei, 75; Porta de' Borsari, 86; Roman Theatre, 84; S. Bernardino, Capp. Pellegrini, 29.
Vicentini, Antonio, 88.
Vicentino, Andrea, 88, *88*.
Vicenza, Palazzo della Ragione, 75; Loggia del Capitanio, 86, 87; Palazzo Angarano, 124; Chiericati (Museo Civico), *84*; Civena, 75; Poiana, 76; Porto-Colleoni, 75-82; *77*, 123; della Ragione, 66, 75; Thiene, *78*, 82, *83*, 153; Valmarana, 84, *85*, 86, 89, 94; Teatro Olimpico, 66; Villa at Cricoli, 61, *62*; Rotonda, *69*, 70, *71*.
Vigna, S. Francesco, 140.
Vignola, 82, 117.
Villa Angarano, Nr. Bassano, 73.
Villa Maser, nr. Asolo, 73, *73*, 125, *126*, 127.
Villalpando, G.B., 116, *116*, 117.
Viollet-le-Duc, 143.
Vischer, Hermann, 59.
da Viterbo, Egidio, 34.
Vitruvius, 16, 18, 22, *24*, 25, 31, 32, 41, 51, 61, 64, 65, 76, 80, 91, 94, 95, 104, 107, 108, 113, 116, 123, 127ff., 135, 141, 150, 151, 153; Barbaro's ed. of, see: Barbaro; Cesariano's ed. of, see: Cesariano; later ed. of, 25.
Vittone, Bernardo Antonio, 134.

Walker, D.P., 105.
Weinberger, M., 49.
Whitehead, 155.
Wilde, Johannes, 144.
Willich, 50.
Winterberg, C., 25.
Winthrop Kent, W., 91.
Wittkower, R., 113, 114, 130, 134, 144.
Witzel, Karl, 142.
Wolff, Odilio, 142, 143.
Wölfflin, Heinrich, 143.
Wood, John, 142.
Wotton, Sir Henry, 131, 142.

Yates, Frances A., 105, 114.

Zarlino, 114, 117, 119, 124, 127, 132, 134.
Zeising, A., 142, 143.
Ziani, Sebastiani, 94.
Zocca, 37.
Zorzi, 60, 65, 68, 75.
Zorzi, Andrea, 133.
Zorzi, Francescò, 25.
Zorzi, Giangiorgio, 62, 64, 73, 76.
Zoubov, V.P., 128, 140, 144.
Zucchini, 97.